بسم الله الرحمن الرحيم

THE DARQAWI WAY

Mawlay al-Arabi ad-Darqawi

letters from the shaykh
to the fuqara

Madinah Press

Paper Edition 2005

by **MADINAH PRESS**
Capetown, South Africa

Distributed by :
Madinah Distributor (000866370-K)
4, Jalan Pawang, Off Jalan Keramat Hujung
54000 Kuala Lumpur
Malaysia.
Tel : 603-4257 1675
Fax : 603-4260 4021 / 4260 4016
e-mail : madinah@streamyx.com
Hand Phone : 019-3834541

ISBN NO.: 0 9065 12 06 9

Printed by :
Art Printing Works Sdn. Bhd. (Co.No.9406-D)

THE DARQAWI WAY
letters from the shaykh to the fuqara
by Mawlay al-'Arabi ad-Darqawi

translated by 'Aisha 'Abd ar-Rahman at-Tarjumana

CONTENTS

Letters of the Supreme Name,
from the end-piece of a handwritten
edition of 'The Darqawi Way' in
Ksar Souk, Morocco.

A SONG OF WELCOME

Oh! Mawlay al'Arabi, I greet you!
The West greets the West —
Although the four corners are gone
And the seasons are joined.
In the tongue of the People
I welcome you — the man of the time.
Wild, in rags, with three hats
And wisdom underneath them.
You flung dust in the enemy's face
Scattering them by the secret
Of a rare sunna the 'ulama forgot.

Oh! Mawlay al'Arabi, I love you!
The Pole greets the Pole —
The centre is everywhere
And the circle is complete.
We have danced with Darqawa,
Supped at their table, yes,
And much, much more, I
And you have sung the same song,
The song of the sultan of love.

Oh! Mawlay al'Arabi, you said it!
Out in the open you gave the gift.
Men drank freely from your jug.
The cup passed swiftly, dizzily —
Until it came into my hand.
I have drunk, I have drunk,
I am drinking still, the game
Is over and the work is done.
What is left if it is not this?
This wine that is not air,
Nor fire, nor earth, nor water.
This diamond — I drink it!

Oh! Mawlay al'Arabi, you greet me!
There is no house in which I sit
That you do not sit beside me.
We are both from bel-Habib, the Ghawth,
The Great. How strange! We are
From him — you coming before, and
I coming after. He is our source.
He is our stillness, vortex, seal.
This is one hadra, one circle,
One grain of sand beneath
The sandal of Muhammad.
Salallahu alayhi wa salam.

Shaykh 'Abd al-Qadir as-Sufi ad-Darqawi

THE DARQAWI WAY
THE LETTERS OF SHAYKH DARQAWI

This work is used in the circles of the Darqawi Way not only in Morocco but across North Africa, as well as at Darqawi zawiyyas in England, the United States, Argentina, Spain, Malaysia, and Makkah. The work also serves as a very vivid and clear introduction to the great masterwork of sufic science, 'The Meaning of Man', for its author was Sidi 'Ali al-Jamal, the Master of Shaykh ad-Darqawi.

His letters have never before been translated into English and this translation will help increase knowledge of the great teacher throughout the world. A short extract from the letters has appeared in English but it was an odd performance marred by an intrusive masonic vocabulary that has no place in Islamic sufism. This therefore is the first appearance of the text to contain the complete range of instructions and teachings. Only one or two letters have been omitted which seemed to repeat matters already dealt with and some matters of little interest.

The Darqawi Way has two practices which its adepts perform as part of their discipline. One is the Dance, called hadra or raqs, and the other is the dhikr or invocation of the Supreme Name. Referring to these, Shaykh Muhammad ibn al-Habib, our noble and great Master, said in his 'Diwan':

Here are the ones (meaning the sufis) who have obliterated their selves and plumbed every depth in the oceans of love.

So submit to them for what you see of their ardent love, and their dancing and singing at the invocation of the Beloved.

If you had only tasted something of the meaning of our words you would already be experiencing every (inner) state.

The Dance, which is really the invocation of Allah while standing and swaying, as described in the Qur'an and also in the hadith literature, is usually preceded by the singing from the Diwans of the great sufis. The Diwans of the Darqawi Way are among the most sublime in the literature of the Way. Of these, mention should be made of the Diwan of Shaykh al-Harraq, whose Master was Shaykh ad-Darqawi himself; the Diwan of Shaykh al-'Alawi of Algeria; and the renowned Diwan of Shaykh Muhammad ibn al-Habib which is sung all round the world in the gatherings of the sufis.

The invocation of the Supreme Name is referred to in these letters many times and this work contains passages of great importance for the Darqawi fuqara, for here their Imam refers to both the technique and his own personal enlightenment through its use. The significance of these references is that they refer not to the traditional method of its invocation used in the Shadhili Way, which preceded the Darqawi Way, but because they speak of the technique which Sidi 'Ali al-Jamal taught to him. He, in turn, writes

4

that he found this method in the Shadhili texts passed on to him by his own Masters. This technique involves the visualisation of the letters of the Supreme Name — ALLAH — in the first Station of the Supreme Name, as well as certain changes in the visualisation. Far from being merely a concentration technique this method is very far-reaching in its effects, due to the meanings and secrets which Allah has attached to the letters of His own Name.

The purpose of this great invocation is nothing less than fana' fi'llah — annihilation in Allah. This central theme is expounded again and again, helping and guiding the seekers on their path to illumination. Here is a book for the adept to use. It should be studied and gone over until it is understood and until the promised states and stations of gnosis reveal themselves to the seeker. This is the meaning of the Way and the purpose of the letters. These are despatches from the battlefield of the ruh (spirit) in its war against the self and its ignorance. It is filled with the taste as well as the promise of victory — and to the muslims the word victory and the word opening — inner opening — are the same.

Shaykh 'Abd al-Qadir as-Sufi ad-Darqawi

FOREWORD

These are the letters of the great Shaykh and famous gnostic, high in rank and noble of lineage, who built the supports of his tariqa on the basis of obscurity and adab: Abu 'Abdillah, Sayyidi Muhammad al-'Arabi b. Sayyidi Ahmad al-Hasani ad-Darqawi, may Allah be pleased with him and profit us by him. Amin.

Since they have no opening address or preface they were given an opening address by the Shaykh, the Faqih, Ibn 'Abbas, Sayyidi Ahmad b. Muhammad az-Zagari, al-Hasani, called Ibn al-Khayyat. The discourse contains something about the states of the Shaykh. May Allah give benefit to all by His favour and generosity. Amin.

In the name of Allah, the Merciful, the Compassionate. May Allah bless our Lord and Master Muhammad and his family.

Praise be to Allah who placed in every age one who calls to Allah and is a guide to the treatment of the sicknesses of the selves and to the path of putting hearts right. Whoever answers his call is happy. Whoever is arrogant or shy continues with the hobbling-cord of his sickness. Glory be to Him! He purifies the hearts of whomever He wills of His slaves and makes them Imams in the path of guided conduct. They travel on the Path to Allah and they recognise its states. They have insight into the machinations of the self. They know its actions. Their Master has guided them to His Path after much striving. Their selves have been put at rest after struggle and suffering. They have drawn near to their Master with sincere intention and their Master has drawn near to them as befits the sublime essence.

7

I testify that there is no god but Allah alone, with no partner. He teaches knowledges direct from the divine presence to whomever He wills among His slaves. I testify that Sayyiduna Muhammad is His slave and Messenger. Whoever imitates him has risen through resplendent elevations, may Allah bless him and grant him peace and his family, who did without in this abode, and acted with love for the essence of Allah — glory be to Him! It was not for good in the Garden or fear of the Fire. May He bless him with a blessing and peace by which we enter into the mesh of those who love the dutifully obedient, and by which we obtain the privilege of You along with whoever You love in the Abode of Permanence (the Next World).

These are the letters of the Shaykh, the Imam, the Ghawth who benefits the elite and the common, the famous wali and great siddiq, the perfect realised gnostic, the one who has arrived, who is drowned in the sea of oneness, utterly crushed and annihilated in the immensity of the sublime essence, who is firmly established and firmly rooted, the lofty mountain which joins the shari'at of Muhammad and the reality, bewildered in every station of his realisation, the Cave of mankind and the shelter of the elite and common. He is the sign of the Merciful and the rarity of the age, the word of Allah from His direct presence, and the shelter of His resplendent tajalli-manifestation. He is the Sharif ad-Darqawi al-Hasani, the teacher, endowed with noble qualities, our lord and master al-'Arabi, may Allah give us the benefit of his baraka and send back some of his fragrant breezes to us. He sent the letters to those who had the benefit of his company and entered under his banner and came to his presence. He is loved by those from whom the veils have been lifted and from whom others are distant. With them, the night becomes the awakening of day. The cosmos is crushed and annihilated in their eyes since they see the One, the Conquerer. What a contemplation it is! How sweet it is! What a station it has!

How high they are!

These are letters which tell about the station of their sender and make his gnoses known in what they say. Their drink is clear and pure for the thirsty. Those kept in seclusion with them manifest the splendour of the sun to the eyes. They join words and effects, warnings and signs for consideration. The intellects do not see because of it and all examinations agree that the knowledge of their author is an overflowing sea. In them are the commands and words of the shari'at of Muhammad, and the sunna and actions of the tariqa, and the secrets and states of the reality. All this is in the most concise phrase and exact expression and clearest indication. He wrote them according to events. The answer is according to the question. Each letter is enough for the one who has it with the greatest possible richness. It takes him to the end of hope and desire.

The one who receives these letters does not turn to any other books and means except them. Oh brother! grab on to them and act according to them. Take on their character. All that there is in them is the shari'at of the master of the Messengers, the path of the wayfarers, indications of the realised gnostics who have arrived, and the ecstasies of the beloved lovers. They, like their author, are well-known and famous in every land. They are spread out as this Darqawi order is spread out, the group of the dutifully obedient.

The author of these letters is the Shaykh, the Imam, the Ghawth, the sovereign gnostic, the eternal realised one, the Shaykh of the Shaykhs. He does not seek shelter with other than his Lord and Master. He is the Hasani sharif, possessing noble qualities, our master al-'Arabi b. Ahmad ad-Darqawi. He, may Allah be pleased with him, is among our pure ones, the Sharifs, the people of the House of the Chosen Messenger from whom filth falls away. The sun of their Beloved is not hidden among the group who are entitled the Darqawiyyun. They are spread out in places in the earth and they are respected in their positions, recognised as possessing a noble lineage. There was a guild in this blessed group in the time of Mawlana Isma'il and Sayyidi Muhammad b. 'Abdillah and Mawlana Sulayman as I have mentioned in another place. There is a group of them in Sus al-Aqsa. There is a group of them at Sahil ad-Dakala at the port of Asafi in which is the tomb of the right-acting wali, the famous clear one Abu Muhammad Salih, the Shaykh of the great Shaykh, Abu Madyan al-Ghawth, may Allah profit us by him. Many of them are in the tribe of the Banu Zarwal. All of them are people of modesty, generosity, bereftness and self-restraint. Their ancestor from whom they trace their lineage is the Imam Abu Abdillah Sayyidi Muhammad b. Yusuf, entitled Abu Darqa. He, may Allah be pleased with him, had an immense rank and was very famous. He, may Allah be pleased with him, was a man of knowledge and action, one who did without, who stood up in prayer and fasted and gave sadaqa. He finished the Qur'an every day. He strove in the way of Allah. He had a great shield (darqa) with which he shielded himself in the wars. Because of it, he was called Abu Darqa. His tomb is a famous place to visit. It has a perfect dome over it and it is located at Tamasna at the tribe of Shawiya near the Wadi Umm ar-Rabi'. He was among the descendants of Mawlana Ahmad b. Mawlana Idris b. Mawlana Idris, may Allah be pleased with them.

Shaykh Mawlana al-'Arabi, may Allah be pleased with him, was bewildered concerning his lineage when he was young. Allah-ta'ala showed him his lineage through eyewitnessing and unveiling by a light which was like the light which the common people call the rainbow. It came out as a bow from the Prophet, may Allah bless him and grant him peace, to Mawlana Idris and from Mawlana Idris to Sayyidi Abu Darqa, and from Sayyidi Abu Darqa to Mawlana al-'Arabi, may Allah be pleased with him. Individuals among the people of the House, may Allah be pleased with them, are very often gripped by this bewilderment. Its cause is the intensity of respect for this noble lineage and fear of pretension. This is part of scrupulousness. The Banu Zarwal was the birthplace of Shaykh Mawlana al-'Arabi, may Allah be pleased with him. He grew up there and lived there and died there. His tomb is there. This blessed tribe has many benefits and famous special qualities. Some of those among them are the descendants of the four Khalifs, Abu Bakr, 'Umar, 'Uthman, and 'Ali, may Allah be pleased with them. Among them is the great wali, the famous master, Sayyidi al-Hajj b. Faqira az-Zarwali. He recited the seven variants of Qur'an in order in the Noble Rawda, the meadow of the Prophet, may Allah bless him and grant him peace. When he finished it, the Prophet, may Allah bless him and grant him peace, answered him and said, "It was sent down on me like that, Imam az-Zarwali, may Allah bless you and your Zarwali tribe".

Among them is that Allah has joined agriculture and armour, grapes, olives, fruits and the courage of its people. This Shaykh, Mawlana al-'Arabi, may Allah be pleased with him, said, "People say: 'Whoever has his garment touch the garment of the Zarwali profits and does not lose' ". It is as if he, may Allah be pleased with him, were indicating himself by these words, talking about the blessings of Allah ta'ala and good counsel for the slaves of Allah. The awliya of Allah–ta'ala are the elixir of the hearts. Whoever sees them, has such a happiness by them that he is never miserable after it. The greatest Shaykh and most famous gnostic, Abu'l Hasan ash-Shadhili, said about the firm qualities of his disciple Abu'l-'Abbas al-Mursi, may Allah be pleased with them, "The best man is Abu'l-'Abbas. A Bedouin came to him and urinated on his leg and it made him reach Allah immediately". Shaykh Abu'l-'Abbas al-Mursi, may Allah be pleased with him, said "By Allah, the only thing between me and a man is that I look at him, and when I look at him, I am enough for him and enrich him". It is as he said. Mawlana at-

Tihami b. Sayyidi Muhammad al-Wazzani al-'Alami al-Yamlihi, may Allah be pleased with him said:

Whoever comes to our presence free and clear, leaves with his heart fattened.
Whoever comes covered in bad luck, leaves hollowed out.
The Messenger of Allah is the Guarantor.

I said: Mawlana al-'Arabi ad-Darqawi, the author of these letters, may Allah be pleased with him, was the answer for this world in the heart of the sources. How many people were opened by Allah at his hand, and the hand of his companions and heirs after him, who had blind eyes, heedless hearts, and ears deaf to perception of the divine presence! They were not aware and now their hearts have found a nest and their spirits a residence, may Allah profit us by their baraka. If you said that this gnostic master is from the people of the House of the Messenger and among the most famous of them, so he is not Zarwali, then I say in answer to that that the 'ulama of the hadith say, "Whoever resides in a place for 40 years has a sound connection to it". Mawlana al-'Arabi was born in the tribe of Banu Zarwal after 1150 a.h., may Allah be pleased with him. He grew up with its people in self-restraint, protection, modesty, and manliness. In his youth, he was occupied with recitation of Qur'an and visiting (tombs). He only recognised the good. He was supported and protected. He said, may Allah be pleased with him, "Once I was on the point of an act of rebellion when I was young with someone I desired. My body was covered in many sores when the thought of evil came to my heart. I asked Allah's forgiveness and those sores went away immediately. It was a favour from Allah and a blessing".

He learned the Qur'an by heart in the first order very exactly. He was beloved by all who saw him. He said, may Allah be pleased with him, "I used to clean the student's writing-boards. Very often, I would take the board in my hand and tell its owner before I looked at it, 'This board is heavy. Such-and-such is in it of loss'. or 'It is light. There is only such-and-such in it or nothing'. I always found that what I had told him was true. This was by inspiration from Allah, glory be to Him! When he recited Qur'an, his state was lack of unnatural constraint. He would write the board and then reflect on it a little and then leave it and occupy himself with the writing on the boards of the students and talking with them. He recited the seven variants in that manner after he knew them by heart.

Then he was occupied with studying knowledge at Fez at the al-Misbahiyya Madrasa for a suitable period. Then he met the great Shaykh, the famous gnostic, the lofty Sharif, Abu'l-Hasan, Sayyidi 'Ali, known as al-Jamal, may Allah profit us by him! after many visits to Mawlana Idris b. Idris, may Allah be pleased with both of them. It was said that he recited the Qur'an 60 times at his tomb in search of the Shaykh of guidance. When he completely finished the 60 times he had a bout of intense weeping until his eyes became red. He left the tomb of Mawlana Idris and passed by a sharif, Sayyidi Hamid, who was one of the descendants of the famous Qutb, the great gnostic Mawlana 'Abdu'l-Aziz ad-Dabbagh, through his daughter. He was looking expectantly at him and others with great esteem and said, "Why do I see you in this state?" He pressed him urgently and told him that he needed to take someone's hand. Sayyidi Hamid said to him, "I will lead you to him if you have not taken the advice of the people of inadequate opinion and flabby intellect". Ash-Shustari said in his poem ending in Ra':

'Only ask someone about him who has an inner eye and is free of appetites and not deluded.'

Mawlana al-'Arabi asked him, 'Who is he?' "He is the majestic Shaykh, the noble, sharif, the all-encompassing Ghawth and the vast sea Abu'l-Hasan Sayyidi 'Ali b. 'Abdi'r-Rahman al-'Imrani, entitled al-Jamal (the camel) with the people of Fez, and al-Jamal (beauty) with the angels of the

13

Merciful as I was told by one of the awliya' whom the angels had spoken to and greeted. He said that the angels told him that Sayyidi 'Ali al-Jamal had been entrusted with the office of the Ghawth for 30 years." Sayyidi 'Ali al-Jamal, may Allah be pleased with him! said, "Part of what Allah bestowed on me is that He — glory be to Him! made me such that whenever I mention the Messenger of Allah, may Allah bless him and grant him peace or think about him, I find him present before me with his ten noble, dutiful Companions who were promised the Garden, may Allah be pleased with them. That is in the sensory world itself, not only the meaning. We speak with him and we take knowledge from the source of knowledge and action from the source of action". His state would change, may Allah be pleased with him, and his skin would shiver, and his eyes would become red when he mentioned the Messenger, may Allah bless him and grant him peace, or thought about him, peace be upon him. In the beginning of his affair Mawlana 'Ali was a wazir (government minister). Then he was dismissed from wazirate and went to the gnostic Shaykh, Sayyidi al-'Arabi, the son of the greatest Qutb, Sayyidi Ahmad b. 'Abdillah Ma'n, may Allah profit us by them! He said to him, "Do you give life to a tariqa which has been obliterated since the time of al-Junayd to our time?" He said, "Yes." Therefore, he put on the patched robe and began to beg and take knowledge from him and benefit from him.

Mawlana al-'Arabi, may Allah be pleased with him, said: "He informed me about his Shaykh, but it was my custom never to undertake any matter, great or small, until I had done the Istikhara of the Prophet. That night, I did the Istikhara, asking Allah for good and I spent the night absorbed in wondering about his character and appearance and what my meeting with him would be like. I did not sleep at all that night. When I had prayed the Subh prayer I set out for his Zawiyya at ar-Rumalya between the two towns, beside the river,

on the qibla side, may Allah ennoble it! That is where
his tomb is now. It is famous and a place which people
visit. I knocked on the door and there he was, standing,
sweeping the zawiyya. He always swept it with his
blessed hand every day in spite of his advanced age and
the exaltedness of his rank. He said, 'What do you
want?' I said, 'Sayyidi, I want you to take my hand
for Allah'. He turned on me fiercely and confused me
and hid his state from me. He said, 'Who told you this?
Who takes my hand? Why should I take your hand?'
He rebuffed me and chased me away. All of that was to
test my sincerity. I turned from him and then did the
Istikhara again that night, asking Allah for good. Then
I prayed the dawn prayer and set out for his Zawiyya.
I found him in the same state, sweeping the zawiyya,
may Allah be pleased with him. I knocked on the door
and he opened it for me. I said, 'Take my hand for
Allah'. He grasped my hand and said to me, 'Welcome!'
He brought me to his place in the Zawiyya and was
very delighted about me and completely overjoyed. I
said to him, 'Sayyidi, I have been looking for a Shaykh
for a long time'. He said to me, 'And I have been
looking for a sincere murid for a very long time'. He
gave me the wird and told me, 'Come and go'. I used to
come and go every day. He had me do dhikr with some
of the brothers from the people of Fez, may Allah protect it from every harm!''

He remained close to his Shaykh for two years. When the
clear opening came to him suddenly and he had full mastery
of his state and Allah wanted the slaves to benefit from him,
he broke the reins of his interest in order to move from Fez
to his land, the tribe of Banu Zarwal where he now is. He
asked his Shaykh's permission to travel with his children. He
gave him permission for that in a statement which is too long
to mention.

Mawlana al-'Arabi had a number of Shaykhs. Among them was the great Shaykh, the noble Sharif, the wali of Allah ta'ala, Sayyidi at-Tayyib b. Mawlana Muhammad Biwazzan. He, may Allah be pleased with him, said, "I visited him seven times when I was a young child. Once I found him with a large crowd around him. He, may Allah be pleased with him, opened a way for me among the people and brought me near him so that I could kiss his hand and knee. I put two writing-boards in his room. The sura al-Jumu'a (62) was on one of them. He placed his noble hand on my brow and recited to me what Allah willed. He was delighted with me and asked for good for me. After that, good, memorization of Qur'an, baraka and the secret appeared from me. There was the breaking of norms after I had memorized a little. He was one of my Shaykhs".

He said, "Similarly, I visited his paternal cousin, the great and famous realised wali, the lofty sharif, Abu 'Abdillah Sayyidi Muhammad b. 'Ali b. Raysun al-Hasani al-'Alami at the Jabal al-'Alam at Tazrun, near the tomb of the great Qutb, our cousin Mawlana 'Abdu's-Salam bin Mashish. I went seven times from the tribe of Banu Zarwal, and once or twice from the city of Fez. Once he gave me two warm loaves of bread filled with ghee and some others he had. We did not see him give them to anyone else, he particularly gave them to me rather than the group of students. Another time he hit me with his right hand on my left shoulder and told me, 'May Allah give you strength!' Then he repeated his action three times. Then he left me and pushed me away with his blessed hands and said, 'Go! I have given you the great one'. He meant the office of the Qutb, and Allah knows best". He said, "He was one of my Shaykhs like my master and support, the great Qutb, Mawlay 'Ali al-Jamal, may Allah be pleased with him".

Another of his Shaykhs, may Allah be pleased with him, was the great majdhoub, the famous wali Sayyidi al-'Arabi al-Baqqal, may Allah be pleased with him and profit us by him! Amin.

As for his visits to others like those, both alive and dead, it is impossible to count all of them, especially visits to the noble Qutb, the spring of the thirsty, Mawlana 'Abdu-s-Salam b. Mashish and Mawlay Abu Silham and Mawlay Abu-sh-Shita' al-Khammar, and Sayyidi 'Ali b. Da'ud, and the majestic Qutb Sayyidi 'Abdu-l-Warith al-Yasluti al-'Uthmani and other famous ones, may Allah be pleased with them. He, may Allah be pleased with him, did not cease to do that until Allah took him by the hand in such an extraordinary way that there is no describing it. It was unparalleled. This is because visiting the awliyya contains great virtue and a clear secret, immense importance, and far-reaching consequences. This is recognised by the one who applies himself to it and samples it since it is one of the doors of Allah-ta'ala.

Mawlana al-'Arabi, may Allah be pleased with him, died on Tuesday night, the 28th of Safar in the year 1235. He died at an advanced age, about 80 years old, at his zawiyya in the night, after having lived "a pleasing life in a high garden in which foolish talk is not heard". He was buried at his other zawiyya called Bu Barih on Wednesday night. He was washed by the majestic free lady, the noble precious one who fasts, prays, gives sadaqa and does dhikr, the discerning truthful one, his wife Maryam, the daughter of the shaykh who was the son of his grandmother al-Hasnawi. He was prayed over by the lofty master, the respected scholar, the venerated wali of Allah-ta'ala, His loved one and the dearest of people to him, Abu'l-Abbas, Sayyidi Ahmad b. Muhammad b. 'Abdu-r-Rahman, one of the descendants of the great Shaykh, the clear famous Qutb, Abu'l-Baqa' Sayiddi 'Abdu-l-Warith al-Yasuluti al-'Uthmani. All of that was of his often repeated request, may Allah be pleased with him. The two zawiyyas are both at the tribe of Banu Zarwal at Jabal az-Zabib, may Allah protect it! It is a distance of about two days from the city of Fez which is protected by Allah. They are well-known and places to visit and honour for both the common and the elite.

We will mention something about the life of Mawlana al-'Arabi, may Allah be pleased with him, his beginning, his wayfaring, and a clarification of his transmission and practices. We will mention something about his states which were perceived by his companions. As for his states, may Allah be pleased with him! in his beginning and his wayfaring, the greatest of them was his doing-without in this world and divesting himself of it in the sensory and in the meaning, his realisation of its character, his opposition to his nafs (self) and leaving what was light for it and making it follow what was heavy for it since whatever is heavy for it is none other than the truth. That is the swiftest to the answer and opening as he said, may Allah be pleased with him, "Turn it to the Truth and turn it away from creation. No one should be concerned with creatures whether they praise him or blame him". He clung to poverty and neediness. He preferred abasement and being scorned. He was on his guard about what people put together and gathered and stored. He left nothing of his evening meal for his breakfast, and nothing of his breakfast for his evening meal. He would take what was necessary to support his physical constitution and that of his family, and would leave the rest for Allah's slaves. This is a great road which can only be travelled by the one to whom Allah gives the power to do it. The Shaykh, the great unveiled gnostic, the wali of Allah—ta'ala, Abu'l-Abbas Sayyidi Ahmad b. 'Ajiba al-Manjari al-Hasani, said,"Mawlana al-'Arabi remained in this state for 25 years. He left nothing of his evening meal for his breakfast and nothing of his breakfast for his evening meal, to such an extent that it included the oil of the lampwick. It was by confidence in Allah, reliance on Allah, and seeking refuge with Allah. Opening of provision would come to him from Allah and he would only take of it according to his needs, and the needs of his wife and children. They were a group who were like birds in the nest in the morning and evening until the time when he was given permission by Allah. Then he would take by Allah as he had left for Allah. He began to be increased by everything and not decreased by anything".

At the beginning of his affair, he, may Allah be pleased with him! would wear rough garments like coarse felt and the patched jelaba, and very thick black-striped garments, and the short-sleeved hooded jelaba on its own, and the old clean straw hat. He used to put straw hats on top of each other on his head, three or four of them. He carried two or three cases on his back. At other times he would go bareheaded and barefoot, begging in the markets and other places. He would sit on the rubbish heaps while being careful about impurity and he would sleep in the road. He carried the waterskin on his back and gave water for Allah. He had other states and actions of the malamatiyya which took him far from creation and near to the King, the Real. He only did that to free himself from what did not concern him and so he would not show off to his fellow men. He had most of those states. He had strange states and superogatory actions which were troublesome and difficult for the self. What he says in his letters is filled with things that indicate this.

By these continuous superogatory practices, he, may Allah be pleased with him! received from Allah the fullest portion and the greatest share. He continued to draw near Him with these and other actions until He chose him for His presence by His favour which He gave him. He was a sign of gnosis of Allah, action, nobility, forbearance, steadfastness, deliberateness, self-restraint, fear, awe, serenity (sakina), humility, modesty, generosity, openhandedness, doing-without, scrupulousness, mercy, compassion, contentment, satisfaction with the knowledge of Allah, being at rest with Allah, relying on Him in all states, passion, yearning, resolution, natural inclination, good intention, love, good opinion, true sincerity, high himma, vast capacity, noble character and immense good qualities, the resplendent states of the sunna, lofty stations, gifts direct from the presence of Allah, and divine ecstasies. He possessed obliteration and annihilation, sobriety and going-on, and withdrawal in his Master and seeing that He had control of him. He was drowned in the sea of reality. He was given attraction to Allah (jadhb) in reality. He was given power, firm establishment and firm rooting in gnosis and certainty. He travelled a level road and a straight path from the sunna. He drank a clear limpid drink from the wine of before-endless-time and came from its thirst-quenching pool. His lights were strong and his clear signs and secrets overflowed on the horizons. He let a large number of people drink cups of his wine and filled their hearts and spirits with moons and suns. By that, his will continued and his gift remained with them and they remained with it forever by an immense support. That is a favour from Allah which He gives to whomever He wills. Allah has immense favour.

Part of what he was not concerned with is that there be proof and clear signs given for him, especially with the people of perfect creeds and good intentions. However, the deeds of this lofty master have arrived by many independent definite transmissions, particularly with this noble group, turned to Allah, which spreads out as the sun spreads out on the horizons. In general, this master's outward appearance was, like other gnostics, may Allah be pleased with them, like people in their human states of eating, drinking, sleep, marriage, buying and selling, loans, amazement, laughter at what people laugh at, inattentiveness, forgetfulness, asking about what he did not write down, weakness, illness, need, poverty, incapacity, and other human qualities which are not incompatible with slaveness.

By Allah, their inward and their reality is not like that of other people, even if they have the same form as them. Their witnessing is not restricted to themselves and phenomenal beings. They are like the elixir which inevitably changes the sources in reality. They are the word of Allah which is not restricted or exhausted. Their qualities cannot be counted and their virtues are endless. This is so much the case that Shaykh Abu'l-'Abbas al-Mursi, may Allah be pleased with him, said "If the reality of the wali were unveiled, he would be worshipped". It is enough for the one who has not reached their station nor left the prison of the self nor travelled the road of this tariqa to surrender to its people and to recoil from having thoughts about its people. He enters into the realm of the one who believes in Allah and the Last Day. Let him speak good or be silent since whenever a man's Islam is good, he abandons what does not concern him. He profits by submission as he profits by iman in the unseen. Whoever wants understanding is certainly included under the word of Allah-ta'ala, "They lie about what they do not fully know".

The basis of the tariqa of the People, may Allah be pleased with them! is all based on submission, obedience, embracing iman, and firm trust, not on dhikr and criticism. Shaykh Zarruq, may Allah be pleased with him, said, "The basis of fiqh is investigation and precise determination. The basis of sufism is submission and assent. Success is by Allah-ta'ala."

As far as his 'ibada is concerned, may Allah be pleased with him, it was based on the path of the shari'at of Muhammad without deep penetration or lassitude. It was in the middle without excess or not doing enough. He allowed no indulgence in actions confirmed by the sunna and recommended things, cleanliness, purity, recitation, Istikhara, visiting awliya, the Duha prayer, greeting the mosque, getting up before dawn and waking up his family at that time, visiting the sick, escorting funerals, feeding those leaving and arriving to such an extent that he was a rare jewel in his age. He was well-known and famous in all lands. He gave sadaqa every day and night to such an extent that he also considered it an obligation for him, above and beyond what he did of feeding the common and the elite. He hastened to virtues at every moment. He was humble to Allah with every creature, even the one who was a worthless good-for-nothing. He would honour him, bring him in, sit with him, and be friendly with him more than our esteem and behaviour with 'ulama and the salihun. However, whoever tastes, recognises.

"He taught every group of men their watering-place"

The one who perceives the reality of existence and recognises it by eyewitnessing and seeing is not like the one who sees only heaven and earth, and creatures with different colours and names, attributes, languages and essences. Are those who know and those who do not know the same? Is darkness and light the same? By Allah, no!

In spite of that, he, may Allah be pleased with him, liked coarse clothes, food and beds. He liked to sit on the ground. He said, "Sitting on the ground without a mat brings wealth". He, may Allah have mercy on him, was very conscientious about keeping himself free of blame in word and deed. He urged that more than anything. He did not do wudu until the traces of urine had been completely removed and his heart was at rest about it. He said, "Whoever does wudu before he ascertained that the traces of urine had been removed has no wudu and no prayer and no deen". His companions confirmed perseverance and relentlessness about wudu constantly.

After that was the prayer and after the prayer was supplication. He would pull back his hat and turban in prostration, and touch the ground with his forehead and nose. He would recite the Qur'an and separate the Fatiha and the sura for as long as it takes a man to swallow. He would do the same between the sura and the takbir of bowing. He said the Basmala before the Fatiha in the obligatory and super-ogatory prayers. He would say it silently in the obligatory prayer when the prayer was spoken out loud. Imam al-Mazi and others chose that. The dhikr which he did after his obligatory prayer was:

"I ask Allah's forgiveness" (three times).

"Oh Allah! You are Peace, and peace is from You and peace returns to You. Our Lord, give us life by peace and let us enter the Abode of Peace. You are blessed and Exalted, with majesty and honour. There is no god but Allah, alone, with no partner. He has the Kingdom and He has praise. He has power over everything. Oh Allah! None can bar what You give and none can give what You bar. None can repel what You have decreed and the earnestness of the earnest one does not bring him any profit from You".

Then he would recite the Ayatu'l-Kursi until the end. He would say "Glory be to Allah", "Praise be to Allah", and "Allah is Greater" thirty-three times. He would then raise his hands and ask Allah for guidance and well-being for all the slaves from His favour.

The most exact of his actions, dhikr, and 'ibada, may Allah be pleased with him! was the prayer. He said, "We repeated many actions for several years and we found that all of them had great baraka. By Allah, we found the baraka of the repetition of the prayer above the baraka of every action. Had it not been for the objections raised to us by the words of the shaykhs, may Allah be pleased with them — 'Whoever has no shaykh, shaytan is his shaykh'. and 'Whoever has no shaykh, has no qibla', and 'Whoever has no shaykh, is idle'. we would have said that the prayer is in the place of the shaykh". He was like that with "la ilaha illa'llah", recitation of Qur'an, and other good actions because he, may Allah be pleased with him, believed in being relentless in action along

23

with presence of the heart, completely leaving what did not concern him and guarding the obligatory prayers and the sunna. Perseverance is in the place of the shaykh for the one who does not find a shaykh. As far as the one who finds him is concerned, he said in respect to perseverance that it is whatever benefits the heart, like doing-without in this world and sitting among the awliya. He would insist on the prayer very strongly because of what he saw in it of harmony and intimate conversation and the fact that it is the place of the descent of baraka and mercy. It joins all the acts of 'ibada. He said, may Allah be pleased with him, "Allah knows best, but we think that whenever someone prays the prayer with its conditions and adab perfect − provided that he only does wudu after freeing himself of urine so that not the slightest trace of it remains − he has a great opening which has no like or parallel, Allah−ta'ala willing". He used to say, "Seize the prayer before you miss it by weakness, old age, and death. Whoever has missed prayers should make them up. Otherwise, he will have cause to regret them". In brief, the prayer was the coolness of his eye, the nourishment of his sight, and his sanctuary in ease and hardship, in a group and alone. It was the greatest treasure and store which he had. He did not fail to do it, and he was not lazy and did not toss it aside. He did not slack off at home or on journeys, standing or sitting, in health or illness or when he was very old because prayer is the alchemy of the people of adab. It is what transforms the sources. The Prophet, blessings and peace be upon him, said, "He made the coolness of my eye in the prayer".

He, may Allah be pleased with him, used to quote the books of the sufis, may Allah be pleased with them, according to their ranks: the people of striving, discipline, and wayfaring, and the people of attraction (jadhb) and realities, in the beginning, middle and end. He would pick flowers and lights from their gardens, and pluck all manner of fruits from them. He would read some books of Fiqh as 'ibada, the commentators of the Risala, the commentaries of the shaykh, Miyyaratu-l-Kabir wa-s-Saghir 'ala-l-Murshid al-Mu'in (Provider of the young and old by the helping guide) by Ibn Ashir, the Sharh ad-Daghaliyya (Commentary of the dense jungle) by Shaykh Zarruq, the Tabaqat al-Awliya (classes of the Awliya), may Allah be pleased with them, by Shaykh ash-Shar'ani, the Tabaqat al-'Ulama, may Allah be pleased with them, by Shaykh Sayyidi Ahmed Baba as-Sudani al-Maghribi on the manaqib (qualities) of Shaykh Abu Ya'za and others. He also read books of tafsir like Imam Ibn 'Atiya, Imam al-Khazin, and the two Jalalud-dins. No book could hold him from beginning to end except for the Sahih of Imam al-Bukhari, may Allah be pleased with him, and the Shifa (healing) of the Qadi 'Iyad, may Allah be pleased with him.

He loved divestment and commanded it. He wore the patched robe. He said, "Divestment from this world, out-and inwardly is good for all people. There was no Messenger or Prophet who was not divested of this world and on his guard about following any of it". He said, "Divestment with its people is like the elixir with its people. Only the one who is ignorant of it and does not recognise its value rejects it".

The circle of dhikr spread and was famous with all his companions in the land of the east and the west (i.e. North Africa), the Sahara, the furthest and nearest part of Sus, in the cities and towns, hamlets and tents, in mosques, zawiyyas, and houses, out loud, day and night, standing and sitting, in esteem and respect. All in one voice and one direction in repletion in it, in between, and in deficiency, in la ilaha illa'llah and the name of majesty, by the tongue and heart, according to ranks. The hands are folded in standing and sitting as in tashahhud. More of that is in their adab and composing verses by delicate repetition, and love poems about the reality which the sufis, may Allah be pleased with them, use as a technical term for the essence. It was his habit and his obligation. Part of it was his opening and source of growth. His school and drink revolves around it. The beginner, the one in the middle and the one at the end, the seeker of baraka and the lover are all the same in it like the prayer. Each plucks the fruits of his dhikr according to his position with his Lord and his value, except for women. He did not put them near the men. They were by themselves in a secluded place — then they liked to do dhikr in a group, out loud with one voice as was his circle of dhikr. Success is by Allah.

Many people were trained by his hand, may Allah be pleased with him, and a large number of Allah's slaves profited by him. I was told by our Shaykh, the Faqih and gnostic, Abu Hafs, Sayyidi al-Hajj 'Umar b. Suda al-Mari, may Allah have mercy on him! that Shaykh Mawlay al-'Arabi did not die until he had trained about 40,000 disciples. All of them were prepared to guide to Allah, glory be to Him.

The author, may Allah have mercy on him! said:
In the name of Allah, the Merciful, the Compassionate.
May Allah bless our master Muhammad and his family.

The author said, may Allah pardon us and him:

Allah was kind to His slave al-'Arabi b. Ahmad, the Darqawi sharif from the Zarwali tribe, may Allah defend it from every affliction! by allowing him to meet the lofty shaykh, the noble sharif, the wali of Allah ta'ala, Abu'l-Hasan 'Ali b. Sayyidi 'Abdu-r-Rahman al-Hasani al-'Imrani in the year 1182. That was in the city of Fez. He died in it, may Allah have mercy on him! in 1193. His tomb is at Rumaya (or Ramila). It is famous, may Allah give us the benefit of his baraka. His roots were among the sharifs of the Banu 'Imran, the people of the tribe of Banu Hassan. Then his father moved to the city of Fez and died there, may Allah have mercy on them. It is also said that his grandfather was the one who moved there.

He, may Allah be pleased with him! was given the name al-Jamal (the camel). When he was young, he was very strong and powerful. One day, he was going along one of the roads to Fez when he found a camel asleep there. He lifted it up and put it down off the road. Someone saw him while he was doing it, and said, "This is the camel!" Then he became well-known among the people of Fez as the Camel. This is the reason for his nickname, Sayyidi 'Ali al-Jamal.

He himself was a Hasani 'Imrani sharif as we have said. Allah knows best. He, may Allah be pleased with him, was among the loftiest and most majestic shaykhs of the tariq, may Allah be pleased with them. He had constant intoxication and constant sobriety. He joined both of them and was very strong in both of them. Allah is the authority for what I say. He was also among the people of outward divestment and the people of inward divestment and among the elite people of tawhid like the wali of Allah, Abu'l-Hasan ash-Shustari and his likes among the great, may Allah be pleased with them and give us the benefit of their baraka. My Lord – glory be to Him! honoured me with his love and company for two full years. Then I moved after that to my tribe, the Banu Zarwal where we are right now. I used to visit him two or three times every year. It may have been more than that. Every time we visited him, we would keep his constant company to learn from him for a certain period of time.

I took the wird from him, and it is: "I ask Allah's forgiveness" one hundred times. "Oh Allah, bless Sayyiduna Muhammad, the unlettered prophet and his family and companions, and grant them peace abundantly" one hundred times, and "la ilaha illa'llah" one thousand times, and at the end of each hundred, "Sayyiduna Muhammad is the Messenger of Allah, may Allah bless him and grant him peace". It was done after the dawn prayer and after the sunset prayer. After I took it from him, he said to me, "For us, this is part of the path of the people of the outward, the victorious masters, may Allah be pleased with all of them". Then he taught me the Greatest Name. It is Allah without any specific number. He also told me, "For us, it is part of the path of the people of the inward, the masters, the children of the son of 'Abdillah, the people of al-Makhfiya in the city of Fez." When he finished this, he said to me, "Come and go". I did that every day. We gathered together and did dhikr with some of the brothers from the people of Fez, may Allah rescue them from every harm!

I remained with him in this state of dhikr until he died, may Allah have mercy on him! and be pleased with him! By Allah, his reminding profited me, and I recognised who was in a state of dhikr among the people and who was in a state of heedlessness among them. No one oppressed me by his knowledge or action because some people have much 'ibada while they are heedless in spite of their 'ibada. Some people have very little 'ibada while they remember in spite of their little 'ibada and little knowledge, because they act by what they know, so Allah bequeaths to them a knowledge which they did not know as has come down in transmission. They are better than others because the goal is what they have. It is not with the one who knows a lot and does not act by what he knows.

When I saw the excellence of learning and its secret and good, my love for it caught fire. By Allah, from that moment, I based myself on it along with the people of my love. Allah strengthed them in it and He annihilated them to themselves in it since the one who is not annihilated in Him does not love Him passionately. It is as the Imam of the passionate lovers, the wali of Allah–ta'ala, Sayyidi Abu Hafs 'Umar b. al-Farid said in his poem in Ta', may Allah be pleased with him! :

> You do not love Me as long as you are not annihilated in Me
> You are not annihilated as long as My form has not appeared in tajalli in You.

He did not speak by himself. He spoke by his Lord. As for himself, by Allah, he had gone with those who go and won with those who have won. The people have spoken about annihilation, and they have said many things about it. As far as I am concerned, the most lasting of them – and Allah knows best – are the words of the wali of Allah–ta'ala, Abu Sa'id b. al-Arabi, may Allah be pleased with him, when he was asked about annihilation. He said, "Annihilation is that immensity and majesty appear on the slave and make him forget this world and the next, states, degrees, stations, and dhikr. This annihilates him to everthing – to his intellect, himself, his annihilation to things, and his annihilation be-

29

cause he is drowned in the oceans of immensity." The wali of Allah-ta'ala, Sayyidi Abu'l-Mawahib at-Tunisi, may Allah be pleased with him! said: "Annihilation is obliteration, disappearance, leaving yourself, extinction." There are more statements of that nature. One only comes to Allah by one of two doors – by the door of the greater annihilation which is natural death, or by the door of the annihilation which concerns this Shadhili group may Allah be pleased with it. It is as the wali of Allah-ta'ala Sayyidi Abu'l-'Abbas al-Mursi, may Allah be pleased with him! said, "I said: Oh Allah! Open our inner eyes, illuminate our secrets, annihilate us to our selves and make us go on by You, not by our selves:

> If we are by Him we boast our selves above the free and the slaves.
> If we return to our selves, our abasement is the abasement of the jews."

It says in the Hikam of Ibn 'Ata'Illah, "There is no end to your critics if He returns you to yourself. Your praises are never finished if He manifests His generosity on you."

At that moment, my master ('Ali al-Jamal) ordered me to tether the meanings which came to me. He said to me, may Allah be pleased with him, "Whenever one of the meanings comes to you, hurry to tether it. If not, it will escape you and go. The first time when it comes to you, it is very large like the mountain. If you rush to tether it, you grab it as it has come to you. If you are slow, it comes to you again like a camel. If you are slow, it comes again like a sparrow. If you are slow, it leaves you and goes from you. You must tether it up with the senses in order for it to remain with you, since it is like a sheep. If you tether it with a rope, it remains for you. If not, it does not. If it remains yours, it will come to you again and again. It is like that. In this manner, you and others acquire travelling. If you do not do it, there is no travel. The likeness of that is like the swimmer who pushes his right hand through the water and then his left hand, and travels without stopping as opposed to the one who does not pass his hands through the water and does not move. He does not travel." This is what he told me, may Allah be pleased with him. I used to tether the teaching which came to me, but not all the time. I only did it at some times. If I had always tethered it, I would have had more of it, but we do not like a lot of talk since it has little benefit for people. The least amount of teaching is enough if intention and attention are present. If not, there is none.

Now I want to gather together what Allah wills of the meanings which I tethered so that the people of my love can benefit by them during my life and after my death, Allah willing. I was also moved to gather them together since joining some of them to others possesses baraka and favour because gatheredness has baraka and favour. Our tariq is outwardly manifest and famous for our lovers. The goal is to imitate us. There may be people who are delighted by it when they learn of it. Bringing joy to the believers has an immense wage. Perhaps the people of knowledge who reject this path which we have will find a precious ruby of knowledge in it. If it comes to their hand, they will withdraw from the state of rejection to the state of confirmation, and from the state of heedlessness to the state of dhikr. Then we would be a cause of their being merciful, and Allah shows mercy to the merciful. Allah willing, it is not lacking in jewels of knowledge by the baraka of the people of the tariq, may Allah be pleased with them.

I had a dream while I was in Fez, in the 1200's. One of the kings had given me a paper. I opened it and there were many jewels in it. The king I saw was the master of the people of the west and the master of others, Mawlana Idris b. Mawlana Idris b. Mawlana 'Abdullah al-Kamil b. Mawlana al-Hasan al-Muthanna b. al-Hasan as-Sibt, son of the greatest Imam and famous clear secret, Mawlana 'Ali b. Abi Talib, may Allah honour him! since I was visiting him in knowledge. It appeared to me when I interpreted it, that the king I saw was Allah, the Mighty, the Majestic, and that the jewels were the jewels of knowledge. Allah knows best.

On the night of the day I met the Shaykh and took the wird from him and when he taught me the name of majesty, Allah, I saw that Imam, Mawlana 'Ali, may Allah honour him! at the tomb of Mawlana Idris the younger, may Allah be pleased with him. I took it from his blessed hand and went with it to the Misbahiyya Madrasa intending to give that honour to it. When I reached as-Shama'in, I woke from my sleep. I told the Shaykh what I dreamt, and he said to me, may Allah be pleased with him! "Rejoice in much good! You are among the people of sufism, may Allah be pleased with them." I said, "Because Imam 'Ali, may Allah honour him! is their Imam, may Allah be pleased with him! He is the greatest of them, and he is their Qutb, may Allah honour him!"

Some days after that, the state of contraction oppressed me to the very limit of oppression until it very nearly stripped me of Islam. As for the quality of the elite, it stripped me of that and put me far from it. Allah is the authority for what I say. Then I was hard pressed, in need of my Lord. I went to the tomb of the wali of Allah, Sayyidi Abu'l-Shita al-Khammar, may Allah profit us by him! I spent the night there, reciting the Book of Allah, the Mighty, the Majestic, without any heart. It was only with the tongue. As for the heart, I had it in name only. Then I finished the Qur'an from first to last and asked Allah-ta'ala for the effect to be manifest because of my great need and immense poverty so that He would cure me of what had afflicted me. After I finished it, I fell asleep. Then I dreamt that I was reciting the suratu'l-Qasas with an illiterate man who did not recognise its name on the writing-board with a great slow recitation and a loud voice. When I woke at the tomb, I looked to see if there was anything to be seen about it. I found it and it delighted me greatly since he said, may Allah be pleased with him, "Recitation of the Suratu'l-Qasas in a dream means obtaining knowledge, understanding, and correctness among people." Then that was actualised for me by Allah's favour. Thanks be to Allah!

This teaching of mine is plentiful. I did not mean it for one particular person of the people of my love. Sometimes it was for one of them, and sometimes it was for more than one, and at still other times, it was for all of them, may Allah be pleased with them! The only reason that I put it together is that its excellence, secret, good, and merit appeared to me. Allah is the authority for what we say. The man of intellect should only write that which the intellects of people will accept. Otherwise, he should not write anything since the Messenger of Allah, may Allah bless him and grant him peace, said, "Speak to the people according to what they understand." He should also only write that which his adversary self does not dispute about so that he will not have opponents of his fellow men disputing it. Whatever his opponent the self accepts certainly his fellow men will accept. What it does not accept, they will not accept. There is no doubt that the words of the great like al-Junayd, al-Ghazali, ash-Shadhili, at-Hatimi and their likes, may Allah be pleased with them! were rejected and refuted by those who had not reached their station since their words were only understood by the one who had obtained their station. Only the one who is in their domain surrenders to them. As far as other people are concerned, they cannot do it unless he makes them understand and he sends packing the repugnant matters which they have — like ignorance, deviation from the right way, stupidity, heresy, and kufr. We seek refuge with Allah from falling into that since the only one who falls into it is one whose inner eye is dull and whose inner secret is dark. We seek refuge with Allah.

1

Part of the teaching which I prefer for one connected to me is that he performs the obligatory prayer and confirms the sunna. He should also have his body always clean of filth, or more precisely, its impurity, the hair of the private parts and armpits, the nails of the hands and feet, and his clothes and place. He should leave whatever does not concern him and he should free himself of any traces of urine. He should hold on to that until he is certain of it or his heart is at rest that his urine is completely removed. He should withdraw from following the senses and all habits and appetites. He should not think that unlikely or think it preposterous:

> The self is like the child. If you neglect it, it grows up based on love of suckling. If you wean it, it is weaned.

This is what the wali of Allah-ta'ala, Sayyidi al-Busayri, may Allah be pleased with him! said in his Burda. It is also as the lofty Shaykh, the wali of Allah-ta'ala Sayyidi Ibn 'Ata'Illah said, in his Hikam: "Whoever thinks that it is preposterous that Allah will rescue him from his appetite and bring him out of his heedlessness, has considered divine power to be powerless. Allah has the power over everything."

We think that obligatory things are enough for him when they are accompanied by what we mentioned. It will enrich him greatly. A lot of actions are not enough for him if he does not have that which we mentioned. In spite of this, we prefer that he perform the obligatory actions and the superogatory good deeds which are confirmed by the sunna. Allah gives success.

Peace

2

If you want to travel the Path quickly and to immediately obtain realisation, you must perform obligatory prayers and what is confirmed of superogatory good actions. You should learn outward knowledge as it is necessary since our Lord is only worshipped by means of it. Do not pursue it since it is not desired that you penetrate deeply into it. What is desired is to penetrate deeply into the inward. Oppose your passion and whims. If you do that, you will see wonders. Good character is sufism with the sufis and the deen with the people of the deen.

You should always flee from the sensory as well since it is the opposite of the meanings. Two opposites are not joined together. Whenever you strengthen the senses, you weaken the meanings, and whenever you strengthen the meanings, you weaken the senses. Listen to what happened to our master at the beginning of his affair, may Allah be pleased with him. He had threshed three measures of wheat, and told that to his master, Sayyidi al-'Arabi b. 'Abdillah. He said to him, "If you increase in the sensory, you decrease in meanings. If you decrease in the sensory, you increase in meanings." The matter is perfectly clear because even after you have smelt people for a long time, you will never catch a whiff of the scent of meanings in them. You only smell the smell of sweat on them. That is because the sensory has competely overpowered them. It has seized their hearts and limbs. They think that their profit is in it so they plunge into it and absorb themselves in it alone. They are occupied with it alone and they are only happy in it. They cannot separate from it at all. However, a large number of people have separated themselves from it in order to immerse themselves in the meanings by their separation from it for the rest of their lives, may Allah be pleased with them and give us the benefit of their baraka. Amin. Amin. Amin. It is as if Allah-ta'ala had not given them meanings, although each of them has a part in them as the seas have waves. Had they known that, sensory things would not have distracted them from meanings. Had they known that, they would have found that inside themselves are oceans without a shore. Allah is the authority for what I say.

Peace

3

Dhikr is the greatest pillar and support in the path of Allah as you know. Therefore, you must do it as you have been ordered. By Allah, it will give you strength. We like you to stimulate the slaves of Allah to remember Allah — and Allah likes that too. Remind them of the sunna of the Messenger of Allah, may Allah bless him and grant him peace, and put them on their guard against kufr constantly. Always remind them of humility, and to go without in this world. Order them to be content with a little of it as Allah has commanded.

Know, may Allah have mercy on you! that the first benefit that I had from my master, may Allah be pleased with him, is that he took two baskets filled with excrement and put them in my hands. He did not put them on my back like my fellows. It was very hard for my self and so difficult that I became terribly constricted by it. I was violently shaken and alarmed. I was put into very great turmoil so that I nearly wept because of it. By Allah, I wept because of my humiliation, abasement, and degradation since my self rejected what was happening and had never accepted it. I was not aware of its pride, arrogance, malignancy, and pigheadness. I did not know whether it was proud or not. No faqih had given me any understanding about it, not among all of those with whom I studied Qur'an — and I studied Qur'an with a lot of people. While we were in that bewilderment and distress, suddenly a shaykh from the people of great unveiling and clear secrets was there before me. My pride was unveiled to him as well as my bewilderment and distress. He came to me and took the two baskets from my hands and put them on my back like my fellows who had a better exterior and a better state than me. They were not concerned with themselves, and they were not proud, arrogant, or malignant. When he put it on my back, he said to me, "This is a good measure so that you can expel something of pride." At that, the door was opened to me and I was guided to correctness by it. I recognised the people of pride from the people of humility, the people of earnestness from the people of jest, the people of knowledge from the people of ignorance, the people of the sunna from the people of innovation, and the people of knowledge and action from the people of knowledge without action. After that, no sunni oppressed me by his sunna, no innovator by his innovation, no worshipper by his 'ibada and no person who does without by his doing-without. It was like that because the Shaykh, may Allah be pleased with him, made me recognise the real from the false, earnestness from jest, may Allah repay him with good and shield him from evil.

We would like Sayyidi Ahmad b. 'Ajiba to urge the slaves of Allah to be truthful in their words and actions, and we would like him to urge them to be scrupulous. The Path is brought near them by these two, and realisation is obtained through them. Allah is the authority for what we say.

Peace

4

Know, may Allah have mercy on you! that when the faqir changes the remembrance of all things for the remembrance of Allah, his slaveness for Allah is purified and made sincere. When his slaveness is pure and sincerely Allah's he is the wali of Allah. Remember only Allah and be Allah's alone. Whoever belongs to Allah, Allah is his. How happy is the one who belongs to Allah and Allah is his! His words, may He be exalted! about the virtue of dhikr of Allah is enough, *"Remember me and I will remember you."* The Prophet, may Allah bless him and grant him peace, said in that which he related from his Lord, the Great, the Majesty, "I sit with the one who remembers Me."

My master, may Allah be pleased with him! used to say to me, "I like what I hear said against you." Al-'Arabi ad-Darqawi is like that. He likes what he hears said against you which kills the self and gives life to your hearts, and not the opposite. Only the heedless ignorant man, whose inner eye is dull and secret is dark, is concerned with what gives life to the self and kills the hearts. Man has only one heart. Wherever he turns in one direction, he turns away from the other since *"Allah did not give a man two hearts in his breast"* as Allah-ta'ala said. The lofty Shaykh, Sayyidi Ibn 'Ata'Illah, may Allah be pleased with him, said,

> "Your turning to Allah is your turning away from
> creation. Your turning to creation is your turning
> from Allah."

One of the brothers said to me, "I am nothing." I told him, "Do not say 'I am nothing.' Do not say 'I am something.' Do not say 'Something concerns me.' Do not say, 'Nothing concerns me.' Say 'Allah' and you will see wonders."

Peace

5

Another one said to me, "What is the cure for the self?" I said, "Forget it and do not remember it at all since the only one who remembers his Lord is the one who forgets himself. Your intellects cannot conceive of the fact that it is the created being who makes you forget your Lord. It is our own being which makes us forget our Lord. We are only veiled from our Lord by our preoccupation with our appetites. If we were to forget our own being, we would find the Maker of being and we would lose ourselves and the cosmos altogether. Your intellects cannot conceive of man losing the perception of the cosmos before he has lost the perception of his own self. By Allah that will never happen.

Peace

6

Begging and the patched robe are both part of the Path of the people, may Allah be pleased with them. However, we have seen many who keep our company at this time who do not remember Allah-ta'ala as they remember these two things. One of them took the wird from me and then immediately rushed to put on the patched robe since it is the basis of undertaking begging. This was his goal with me. As a means to that, he used the wird which he took from me, and then put on the patched robe. When I saw him doing that, I said to him, "Stop wearing the patched robe and notoriety will leave you. Remember your Lord. You are in such a state that even your candlestick distracts you. Strengthen your luminosity — then if you put on the patched robe or go around begging, it will not harm you."

There is no doubt that begging and the patched robe are both heavy for the self and light for it. Whoever finds them light, should abandon them. Whoever finds them heavy, should take them. He should not take the direction which is light since sincerity lies in that which is heavy. Sincerity is that which is needed. He should not take the direction in which there is less sincerity than in the other direction. He should take the direction in which there is more sincerity. It is like that until he finds that the heavy and the light, and praise and blame are the same for him. There will be sincerity in all directions. Then he will be free. By Allah, whoever is free, is a wali.

I scrutinised one who had left all attachments except for begging, which is the weakest of the means of subsistence, because he had not tasted that which the one who abandons attachments tastes and he had not smelled His scent. It was clear to me that the reason for that was his reliance on the appetite of his self. That was what the self was given. Had he been purified of it, his luminosity would have become strong and his humanness would have become weak and he would have tasted what the Rijal have tasted, may Allah be pleased with them. Al-Junayd wrote to one of his brothers, "Whoever points to Allah while he relies on other-than-Allah, Allah will put him to the test and veil his dhikr from his heart and make it go only on his tongue. If he takes note and cuts himself off from what he was relying on and returns to what he indicated, then what he had of distress and affliction will be lifted from him. . . . . etc."

Your intellects cannot conceive of a faqir who, having nothing at all, is not in the presence of Allah. That is impossible. Whoever has himma which has risen above phenomenal beings reaches the Maker of being. To reach Him is to reach knowledge of Him. Therefore, set out with firm resolution and leave whatever you rely on, whatever it may be, and do not rely on it.

The one who is pleased with the other-than-You as a substitute is disappointed.
The one who remains with that which turns its back on You is lost.

Everything you part from can be replaced.
There is no replacement for Allah if you separate yourself from Him

I have no desire in anything except Your essence – not in any form of tajalli-manifestation nor any gem which is obtained.

What a difference there is between the one whose himma is for the houris and the castles (of the Garden) and the one whose himma is for the removal of veils and constant presence as the wali of Allah–ta'ala, Abu Madyan said — may Allah be pleased with him: "Beware of hoarding as the goal of your striving since one of the benefits of disregard for the outward and the inward is the breaking of norms (miracles). We only see the one who is constantly and eternally respectful to them (the outward and inward)."

Peace

7

Know, may Allah have mercy on you! that once I was with my brother in Allah, the right-acting wali, the Hasani sharif, Abu'l-'Abbas Sayyidi Ahmad at-Tahiri, may Allah have mercy on him! in the Qarawiyyin Mosque, may Allah preserve it! Both of us were strongly involved in witnessing. Then suddenly he became lukewarm and slackened — or we could say that he weakened — until he began to fall into conversation like common people. I said to him with severity and anger, "If you wish to win, then strike and send it packing!"

When one of the brothers told me that he had hit a jew without any reason, rather by vanity and injustice, I told him, "Do not hit a jew or a christian or a muslim, strike your self and keep on beating it until it dies. It is necessary!" My brothers, you must also stop plunging into conversation since it is one of the greatest temptations, and it is not compatible with your station and not in harmony with your state. Only mention good about people since the Prophet, peace be upon him, said, "Whoever is not thankful to people is not thankful to Allah." We think — and Allah knows best — that the one who does not see people — i.e. who has withdrawn from seeing them, does not witness Allah with a perfect witnessing since the perfect one is the one who is not veiled from the Creator by creation, nor from creation by the Creator. He is not veiled by separation from gatheredness nor from gatheredness by separation. He is not veiled from the effect by the cause nor from the cause by the effect. He is not veiled from the reality by the shari'at of Muhammad nor from the shari'at of Muhammad by the reality. He is not veiled by travelling from attraction nor by attraction from travelling, and so forth. He has arrived. He is perfect. He is the gnostic. His opposite is destroyed except for the majdhoub who has withdrawn entirely from his senses. He is not destroyed.

Peace

8

Occupy yourselves with what your Lord has commanded and not with yourselves when someone directs abuse towards you, whether he is one of you or not. If you do not come to your own assistance, Allah-ta'ala will help you and take care of your affair. If you come to your own assistance in it and take charge of your affair, Allah — glory be to Him! will let you take care of it. You have no power to do anything, and "Allah has power over everything."

The shaykh, the wali of Allah–ta'ala, Sayyidi Qasim al-Khassasi, may Allah be pleased with him! said, "Do not be occupied at all with the one who abuses you. Be occupied with Allah and He will drive him away from you. He is the One who makes him move against you in order to test your claim to true sincerity. Many people have erred in this matter. They are occupied with the abuse of the one who abuses them so the abuse will continue along with wrong action. Had they returned to Allah, He would have driven them away from it all and their proper business would have been enough for them."

Peace

9

May Allah have mercy on you! Take that which will kill
your self and give life to your heart. The root of good things
lies in freeing the heart from love of this world as the root of
ugly things lies in filling it with love of this world. I wrote to
one of the brothers: "The cause of deviation from right
action is love of this world. The one who turns to it with his
heart and limbs is the one who turns away from Allah with
his heart and limbs. The one who turns away from Allah with
his heart and limbs is the one who is very much wantonly
astray and a great wrongdoer. Had it not been that iman is
firm in his heart, we would have judged him to be a kafir."
May Allah have mercy on you! Take that which will kill your
self and give life to your hearts as we told you since there is
no way for us to reach the presence of our Lord except after
the death of our selves, no matter what we do. The shaykh,
the wali of Allah–ta'ala, Sayyidi Abu Madyan, may Allah be
pleased with him! said, "Whoever does not die, does not see
Allah."

One of the brothers complained to us about someone who
was acting hostilely towards him with injustice. We told him,
"If you wish to kill the one who oppresses you, then kill
your self. If you kill it, you will kill all your oppressors
with that one blow. May the curse of Allah be on those
who lie!"

Then we said to one of them, "Disappointment, all disappointment is that the form of your self appears to you
and then afterwards its abode is still full and its traces have
not been obliterated. You should always burden it with
whatever is heavy for it until you kill it since the life of the
heart lies in killing it as one of the masters said, "The life of
the heart is only in killing the self." One of them said,
"Love is a bride, and the self is the bride-price. The hearts
only have life after the death of the self." There are many
more statements to this effect. When one of them struck a

jew because of vanity, injustice, and oppression, and told us about that, we said to him, "Do not strike a jew nor christian nor anyone else. If there must be blows then strike your self, and keep on beating it until you kill it. Do not leave it a single snake." We like our brothers to be like that since all faults lie in the faqir with the live self. As for the faqir with the dead self, he is safe from faults and he always sees the unseen worlds. He is the master of all people in spite of them. Allah ta'ala has given to him.

We urge you with every possible means to always have cleanliness, bereftness, and contentment. Truly, none is bereft unless he has killed his self and recognised his Lord. Whoever has not done that, he is not bereft. Gathering concentration on Allah gathers one to Allah. Gathering concentration on other-than-Allah gathers one to other-than-Allah. We seek refuge with Allah from other-than-Allah being with Allah! *"Allah was, and nothing was with Him. He is now as He was."*

Peace

10

Praise Allah–ta'ala for what you possess in the way of turning to Him in this moment. Now this world has snatched the hearts and limbs of people — except for the very rare exception among them. Recognise the value of the state which you have. It is the state of divestment since it has great excellence and a clear secret. None is ignorant of that except for the one whose inner eye is dull and whose inner secret is dark. By Allah, had it not been for its baraka, all of us would still be absorbed in the wanton deviation which we had before the baraka existed. There is no harm for us in it since it is an act of obedience which Allah has commanded us to do. Allah has rescued us. Praise be to Allah for the gnosis of the people of Allah since there is no failure for the one who gives up the means of subsistence, wearing good clothing, and being on familiar terms with his companions and loved ones. He must be adorned with that which adorns the people of the Path, may Allah be pleased with them! We said, "Whoever wants to be adorned, must give up passion and whim." Many of our North African brothers and our brothers in the East, may Allah be pleased with all of them, have been reminded because of our divestment and the divestment of our brothers. Many of them have left this world and turned back to their Lord. That is all because they saw our state which is the state of the openhanded — may Allah provide us with their love and pleasure! Amin. They acknowledge it and live by it and cling to Allah. Whoever clings to Allah has been guided to a straight path. There is no doubt that the one who clings to Allah does not lack Allah's help — or might we say, Allah's delegation and representation.

Peace

11

One only comes to Allah by the door of the death of the self as the People have said, may Allah be pleased with them. Allah knows best, but we think that the faqir will not kill his self until he has seen its form. He will not see its form until he has separated himself from this world, and his companions, loved ones and habits.

One of the fuqara said to me, "My wife has overcome me." I told him, "It is not she who has overcome you, but it is your self which has overcome you. If you overcome it, you will overcome all phenomenal being in spite of its defiance to you, or to be more precise, your wife in this case. It is only our self which overcomes us and acts with hostility to us. If only we could kill it, we would kill all the oppressors with that one blow.

My brother, we urge you by every possible means, as well

as all of the brothers in that sphere, not to be extravagant with breaking norms (miracles) as this news reached us regarding them. They should have whatever kills the self and gives life to the hearts. We are alarmed by what they have of miracles and divulging the realities. We are very much afraid for them and ourselves since Allah-ta'ala said, "Let those who are in conflict with Our command beware lest they be struck by temptation, trial, or a painful punishment strike them." We also fear that their luminous reality may be transformed into a dark reality. May Allah rescue us and them from every error.

Peace

12

Whoever wants the distance to become short for him, and to have something of election which no one else has, should take just a little of this world without hardship or trouble and without being deluded by the knowledge or action of anyone who loves it whoever he may be. He will only have ignorance. As for knowledge, he will have nothing of it. He should take just a little of it from the knower of the sunna who hates this world. This is in imitation of our Prophet, may Allah bless him and grant him peace. As for the one whose heart is filled up with love of this world while his limbs are engaged in gathering it up, he has neither knowledge nor action. He has ignorance. "Allah does not look at your forms or your bodies. He looks at your hearts." As has come in the Book of Allah-ta'ala: *"The eyes are not blind, but the hearts in the breasts are blind."*

Peace

13

The self is an immense business. It is the whole cosmos

since it is a copy of existence. All that is in the cosmos is in it, and all that is in it is in the cosmos. Whoever has control of the self inevitably has control of the cosmos as whoever is ruled by his self is certainly ruled by the cosmos. Listen to some of what its master has of good, excellence, the secret and baraka!

It happened that the dates of the people of the Tafilalat did not turn out well. Then, when they were in the Hijaz — and I suppose they were intending to go on Hajj — their attention was drawn to an immense business. They said, "Our dates are not doing very well. They will only profit us if we take back a sharif from here to be a reminder for us, our dates, and our land. They agreed to go to one of the sharifs, may Allah be pleased with them and provide us with love of them! and ask him to give them one of his sons. Then he called one of his sons to come before him and said to him, "What would you do to someone who was good to you?" He said, "We would be good to him as he was good to us." He said, "What about the one who was evil to you?" He said, "We would be evil with him as he was evil to us." He left him and called his brother. The same thing that had happened with his brother took place. Then he called another of them and he answered him as his brothers had answered. It was like that until the youngest of them came, may Allah be pleased with all of them! He addressed him and said to him, "What would you do with someone who acts well towards you?" He said, "We would act well with him." He said, "And with one who acts badly towards you?" He said, "We would act well with him." He said, "How? He acts badly with you and you act well with him?" He said, "Yes. He has his evil and I have my good so that my good will overcome his evil." Then he gave him to them, and he made a supplication asking good for him and them. The breaking of normal means of profit is contained in that. This is because Allah would improve the land and the slaves by the sharif. The root of the matter is love of the Prophet, may Allah bless him and grant him peace. Because of that love, Allah made the sharif better. Part of his nature was that people could act badly towards him while he, may Allah be pleased with him, would act well towards them until his good overcame their evil. Such is the property of the self, such is the quality of the sharif, and such is good character. Allah brought many sharifs from him — awliya, 'ulama, emirs, and heroes who resembled the Companions, may Allah be pleased with them. As far as generosity, modesty, high himma, good character, and humility are concerned, that is their concern and their habit, may Allah be pleased with them and provide us with love of them.

Peace

14

The fuqara of earlier times, may Allah be pleased with them, were intent on, or we might say that they strove after only what would kill their self and bring their hearts to life. Now we are the opposite of them. We are only intent on what will kill our hearts and give life to our self. They were only intent on abandoning their appetites and overthrowing the position of the self. We are only intent on fulfilling our appetites and elevating the position of the self. We have put the door behind us and the wall in front of us. I was only moved to tell you this because of what I have seen of the gifts which Allah gives to the one whose self is dead and whose heart is alive. We are content with less than that, but only the ignorant person is content with anything less than arrival. I looked closely to see whether anything besides what I mentioned about our appetites and elevating the position of the self keeps us from the gifts. By Allah, another impediment was obvious to me. It was lack of natural disposition. Generally speaking, the meanings only come to the one who has a great natual disposition in his heart and a strong attachment to seeing the essence of his Lord. This is the one to whom the meanings of the essence of his Lord come until they annihilate him in the essence and annihilate him to the illusion of the existence of anything other-than-it. This is the nature of the essence with the one who is attached to it constantly. This is different from the one whose natural disposition is to acquire knowledge alone or action alone. The meanings do not come to him and he would not be happy with them because his himma is directed to other than the essence of his Lord. Allah-ta'ala provides for the slave according to his himma. There is no doubt that every man is part of the meanings as the sea has waves. However, the sensory has overwhelmed them and snatched their hearts and limbs. It does not leave them open to the meanings since the sensory is the opposite of it. Two opposites are not joined together.

We think that arrrival is not obtained by many actions, or by few of them. It is obtained by pure generosity as the wali of Allah-ta'ala, Sayyidi Ibn 'Ata'Illah, may Allah be pleased with him! says in his Hikam: "If you were only able to reach him after the obliteration of your bad qualities and the obliteration of your pretensions, you would never reach Him. However, if He wishes to bring you to Him, he covers your attribute with His attribute and your quality with His quality. He brings you to Him by what is from Him to you, not by what is from you to Him."

Part of the overflowing favour, generosity and openhandness of Allah is the existence of the teaching shaykh. Had it not been for that favour, no one would find him or reach him because as the wali of Allah-ta'ala Sayyidi Abu'l-'Abbas al-Mursi said, "Recognition of the wali is more difficult than recognition of Allah." It says in the Hikam of Ibn 'Ata'Illah, "Glory be to the One who directs people to His awliya in order to direct them to Him, and who only leads one to them when He wants to bring him to Him." There is no doubt that the master of the people of the heaven and the master of the people of the earth, our master, the Messenger of Allah, may Allah bless him and grant him peace, was openly and clearly manifested, like the sun on a guidepost. In spite of that, not every one saw him. Only some saw him. Allah veiled him from others as He veiled some people to the prophets, peace be upon them, and the the awilya among the people of their time. This is so much so that they cry lies to them and do not accept them. The testimony to that is in the Book of Allah, *"You see them looking at you and they do not see."* *"They said: What is this Messenger who eats foods and walks in the markets?"* and more of what is in the Book of Allah. Almost two-thirds or more is about crying lies to the prophets, peace and blessings be upon them. One of those who did not see him, may Allah bless him and grant him peace, was Abu Jahl — may Allah curse him! He saw him as the orphan of Abu Talib. It is like that with the teaching shaykh who is majdhoub/salik, constantly intoxicated/constantly sober, who joins both of them — only a few find him. When the teaching shaykh is found, sometimes he sees that the liberation of the meaning for the murid lies in hunger, and so he makes him hungry. Sometimes he sees that it lies in satiety, so he fills him up. Sometimes it lies in a lot of wordly means and sometimes in a little of them. Sometimes it lies in sleep and sometimes in staying awake. Sometimes it is in fleeing from people and sometimes in associating with them and being friendly with them, and so forth. This is because his luminosity may become too strong for him so that the teacher fears that it may obliterate him as it has obliterated many murids, past and present. Because of that, he brings him out of retreat to be sociable with people so that his state may be diminished and thereby he becomes safe from obliteration. Similarly, if his luminosity weakens, he returns him to the state of retreat so that it can increase in strength, and so forth. The end is to your Lord. Teaching has become practically impossible because of the scarcity of people who have a heart with a natural disposition to follow, yet the wisdom of Allah is not cut off.

We think that the tariqa is established by the strength and power of Allah since it is taken from our shaykhs, may Allah be pleased with them, who took it from the Messenger of Allah, may Allah bless him and grant him peace, who took it from Sayyiduna Jibril, peace be upon him, who took it from Allah, the Mighty, the Majestic. Whoever is sent to lead it, that is by permission from Allah and His Messenger, may Allah bless him and grant him peace, and the shaykhs, may Allah be pleased with them! As the wali of Allah–ta'ala Sayyidi al-Mursi said, may Allah be pleased with him, "No master puts himself in the front unless waridat have poured upon him and he has permission from Allah and His Messenger. The baraka and secret of the permission is what supports our affair and keeps the state of its people in order. Allah knows best."

Now, about what we were discussing with regard to the attachment of the heart in seeing the essence of our Lord. None of us has that at all until after the annihilation of our self — its obliteration, disappearance, departure, and extinction. As the wali of Allah ta'ala, Sayyidi Abu'l-Mawahib at-Tunisi said, may Allah be pleased with him, "Annihilation is obliteration, disappearance, leaving yourself, extinction." So has the wali of Allah–ta'ala, Sayyidi Abu Madyan, may Allah be pleased with him, said, "Whoever has not died has not seen Allah." This is what all of the shaykhs of the tariqa say, may Allah be pleased with them! Be careful that you do not believe that it is subtle and dense things which veil you from your Lord. By Allah, no! Illusion is what veils us from Him. Illusion is false and useless as the wali of Allah ta'ala, Sayyidi Ibn 'Ata'Illah, may Allah be pleased with him, says in his Hikam,

> "You are not veiled from Allah by the existence of something that exists with Him since there is nothing which exists with Him. You are veiled from Him by the illusion that something exists with Him."

We think — and Allah knows best — that annihilation is obtained in the shortest possible time, Allah willing! by a particular means of invocation of the name of majesty: Allah. I found it with the shaykh, the wali of Allah-ta'ala, Sayyidi Abu'l-Hasan ash-Shadhili, may Allah be pleased with him! In some books owned by a faqih from our brothers, the Banu Zarwal. My master, the teaching sharif Abu'l-Hasan Sayyidi 'Ali, may Allah be pleased with him, taught it to me in a different form which is more exact and more to the point. It is that we were to visualize the five individual letters of the Name when we said "Allah, Allah, Allah." Whenever I let their visualisation fade away, I visualised them once again. If I let them fade away a thousand times at night and a thousand times in the day, I would return to them a thousand times at night and a thousand times in the day. This particular means resulted in immense reflection for me after I had done it for a little more than a month at the beginning of my affair. It brought me knowledges and a great deal of awe. I did not occupy myself with them at all since I was occupied with invocation of the Name and visualising its letters. After a month had passed, a statement came to me, "Allah-ta'ala says: 'He is the First and the Last, the Outward and Inward.'" I turned away from this statement as I was accustomed to do and occupied myself with what I was doing. It did not leave me. It imposed itself on me and did not accept my turning away from it at all as I did not accept its knowledge and I would not listen to it. However, since it would not leave me alone, I said to it, "As for His words that He is the First and the Last and the Inward, I understand them. As for His word 'the Outward', I do not understand it since we only see created being outwardly manifest." Then it said to me "Had He meant by His word, may He be exalted! 'the Outward', something other than the outward which we see, that would have been 'inward' and not 'outward.' I say to you, 'The Outward.'" Then I realised that there was nothing in existence except Allah, and there is nothing in created beings except Him. Praise and thanks be to Allah!

Annihilation in the essence of our Lord is quickly obtained, Allah willing, by the particular means which we described because it results in reflection from morning to night if your resolution is strong. My reflection resulted from it after a month and some days, and Allah knows best. There is no doubt that if anyone obtains reflection — even if it is after a year, or two or three years — he has obtained great good and a clear secret since it says in Prophetic tradition, "An hour of reflection is better than seventy years of worship." There is no doubt that it moves one from the world of turbidity to the world of purity, or we might say, from the presence of creation to the presence of the Creator. Allah is the authority for what we say.

We urge everyone who returns from the state of heedlessness to the state of dhikr to constantly attach his heart to seeing the essence of his Lord so that it can supply him with its meanings as is its nature with the one who is attached to it. He should not be content with the waridat from any wird for that might prevent him from obtaining the real Desire.

Peace

15

Oh faqir! The sickness which has befallen your heart has come to it because of the appetites which have made inroads into you. Had you abandoned them and occupied yourself with the command of your Lord, that which has befallen your heart would not have happened. Listen to what I tell you. May Allah take you by the hand! Whenever your self tries to get the better of you, hurry to your Lord's command and strip away your own will for Him. The thoughts of the self, shaytan and every affliction will inevitably leave you. If, when your self tries to get the better of you, you occupy yourself with management and choice, and absorb yourself in close examination, the thoughts of the self and shaytan with all their armies will pile up, overwhelm and surround you. Then you will have no good at all. You will only have evil. May Allah make us and you travel the road of His awliya. Amin.

Shaykh Ibn 'Ata'Illah said in his Hikam, "Since you know that shaytan will never neglect you, do not neglect *'the One who has your forelock in His hand.'* " Our master, may Allah be pleased with him, said, "The real attack against the enemy is your occupation with the love of the Beloved." We say that all good is in dhikr of Allah. The only path to Him is by the door of moderation with this world and alienation from people, and disregard for the inward and the outward. "Nothing helps the heart like retreat by which it enters the arena of reflection," as Shaykh Ibn 'Ata'Illah, may Allah be pleased with him, said in his Hikam. We said, may Allah be pleased with us! "Nothing helps the heart like doing-without in this world and sitting in the presence of the awliya, may Allah be pleased with them. As for our wird which we took from our master, may Allah be pleased with him! we have already mentioned it.

Overthrowing the position of the self, according to us and to our shaykhs and to all the shaykhs of the tariqa, is a necessary condition. One of them said, may Allah be pleased with them, "That which you dislike from me is that which my heart desires." However faqir, you should only say this to someone after you have said it to yourself and made your self travel that way and no other.

Peace

16
Attacks by the self and shaytan do not get the better of us from any direction as much as that of concern for provision. Yet our Lord — glory be to Him! has sworn to us by Himself

in His Book, *"It is true as you have speech"* and *"Command your family to do the prayer and persevere in it. We do not ask you for provision. We provide for you, and the end belongs to taqwa."* There are many ayat with this meaning and many hadith of the Messenger of Allah, may Allah bless him and grant him peace. The great wali of Allah, Sayyidi Abu Yazid al-Bistami, may Allah be pleased with him, said, "I must worship Him as He has commanded me, and He must provide for me as he has promised me." There are more statements to this effect. I only mention this to you out of the fear that what has happened to most people will happen to you. We see most of them have many means – in the deen and in this world, and yet they are intensely afraid of poverty. If they knew the good things contained in being occupied with Allah, they would have abandoned wordly means altogether and would have occupied themselves with His command. Since they are ignorant and have no knowledge, they gather up the means of this world and the deen, and yet their alarm about fear of poverty and fear of creatures is not stilled. This is great heedlessness and a blameworthy state. Most people have this state – almost all of them. We seek refuge with Allah! My brother, watch out for it, and give yourself completely up to your Lord, and you will see wonders. Do not give yourself to this world like most people or what happened to them might happen to you. By Allah, were our hearts with Allah, this world would come to us, even inside our houses, let alone to their outside, since our master, – glory be to Him! said to it,

"This world!
Serve whoever serves Me and exhaust whoever serves you."

By Allah, if we belonged to our Lord, the cosmos and whatever is in it would be ours, as it has belonged to others, since Allah – glory be to Him, made it our servant and He made us His servants, glory be to Him! Then we have exchanged our Lord and Master – glory be to Him! for that over which we are lords and masters, and we are not ashamed of it. There is no power nor strength except by Allah!

By Allah, it is the means of the deen which one should be concerned with in every age, and in this time in particular since concern with matters of the deen without this world is almost as if it had never existed. Yet it did exist by Allah, even if it does not exist now. Allah is the authority for what we say. We think — and Allah knows best — that one can no longer say to most of the salihun of our time: "Do with but a little of the means of this world and a lot of the means of the next world. Allah will replace it for you as He has replaced it for other people." Today — and Allah knows best — nothing will be accepted from you unless you say, "Cultivate, earn, trade" and the like of that. If you say, "Abandon, do without, be content " very few will listen to that among the elite of the people of this time, not to mention the common people. Listen to what the wali of Allah–ta'ala, Sayyidi Abu'l-'Abbas al-Mursi, may Allah be pleased with him, said: "People have their means of subsistence. Our means are iman and taqwa. Allah, the Mighty, the Majestic, said, *'Had the people of the cities believed and had taqwa, we would have opened upon them baraka from the heavens and the earth.' "* Another time he said, "People have means of subsistence and our means is Allah."

Peace

17

This world is what puts us far from our Lord in spite of our nearness to Him — except for the very rare person among us. I heard my master, may Allah be pleased with him, say, "This world is introduced into the knowledge of the 'ulama and the poverty of the fuqara. It strips them of the reality of what they have." The matter is as he said, may Allah be pleased with him. By Allah, it can even strip the Rijal. What is your concern about your family? Listen and hear what we had when we turned from it and turned to our Lord. By Allah, we did not look at anyone with the intention of having him return from the state of heedlessness to the state of dhikr, without his state being immediately transformed to what was desired. That was not by our choice or his choice. It was by the choice and command of Allah. So, when we returned to the world and occupied ourselves with it, by Allah, we were stripped of station — and it was like the station of the wali of Allah–ta'ala Sayyidi Abu Madyan al-Ghawth, may Allah be pleased with him. We went back to the way we were in the days of heedlessness, or even worse still, so take note, you who have eyes! However, its business was not easy for us and none of it turned out well for us by the baraka of one of the people of the Path to whom we were attached. I saw two great men after they had been honoured with arrival. This world caught their attention and brought them back to it. However, Allah rescued them from it after it had snatched them. Both of them then fled from it and abandoned it. That was by the baraka of one of the people of the Path may Allah be pleased with them to whom they were attached. I saw a great man, and we recognised that it had truly taken him. He did not turn back from it and he died while he was in its power. However, his shaykh was dead and not alive. I do not know whether or not it is valid to take a dead shaykh. There is no doubt that I have seen many people who affiliated themselves with the great wali and famous gnostic, Mawlay 'Abdu-l-Qadir al-Jilani, may Allah profit us by him. They claimed that he was their shaykh although they were alive and he was dead, may Allah be pleased with him. However, we think that what they intended by that was for Allah–ta'ala to show mercy to them because of his love and their dependence on him. This is a good intention. One hopes for good from it because a man's intention is better than his action as is related in the Sahih. "Actions are by intentions. Every man has what he intends."

If they intend other than what we mentioned by that, then their intention is like the one who attaches himself to the living who have arrived in order that they should make them reach their Lord as is the business of the living who have arrived. Only the one who has no knowledge is deluded by that. Had that been valid, our master, the Messenger of Allah, may Allah bless him and grant him peace, would have been enough for all of us and we would have no need of anyone since he is the worthiest person for our affairs. No one can dispense with the shaykh in any of the disciplines, especially the discipline of sufism. The People, may Allah be pleased with them, said, "Whoever has no shaykh, shaytan is his shaykh." Ibn Shiban, may Allah be pleased with him, said, "Whoever has no master is idle. Dropping off the means (of arrival) is lack of proper balance. Basing action on them is misguidance," etc. Whoever claims that he has no need of the shaykh, has turned away from the door and turned toward the wall. If we had kept what the Messenger of Allah brought us, may Allah bless him and grant him peace, and our hearts and limbs had not opposed it at all, we would have no need of the Messenger of Allah, may Allah bless him and grant him peace, nor, by Allah, the shaykh. We have altered and changed until our hearts and limbs have been soiled and polluted and we have fallen into turbidity. How then can we not have need of the shaykh? This is only said by one who is arrogant, ignorant, or pleased with himself.

Peace

18

The true lover must not neglect the prayer on the Prophet, may Allah bless him and grant him peace in the obligatory and superogatory prayer because it is the place of baraka, good, and overflowing favour. Our Prophet, peace be upon him, is worthy of mention there and in every noble place. He must visualise him, peace be upon him, as he calls to mind the prayer on him. It is always like that in the place which we mentioned and in other great moments. I saw many people who greeted him as they prayed and did not know that they were greeting him at the moment of their greeting, They know the prayer, but the one who knows what he does is not like the one who does not know what he does. There is a great difference between them. Allah–ta'ala said, *"Are they equal – those who know and those who do not know? or are they equal – the darkness and the light?"* He should only bless his Prophet and the best of his Lord's creation with his body, clothes and place pure, and his belly free of haram food and his tongue free of lies. He should call his noble essence to mind with his heart, may Allah bless him and grant him peace.

Peace

19

Resistance to the fuqara, the people affiliated with Allah, and to all the slaves of Allah comes from great ignorance and dullness since the people of beginnings must err. The people of the ends have no protection, let alone those who are at the beginning. The Prophets, peace be upon them, have protection, peace be upon them. Whoever sees himself among them is mistaken, so we should remind him with kindness and gentleness. If he is reminded, blessed is Allah! If not, our Lord knows us all better since He, the Exalted! said, *"You who believe! Watch out for yourselves. The one who is misguided will not harm you if you are guided."*

Peace

20

The prayer on the Prophet, may Allah bless him and grant

him peace, which you say at the moment of shaving the head, has good virtue without a doubt as the Prophet said, may Allah bless him and grant him peace. If you like to say it, blessed is Allah! If not, our Prophet, may Allah bless him and grant him peace, tells us that wrong actions fall away from us by the prayer on him and other actions. They fall away from us by leaving what does not concern him, and they fall away from us by pure generosity from Allah. This is part of what one must beleive.

As for your statement about whether the recitation of Warsh is nearer for reaching contemplation then all the variants, we think — and Allah knows best — that contemplation is obtained by all the variants if the reciter leaves this world, people, and what does not concern him. It is not acquired with any recitation if he does not leave this world, people, and what does not concern him. My brother, leave this world, people, and what does not concern you and recite all the variants. Then the contemplation and meanings which come to the hearts from the presence of the Beloved will not leave you and will not let you leave since they will love you intensely and passionately, and yearn for you with the strongest possible yearning. What you possess of them is like the waves the sea possesses. However, the sensory has overwhelmed you and us and all people. It has snatched our hearts and limbs since it is the opposite of meanings. Two opposites are not joined together except for the man whose foot is on the foot of the Messenger of Allah, may Allah bless him and grant him peace. He is extemely rare in every age, and even more so in our time since he is like the Philosopher's Stone. Allah is the authority for what I say.

Peace

21

As for the man you mentioned, bewildered about whose
hand to take among the people of this time, may Allah be
pleased with them, and who does not know what to do, tell
him to do a retreat in an empty mosque or the tomb of a
great wali for a week, or two or three. His body, clothes, and
place should be pure, and his tongue should be free of lies
and his belly free of haram things. During this period, he
should either pray, recite Qur'an, or do the prayer on the
Prophet, may Allah bless him and grant him peace — or as
much prayer as Allah wills or as much recitation as Allah
wills or as much of the prayer on the Prophet, may Allah
bless him and grant him peace, as Allah wills. That should be
without constraint or exhaustion. Then Allah-ta'ala will confirm the truth for him and nullify the false. Allah is the
authority for what we say.

Peace

22

Had you contemplated our teaching which we have directed to you, in it you would have found what you desire
of healing, good, and baraka since the illness and the cure
have been directed to you. If you do not know it, then we
will give you another one which has the same thing the other
one had. Listen to what I tell you. Leave your self, and do
not be charmed by it — not for the sake of this world nor for
the sake of the next world. That might increase the hardness
of your heart. That which now afflicts it has only come to it
because the appetites of your self have made inroads into
you. Had you abandoned them and occupied yourself with
the command of your Lord, your heart would have been
freed of its illness. Then whatever afflictions it encountered
would not result in its becoming turbid or changed. Rather,
it would be refined, brought to its own jewel-like essence,
and purified of turbidity. Had it not been that you remain

with your own portions, you would have reached your Lord. Your reaching him is your reaching knowledge of Him. It is necessary. If your self tries to get the better of you, then turn from it and turn to your Lord and strip away your own will for Him. Then the thoughts of the self and shaytan will leave you, and they will only come to you if you turn your back on invocation of your Lord and do not strip away your own will for Him.

Peace

23

It is only fitting that we should abandon the cause which tempts us away from our deen. Furthermore, it is better to leave that which does not tempt us away from it if doing that will be more likely to preserve it. If not, then do not do it. That which you have is the deen itself. We need only the deen. Therefore, cling to your mosque and do not leave it. Ask Allah-ta'ala for me that both my life and my death be in the mosque of Allah and ask that for all your loved ones.

Peace

24

We hope that Allah-ta'ala will give the pregnant woman a boy and his name should be based on the name of the Prophet, peace be upon him. If it is a girl, then I would like the name of the Hashimi lady (i.e. Fatima). All that the beautiful gives is beautiful. Allah provides for all. Do not burden us with anything since He is enough for us. You love us and we love you for Allah. Listen to what I told one of the brothers, may Allah be pleased with them, "Do not burden us with anything since you will find nothing. It is best that you have a little of what will bring you to Him. Allah is blessed! If not, then come to us for Allah and accept from us for Allah so that the action might be purely for Allah from both aspects. That is the great booty and famous guidance, and Allah knows best. As for putting your wife at ease when she comes, her Lord has better knowledge of her. However, remind her with gentleness and kindness. Perhaps Allah will give her strength as He is the Generous, the Master of great overflowing favour.

In regard to the master who told you that he does not find presence, tell him to stop looking at the past and the present, and to be the son of the moment. He should put death in front of his eyes. Then he will find it, Allah willing.

We told one of our brothers, may Allah be pleased with them, "Whoever desires constant presence should restrain his tongue from speech." We urge you not to hurry to cling to anyone in the moment of your bewilderment — not by writing or anything else for fear that you will close the need by your own hand. This is in the same station as the Greatest Name, and Allah knows best. Bewilderment and poverty designate intense need, and Allah knows best. Ibn 'Ata'Illah said in the Hikam, "The arrival of poverty means feast days for the murids," and "in poverty you may find increase which you do not find in fasting or prayer." When it overwhelms you, do not try to help yourself and do not give it life by any means, or the good might be driven away from you after it has come to you as a divine gift. Surrender your will to your Lord, and you will see wonders. Our master, may Allah be pleased with him, used to say to the one in bewilderment, "Relax your self and learn to swim."

Peace

25

Our master, may Allah be pleased with him, did not consider the words of the fuqara. He considered their states. He used to say, "The two most difficult actions are better than 100 cubits of knowledge." The matter is as he stated since we have seen very many people whose hearts practically did not exist at all. Yet baraka will not be cut off, Allah willing, for as long as the kingdom of Allah lasts. The gnostic of Allah, the shaykh of our shaykhs, Abu 'Abdillah Sayyidi Muhammad b. 'Abdillah al-Fasi, may Allah be pleased with him, used to give him a lot of counsel: "Purify the morsel of food. Abandon the company (of people). Avoid the needs of the moment or passion will overpower you. Very few indeed are the truly sincere among you, and very many are those who are incapable of that." He said that in a counsel to one who wanted to visit him and keep his company. He, may Allah be pleased with him, strongly encouraged blocking the pretext in everthing.

Peace

26

As for the brother who is bewildered in his affair, tell him to perform the obligatory prayer and the confirmed sunna. After that, he should say, "Allah is enough for us, and He is the best Protector" three times. "There is no power nor strength except with Allah, the High, the Great" three times. "Allah will be enough for you against them, and He is the Hearing, the Knowing" three times. "Our Lord, give us mercy from You." to the end of the ayat three times. "Oh Allah, bless Sayyiduna Muhammad, the unlettered Prophet, and his family and Companions, and grant them peace abundantly" morning and evening, and he will see wonders, whether he is at home or on a journey. If he does what we have mentioned, it will strengthen his resolution to go in the direction in which good lies, Allah willing, so strongly that he will not be able to repel it. I ordered one of the brothers, may Allah be pleased with them! to do this. He did it and he had a great blessing and clear secret. Allah is the authority for what we say. We would like whoever is at home or on a journey to do it as long as he is alive.

My brother, do not dislike the fact that your self is based on you. Had it not been for it, you would not have found the way of the travellers. A certain faqih from our brothers, the Banu Zarwal, said to me, "Appetite has entered me." I told him, "It is that which benefits me, and it is that which profits me. It is that which makes me great and it is that which makes me mighty. I only possess the overflowing favour of Allah, its favour, and the favour of our masters, the shaykhs of the tariq, may Allah be pleased with them." Faqir, if you said "How can that be?" I say, "Because of abandoning the self, the one who profits has his profit. Because of keeping hold of the self, the one who loses has lost." The shaykh, Ibn 'Ata'Illah, may Allah be pleased with him, said in his Hikam, "Abuse is channelled through them so that you will not rely on them. He wants to rouse you and move you away from everything so that nothing distracts you from Him." The shaykh, Sayyidi Ibn Banna, may Allah be pleased with him, said in his Mabahith:

"Whoever allows his self what it desires,
his idol is then his own passion."

Peace

27

Faqir, nothing is more beneficial to you than true sincerity with your Lord in what he has commanded you to do and in what He has forbidden you. By Allah, if you were like that with Him, you would see wonders since Allah-ta'ala said, *"Had they been true to Allah, it would have been better for them."* By Allah, if we were true with Him, our enemy would be true with us. By Allah, if we were to restrain our abuse of Allah's slaves, our Lord would restrain every harm and abuse from us. Then we would only see good from everything, and we would not see any evil in anything. The one who used to harm us would not harm us and the one who used to cut us would not cut us. We only have this after the death of our self and its obliteration, disappearance, departure, and extinction, and after our annihilation to our annihilation.

28

Faqir, safety lies in fleeing from all people except for the one whose state is uplifting and whose words direct one to Allah because people are ignorant of the sunna of their Prophet, may Allah bless him and grant him peace, and ignorant of their ignorance. We seek refuge with Allah! This ignorance is so great and immense that whenever they see someone who abuses his self, demeans it, humbles and humiliates it, and who is not concerned with it and turns away from this world and its people, they look down on him, belittle him, are repulsed by him and despise him, and put themselves far from him and hate him because they do not think that he is acting according to the sunna. They think that he has innovation. They do not know that the door of the Muhammadan sunna is that which he has, may Allah be pleased with him, and that what they have is the innovation. The cause of this state of theirs is that the sensory has overwhelmed them and snatched their hearts and limbs. It has left them deaf, dumb, and blind. They have no intellect. How remarkable! The realities are turned upside down so that the sunna becomes innovation and innovation becomes the sunna! The blind man starts describing the Path to the one who is just like him. *"We belong to Allah and we return to Him."* There is no power nor strength except by Allah, the High, the Great.

29

Faqir, do not increase your self so that its reality increases. Do not cultivate all that is formed by your heart. Stop it! Do not let your preoccupation with it distract you from your Lord as most people do. They wander astray, lost in misguidance, and are swallowed up in the mirage. Had they understood, they would have said, "The business of the heart is incredible. In one moment, it gives birth to many children — some permitted, and some forbidden, and some whose quality is not recognised." How can the one who is occupied with its cultivation be free for his Lord? How sad is this son of Adam! He annihilates the cosmos until not a trace of it remains, and the cosmos annihilates him until not a trace of him remains except for a slight odour which lasts a very short time.

Peace

30

Faqir, if you love your master, abandon your self, this world, and people, except for the one whose state lifts you up and whose words guide you to Allah. Watch out! be careful that you are not deluded by one of them who you think guides to Allah while he only guides to his own passion. The wali of Allah–ta'ala Sayyidi Abu'sh-Shita al-Khammar, may Allah profit us by him, said, "By Allah, we only say, 'Sayyidi' to the one who breaks our fetters." Faqir, it is not hidden from you that what imprisons man in this world — which is the world of impurities — and leaves him a prisoner in it, is only illusion. If he were to banish it, then he would travel to the world of purity from which he came. Allah returns every exile to his homeland.

Peace

31

Things are hidden in their opposites without a doubt. Finding in loss, giving in withholding, might in abasement, wealth in poverty, strength in weakness, expansion in constriction, elevation in descent, life in death, victory in defeat, power in incapacity, and so on. Whoever wants to find should be content with loss. Whoever wants a gift should be content with refusal. Whoever wants might should be content with abasement. Whoever wants wealth should be content with poverty. Whoever wants strength should be content with weakness. Whoever wants expansion should be content with constriction. Whoever wants elevation should be content with descent. Whoever wants life should be content with death. Whoever wants victory should be content with defeat. Whoever want power should be content with incapacity. In brief, whoever desires freedom should be content with slaveness as his Prophet, beloved, and master, may Allah bless him and grant him peace, was content with it. Let him choose it as the Prophet, may Allah bless him and grant him peace, chose it. He should not be arrogant or proud and exceed his attributes, for the slave is the slave and the Lord is the Lord. The Shaykh Ibn 'Ata'Illah, may Allah be pleased with him, said in his Hikam, "He forbids you from claiming anything that is not yours from that which creatures possess. Then how can it be permitted for you to claim His attributes when He is the Lord of the worlds?" The people, may Allah be pleased with them, say, "This Path of ours is only useful for people who sweep the rubbish heaps with their spirits"

Peace

32

By Allah, had we left this world, it would come to us and search for us and find us as we search for it and do not find it. It would run to us and overtake us as we run to it and do not overtake it. It would weep for us and we would soothe it as we weep for it and it does not soothe us. It would love us passionately and fulfill its need of us as we love it passionately and do not fulfill our need of it, and so forth. Allah is the authority for what we say. It is said that this world comes to whoever is truly sincere in his doing without it, in spite of itself. If a hat were to fall from the sky, it would only land on the head of the one who does not want it.

Peace

33

Faqir, election possesses excellence, beauty, stature, and harmony. It is like the beautiful bride whose form is unrivaled in its beauty. None takes her and enjoys her excellence, beauty, and what charms she has except for the one who has abandoned his passion. He puts hunger in the place of satiety. He puts silence in place of speech, staying awake in place of sleep, abasement in place of might, descent in place of elevation, poverty in place of wealth, weakness in place of strength, and incapacity in place of power. We might say he puts praiseworthy qualities in place of blameworthy ones. This is the one who enjoys her excellence, beauty, and the charms she has. This is the one who sees his Lord – glory be to Him! and His Prophet, may Allah bless him and grant him peace. This is the one who lives in this world and obtains benefit in it. This is the one who is of the people. This is the one who is Adamic. This is the one who is the knower. This is the one who is the sunni. This is the one who is the gnostic. This is the one who is the sufi. This is the one who is the rajul. This is the one who rejoices at time's misfortune and time does not rejoice at his misfortune.

As for the one whose heart is filled up with bad qualities, he does not enjoy election, and he does not expect to see his Lord – glory be to Him! or to see his Prophet, may Allah bless him and grant him peace. The path to that is in one direction. It is the Lutf of Allah to us and him. Whoever loves Allah and His Messenger, may Allah bless him and grant him peace, must purify his heart of every blameworthy quality as we said. Then, if Allah wills, he will have what he desires.

Peace

34

The strong man is the one who is happy when this world leaves his hands, departs from him and flees from him, and he is happy when people blame him and accuse him. He is content with it because of his knowledge of Allah. Shaykh Ibn 'Ata'Illah, may Allah be pleased with him, said in his Hikam, "If you are pained because people do not turn to you or direct blame towards you, then go back to the knowledge of Allah in you. If you are not content with His knowledge, then your affliction by your lack of contentment with His knowledge is worse than your affliction by their abuse. Abuse is channelled through them so that you will not rely on them. He wants to rouse you and move you away from everything so that nothing distracts you from Him."

Peace

35

Our master, may Allah be pleased with him, left you on the pure Shadhili tariqa which he followed. Today you are on something other than it and it has completely escaped as if he did not leave you on it. By Allah, you yourselves are not on the Shadhili path. You are on something else. If you say, "How is that?" I say that his path, may Allah be pleased with him, descends below and does not rise above. That which you are on rises above and does not descend below.

This is because his path was low and terrestrial outwardly, high and celestial inwardly. Your path is high and celestial outwardly, low and terrestrial inwardly. We might say that his path, may Allah be pleased with him, was majesty outwardly, beauty inwardly. Your path is beauty outwardly, majesty inwardly like the path of the common people. We seek refuge with Allah from the path of the elite being like the path of the common!

Also, staying with papers is not part of the business of the people of tastes. That is their only occupation. There is only one shaykh as well, while you have many shaykhs. This is what I have seen of your state and I think that your ship will not sail. It might be said, it will not even move from its place unless you descend lower and do not ascend higher. You should also leave your preoccupation with papers and follow only one shaykh. If you are not like that, your ship will not be rescued or safe. It will be sunk and seized inevitably.

Peace

36

I strongly advise you always to follow the Muhammadan sunna and to remember your Lord whenever your state is constricted and whenever it is expanded. You should also bless your Prophet, may Allah bless him and grant him peace. This is because if you are as we have told you, you will truly be Allah's slaves. Whoever is truly Allah's slave is not the slave of his passion. He is a wali of Allah.

Watch out! Again — watch out! Be careful not to let anything distract you from your Lord since there is nothing in reality except Allah. *"Allah was and nothing was with Him. He is now as He was."* Know that when a man has need of something, that is because of his ignorance and lack of knowledge. Had it not been for his ignorance, he would not need anything except Allah. The Immense Qur'an and the

Prophetic hadith both testify to this. Listen to the answer of the wali of Allah-ta'ala, Sayyidi Sahl at-Tustary, may Allah be pleased with him! to one of his murids when he said to him, "Master — food!" He told him, "Allah." The murid was silent awhile and then said, "We must have food." He told him, "We must have Allah." I said, by Allah, in reality, we and others have no need except Allah. If we are His, He is ours as in the past with others — He was theirs if they were His.

I also advise you always to keep together and remind each other in your Path throughout your entire lifetime as those before you have done. Watch out! Again — watch out! Be careful not to hasten opening as some of you and others seek to hasten it. By doing that, you will miss the excellence of the Path and its blessing, secret, baraka, and bliss because whoever wants to pluck something before it is permitted to him, is deprived of it as a result. It is absolutely necessary that you keep together and respect each other. You should honour each other and show esteem for each other. Seal your business with modesty towards each other. Fulfill the contract of Allah when you make a contract. Love each other and show affection to each other as the Prophet said, may Allah bless him and grant him peace. Be on your guard against being foolish and insolent, against treachery, dishonesty, or leaving the Path. Allah gives success.

Know that concern for a thing is great. We and you have no concern except for Allah's favour to us. The rajul is the one who does not lack strength, is not lazy and does not slacken off. He fights his self. He gives it a little of the things which it hates and are heavy for it until it is annihilated. "Annihilation is obliteration, disappearance, leaving yourself, extinction" as the wali of Allah ta'ala, Sayyidi Abu'l Mawahib at-Tunisi, may Allah be pleased with him, said in his Qawanin.

Peace

73

37

The believer acquires peace of mind by dhikr until even the Greatest Terror on the Day of Rising does not grieve him. What then do you think about whatever trials and afflictions come to him in this world? My brother, always cling firmly to the dhikr of your Lord as we have told you — you will see wonders. May Allah give us and you success. As far as we are concerned, dhikr is not that the one doing it should say "Allah, Allah" constantly, pray and fast, and then, when some affliction befalls him, should search for whatever means he has to hand and then not find anything. With the people of realisation, may Allah be pleased with them, dhikr is based on the fact that the one doing dhikr follows well-marked commands. The most confirmed of them is that he always leaves what does not concern him. That if his Lord acquaints him with Himself — or we might say, with a tajalli-manifestation from his Lord by the names of majesty or the names of beauty, he recognises Him and is not ignorant of Him. This is the dhikr of those who truly do dhikr, not of the one who constantly worships Allah, and when his master gives him a tajalli-manifestation in what conflicts with his passion, is ignorant of Him and does not recognise Him. Understand! May Allah make us and you understand! Amin.

Be steadfast with your Lord and cling firmly to steadfastness. Then He — glory be to Him! will cover your weakness with His strength by His might, and your poverty with His wealth by His power, your ignorance with His knowledge, your anger with His forbearance, and so forth. Then you will live the life of after-endless-time in this world before the Next World and the life of after-endless- time will not be hidden from you since Allah-ta'ala said about its people, *"We remove whatever rancour is in their breasts."* Our brothers face each other on couches. Fatigue does not touch them in it and they do not leave it.

Peace

38

If you wish to obtain what you desire, then bless the noble Prophet, may Allah bless him and grant him peace, even if only 100 times a day because a little bit of action which is constant is better than a lot which lapses. Action is only small if the person is based on something other than the Muhammadan sunna. If one follows the sunna, then only action is abundant. There is no doubt that the one who holds to the sunna does not miss the prayer on the Prophet, may Allah bless him and grant him peace, even if he does not bless him with his tongue. If he follows his sunna and blesses him with his tongue, then that is light upon light. There is no doubt that the one who clings truly to his sunna blesses him with his entire being. The preoccupied person who is not concerned with the sunna blesses him with his tongue alone rather than with his limbs. A little action in the sunna is better than a lot of action in innovation, so understand! May Allah give us and you understanding! Cling firmly to this blessed teaching and may Allah enrich you by it! Amin.

Peace

39

Faqir, only the man of intellect and inner core is rescued from people, especially the people of this time. Always be on your guard against them. Fear their evil, even when they greet you. When one of them greets you, and you recognise truly that he greets you in order to enter into conversation with you about yourself, then you would end up in his power by doing this. Therefore, return his greeting since it is obligatory to return the greeting and go about your occupation. If he goes on his way, then blessed is Allah! If he does not, then say to him, "Employ me for a dirham or two for Allah." That is exactly the turn of affairs which will rub him the wrong way and so it will irritate him. This is what will drive him off. There is no doubt that it is difficult to free

75

oneself of them. Similarly, there is no doubt that the mastery
that people have over the awliya of Allah in their beginning is
the sunna of Allah in His creation. As Allah-ta'ala said, "You
will not find any change to the sunna of Allah." Shaykh Ibn
'Ata'Illah, may Allah be pleased with him! said in the Lata'if
al-Minan, "Know that the rule with the awliya of Allah-ta'ala
in their beginning is that creation has mastery over them.
Then they are purified of residues and virtues are perfected
in them. This is so that they will not place any dependance
on this creation or incline to them with confidence. Whoever
injures you, has freed you of the bondage of his kindness.
Whoever is kind to you has robbed you because of the favour
which makes you indebted. For that reason, the Prophet,
may Allah bless him and grant him peace, said, "Whoever
does you a kindness, repay it. If you cannot, then make supplication for him." All that is in order to purify the heart
from the bondage of creation's kindness and to attach it to
the Real King." Shaykh Abu'l-Hasan, may Allah be pleased
with him, said, "Flee from the good of people more than you
flee from their evil because the good of people strikes your
heart and their evil strikes your body. It is better to be struck
in your body than in your heart. The enemy who brings you
to Allah is better than the friend who cuts you off from
Allah. Consider their turning to you at night and turning
away from you in the day. Do you not see that when they
turn to you, they tempt you?" The mastery of creation over
the awliya of Allah at the beginning of their Path is the sunna
of Allah with His lovers and friends. I said that we do not see
them rejecting any of the people of the Path, may Allah be
pleased with them, the way that they reject the people of
divestment and the people of begging among them. There is
no doubt that divestment is opposite means, and both of
them are in the shari'at of Muhammad. Whoever attacks
divestment, has attacked reliance (on Allah). Allah-ta'ala
said, "Whoever relies on Allah, He is enough for him. The
command of Allah reaches the point." The wali of Allah

ta'ala, Sayyidi Ibn al-Banna, may Allah be pleased with him, said in his Mabahith:

Occupation with 'ibada without earnings is pure reliance and the proper view of the masters.

Whoever attacks means of subsistence, attacks the sunna. Begging is also permitted in the shari'at of Muhammad since Allah-ta'ala said to his Prophet, may Allah bless him and grant him peace, "As for the beggar, do not rebuff him." He said, may Allah bless him and grant him peace, "Give to the beggar, even if he comes on a horse." I said: Whoever lies, has his lie, as Allah-ta'ala said. Whoever changes or alters, Allah is enough for him.

Peace

40

Faqir, the secret action is seventy times better than the public action as has come in tradition. Allah knows best, but we think that the circle of dhikr which our brothers, the fuqara have publicly – standing and sitting, in zawiyyas and in houses, in isolated places and inhabited places, is in the same position as the secret action since this age is an age of heedlessness. Heedlessness has overwhemed people and seized their hearts and limbs. It has left them deaf, dumb and blind. They have no intellect. Fervour for the deen is like that – making it public and well-known is better than concealing it, especially the circle of dhikr. It has great excellence and a clear secret since the Prophet, may Allah bless him and grant him peace, said, "When you pass by the meadows of Paradise, graze there." It was said, "Messenger of Allah, where are the meadows of Paradise?" He said, "Circles of dhikr." He said, may Allah bless him and grant him peace, "There is no group of people who gather together to do dhikr of Allah, only desiring Allah's face by that, but that a caller calls to them from heaven, 'Arise forgiven! Your evil actions have been

77

changed into good actions." " I told this to our brother in Allah, the sufi scholar, the realised sharif, Abu'l-'Abbas Sayyidi Ahmad Ibn 'Ajiba al-Manjari, may Allah have mercy on him. He found it excellent and did not dislike it, may Allah be pleased with him.

Peace

41

Whoever wants to recognise how many of the days of his life have passed aimlessly, let him devote a moment always for his Lord, and not for any of his portion — provided that he is pure in body, clothes, and place, and his tongue is free of lies and his belly of haram food. By Allah, if his action is for his Lord and not for himself as we have stated, he will recognise what we have said and travel with his heart to his Lord, leaving all the appetites of his self.

Watch out! Watch out! Be on your guard against being deceived by the words of the one who says, "I have many moments for my Lord. I am myself. I have not seen anything and I have not left any appetite nor any of the things which I have." There are many who say this now and have said it in the past. Allah is the authority for what we say. There was one whom we thought good and we believed that he had baraka and a secret, and that he was a man from among the elite, not the common people. He was a great man, a great faqih and a very devout person. He was more than 80 years old. In spite of that, when he saw that the state of some of our brothers, may Allah be pleased with them, had been transformed as soon as they recognised us and that a certain intoxication had occured to them — and Allah is the authority for what we say — he, may Allah have mercy on him, said, "What do these people do in their business in order to obtain intoxication in a minute? We have visited the greatest shaykh, Mawlana 'Abdu-s-Salam b. Mashish, may

Allah profit us by him! more than twenty times for the benefit of a plan about provision. Nothing was realised for us, and since the time I was created and was a membrane in the water, nothing has appeared to me of what has appeared to these people." There is a lot of this sort of thing in the world. There is no power nor strength except by Allah. The matter is not as they claim. Had they not been their Lord's and not belonged to the portion of their selves, and had they followed the sunna of their Prophet in reality, their hearts would have travelled from this world and the Next, and they would not stop or be pleased until they reached the presence of their Lord because the one who has the sunna is not disappointed and does not fall short. Good is never far from him. This is what we believe, and we will believe it until the meeting with our Lord.

Watch out! Watch out! Be careful that illusion does not cut off the path for you as it has cut off the Path for many of your companions, some of whom were greater than you in the sunna and knowledge. You must absolutely be on your guard against illusion since it is baseless. However, in spite of that, whoever affirms it and listens to it is deprived of good by it. We seek refuge with Allah! This is even if it is with someone aware, like the shaykh. It is even more so with his self. It offers him opinions and he writes down the opinions. He does not abandon them or oppose them. We seek refuge with Allah.

Peace

42

Faqir, illusion is baseless as you know. However, if you have regard for it, it will stop you from travelling to your Lord, Allah. It will keep you alone with it, engrossed in it, wandering lost away from your Lord. We seek refuge with Allah. If you do not have regard for it, its evil leaves you and its good comes to you since it is the opposite of its opinion, the opinion of the self, and the opinion of shaytan that the travellers are able to travel, and their every moment is good.

Peace

43

The one who is exclusively devoted to Allah has a great sign by which he is recognised. It is that all matters, great and small, obey him, and are under his full command since in existence, he is like the heart in the body, and Allah knows best. When the heart moves, they move, and when it is still, they are still. If it stands, they stand, and if it sits, they sit. If it is contracted, they contract, and if it is expanded, they expand. If it is weak, they are weak, and if it is strong, they are strong. If it is humble, they are humble, and if it is proud, they are proud, and so on. Similarly, the one who is exclusively devoted to his Lord is annihilated in the contemplation of His immensity from the illusion of the existence of other-than-Him. All existence follows him and is under his full command. Wherever he goes, existence goes. Allah is the authority for what we say.

Peace

44

The spirit is luminous and comes from the world of light — and Allah knows best. There is no doubt that Allah-ta'ala *"Took a handful of His light and said to it, 'Be Muhammad!'"* It was. Everything took on form from his light, may Allah bless him and grant him peace, so understand! The spirit is the self. It only became turbid because of its reliance on the world of turbidity. Had it left this world and alienated itself from it, it would have returned to its homeland from which Abu Zayd Sayyidi 'Abdu-r-Rahman al Majdhoub, may Allah be pleased with him, said:

From where do you come, Spirit, beside yourself with
love, ruhani,

Perfectly still on the carpet of might, with states of
lordship?

Peace

45

If you say to me, "Our master, Sayyidi 'Ali, may Allah be
pleased with him, was wide while you are narrow," I say he
was wide and he was narrow. He was tender and he was
rough. He was strong and he was weak. He was rich and he
was poor. He was a sea without a shore because his knowledge was sweeter than sugar and his knowledge was more
bitter than colocynth. He was always uttering the words of
the wali of Allah–ta'ala, Sayyidi Abu'l-Mawahib at-Tunisi,
may Allah be pleased with him: "Whoever claims to witness
the beauty before he has learned adab with the majesty, reject him, for he is a dajjal (imposter)."

Peace

46

The sincere one can wear whatever clothes he likes, high
or low since the state of elevation and the state of lowness
are the same for him. There is no difference between them.
The one who is not sincere should only be like the common
people. Faqir, leave forbidden and disliked things, and wear
what you like. Marry whom you like. Ride what you like.
Earn what you like. Dwell where you like. Be as you like. If a
proof is established against you, I will take the blame, sincere one!:

If a man does not wear the garments of taqwa, he is stripped naked, even if he wears clothes.

The best clothes a man has are obedience to his Lord.
There is no good in the one who rebels against Allah.

Had this world lasted for its people, the Messenger of
Allah would still be alive.

However, it is annihilated and its bliss is annihilated.
Wrong actions and acts of rebellion go on as they are.

Peace

47

Faqir, listen. I was bewildered about a certain matter of
mine for several days until I was extremely exhausted because of it. That state forced me into a very strong need of
my Lord. Then I found the matter in the Book of Allah before and after: *"The matter belongs entirely to Allah, and
the whole affair returns to Him."* I surrendered His affair to
Him and cast myself down before Him. I did not carry it
since it is carried as was stated by the shaykh of our shaykhs,
Abu 'Abdillah Sayyidi Muhammad b. Sa'id al-Habari at-
Tarabulisi, may Allah be pleased with him! "Leave the house
to its builder. If He wishes, He will set it up, and if He wishes,
He will destroy it." It is as the wali of Allah-ta'ala, Sayyidi
al-Hadrami, may Allah be pleased with him, said,

Surrender to Salma, and go where she goes.
Follow the winds of the Decree, and turn wherever
they turn.

I found rest from my exhaustion and enjoyed myself. My
moment was pleasant. Praise and thanks be to Allah! The
entire secret lies in abandoning the self. As far as killing it is
concerned, the Garden (is obtained) by its payment!

Peace

48

When the slave recognises his Lord, all creatures recognise

him and all things obey him, and Allah knows best. The noble shaykh, our master, may Allah be pleased with him, said, "When your inward is free of beings, it is filled by the Maker of being, and love grows between you and all beings. When your behaviour with the Creator is pure, all creatures are fond of you." We said, may Allah be pleased with us, when you are true in witnesssing your Lord, all His modes of recognition will try to get the better of you, and they will come to you in every description. If you still recognise and are not ignorant, then existence and what is in it will recognise you, love you, respect you, honour you, pay homage to you, obey you, yearn for you, be pleased in remembering you, care about you, boast of you, leap to you, and brag while you see it with your eyes. If you are ignorant of Him when He makes himself known to you, then everything will be ignorant of you, everything will reject you, everything will abase you, everything will humiliate you, everything will push you away, everything will gloat over you, everything will be ignorant of you, everything will flee from you, everything will meet you in competition, and everything will defeat you.

Faqir, if you want your wind to be over all the winds and all your opponents, then be firm in witnessing your Lord at the moment when He makes himself known to you. Then He — glory be to Him! will change your ignorance into knowledge, your weakness into strength, your incapacity into power, your poverty into wealth, your abasement into might, your loss into finding, your loneliness into intimacy, and your distance into nearness. We can say that He — glory be to Him! will cover your attribute with His attribute, and your quality with His quality. He is Generous with immense overflowing favour — glory be to Him and may He be exalted!

Peace

49

If you entrust your affair to your Lord, faqir, and surrender your will to Him when anyone injures you, then be on
your guard against helping yourself and enslaving your heart
to him so that the one who injures you satisfies his desire
in you. If you do that, then a secret which has never occured
to you will come to you so that you see it with your eyes
and hear it with your ears. Allah is the authority for what
we say.

Peace

50

By Allah, my brothers, I did not think that any of the
people of knowledge, may Allah be pleased with them,
would deny seeing the Prophet, may Allah bless him and
grant him peace, while awake until one day I met some of
them at the Qarawiyyin Mosque. We spoke about it with
them. They told me, "How can it be true that one can see
him while awake when he, may Allah bless him and grant
him peace, has been dead for 1200 years and more. It is possible to see him in a dream since he said, may Allah bless him
and grant him peace, ' Whoever sees me in a dream, has truly
seen me. Shaytan cannot take my likeness.'" I told them,
"Certainly he can only be seen when one is awake, when the
meanings — or we might say the thoughts — have moved him
from the world of forms to the world of spirits. He sees him
there without any doubt, and he sees all of his loved ones."
Then they were silent and did not speak. I said, "He can be
seen in the world of spirits." After a moment, they said to
me, "Tell us how that is." I told them, "You tell me — where
is the world of spirits in respect to the world of forms?"
They did not know what to say. I told them, "Where the
world of form is, there is the world of the spirits. Where the
world of turbidity is, there is the world of purity. Where the

world of the Kingdom (Mulk) is, there is the world of the Dominion (Malakut). Where the lower worlds are, there are the upper worlds, and there are all of the worlds. It is said that Allah has 18,000 worlds. Each world is like ours. This is in the 'Hilyatu'l-Awliya', may Allah be pleased with them! All is contained in man while he is not aware of it unless Allah takes charge of him. Then He covers his attribute with His attribute, and his quality with His quality. Allah — glory be to Him! has taken charge of many of His slaves and He still takes charge of them and will do so until their seal, may Allah be pleased with them. The Shaykh Sayyidi Ibn al-Banna, may Allah be pleased with him, said in his Mabahath:

Understand, you are a copy of existence for Allah, so no existent is higher than you.

Is not the Throne and Footstool in you, the celestial world and the terrestrial world?

The cosmos is only a great man, and you are its like in miniature.

The Shaykh Sayyidi al-Mursi, may Allah be pleased with him, said,

Oh you wandering lost in the desert of your secret, look! you will find all existence in you.

You are perfection, in the Path and in the reality, oh you who join together all the secrets of the divinity!

I said: seeing the Prophet, may Allah bless him and grant him peace, is not far from the one who holds to his sunna and takes on his character. He is not disappointed and does not fall short. Good does not go far from him. This is my belief, and we will believe it until we meet our Lord. Good is very far from the one who turns away from the sunna and turns to innovation. He puts blameworthy qualities in the place of praiseworthy qualities. He is absorbed totally in appetites so that he cannot distinguish between good deeds and bad deeds.

As for the one who leaves that and travels on the best of roads, good is not far from him. How can good be far from him when he is doing what his Lord commanded him to do. No, by Allah, and again by Allah, and again by Allah! There is no doubt that the people of meanings, may Allah be pleased with them! are those who desire to see him, may Allah bless him and grant him peace, since they break the habits of their self and leave all their attachments. Because of that, meanings come to them. As for the people of the sensory, they do not desire this vision and they do not hope to obtain it since hope is that which is accompanied by action. If it is not, it is fantasy. How can they expect it when the senses are the opposite of the meanings, and two opposites are not joined together. Whenever the sensory is strong, the meaning grows weak, and whenever the meaning is strong, the sensory grows weak. By Allah, whenever people are overpowered by the sensory, they are occupied with it alone, and they only talk about it and they are happy only with it. We seek refuge with Allah. Only a very few leave it. Allah is the authority for what we say. If someone is like this, then by what door will the meanings come to him? They only come to the one who has left the sensory and renounced it for himself. Indeed, if he abandons it and renounces it for himself, the meanings must inevitably come to him as they have come to many others. Then they will make him travel from world to world — if he does not remain with them — until they bring him to the two noble presences: the divine presence of the Lord and the presence of the Prophet.

There is no doubt that this vision is only obtained by someone after he has been purified of all his faults and refined of all his turbidities. How remarkable! How can you reject and find preposterous and farfetched that the Prophet, may Allah bless him and grant him peace, can be seen? Many of the awliya, may Allah be pleased with them! have seen him while awake, and they see him like the sun on a guidepost. By Allah, the aim of the wali of Allah-ta'ala, Sayyidi al-Busayri, may Allah be pleased with him, was true when he said:

The eye rejects the light of the sun because of ophthalmia.
The mouth rejects the taste of water because of illness.

I said: Whoever wants to recognise whether or not the Prophet, may Allah bless him and grant him peace, can be seen while awake, should look into the books of the People, may Allah be pleased with them, like Imam ar-Rassa', Imam Abu Nu'aym al-Isfahani, Imam as-Suyuti, and others, may Allah be pleased with them. In them he will find that the awliya saw the Prophet, may Allah bless him and grant him peace, both awake and asleep, like the sun on a guidepost. It is like that when they saw other prophets and angels, peace and blessings be upon them. Shaykh Jalalu'd-din as-Suyuti, may Allah be pleased with him, said in his Tanwir al-Halak (Illumination of Pitchblack Darkness) something about the possibility of seeing the Prophet and angels. The same was said by Shaykh 'Abdu-l Ghaffar b. Nuh al-Ghusi in his book, Al-Wahid, about the companion of Shaykh Abu Yahya, Abu 'Abdillah al-Aswani who lived in Akhmim. He used to see the Prophet, may Allah bless him and grant him peace, every hour so that there was practically no hour in which he did not see him. He also said in Al-Wahid that Shaykh Abu'l-Abbas al-Mursi had a connection to the Prophet, may Allah bless him and grant him peace. When he greeted the Prophet, may Allah bless him and grant him peace, he would return the greeting to him, and he would answer him when he spoke with him. Shaykh Taju'd-Din Ibn 'Ata'Illah said in the Lata'if al-Minan, "A man said to Sayyidi Abu'l-'Abbas al-Mursi, may Allah be pleased with him, 'Sayyidi, shake my hand. You have met many men and been to many lands.' He said, 'By Allah, I have not shaken anyone's hand with my hand except for the Messenger of Allah, may Allah bless him and grant him peace.' " He said that the Shaykh said, "Had the Messenger of Allah, may Allah bless him and grant him peace, been veiled from me for the blink of an eye, I would not count myself among the muslims."

Shaykh Safiyyud-Din Ibn Abi'l-Mansur, in his Risala, and Shaykh 'Abdu-l-Ghaffar ibn al-Wahid related a story from Shaykh Abu'l-Hassan al-Warqani. He said that the Shaykh Abu'l-'Abbas at-Tanji told him, "I came to Sayyidi Ahmad ar-Rifa'i and he told me, 'I am not your shaykh. Your shaykh is 'Abdu-r-Rahim at Gana. Go to him.' So I travelled to Gana, and came to Shaykh 'Abdu-r-Rahim. He said to me, 'Do you know the Messenger of Allah, may Allah bless him and grant him peace?' I said, 'No.' He said, 'Go to Jerusalem until you know the Messenger of Allah, may Allah bless him and grant him peace.' So I went to Jerusalem. When I set foot in Jerusalem suddenly the heaven and the earth, the Throne and the Footstool were filled with the Messenger of Allah, may Allah bless him and grant him peace. I returned to the shaykh. He said to me, 'Do you know the Messenger of Allah, may Allah bless him and grant him peace?' I said, 'Yes.' He said, 'Now your Path is perfected. The aqtab are only aqtab, the awtad are only awtad, and the awliya are only awliya by recognising him, may Allah bless him and grant him peace.' "

All of this is in the Tanwir al-Halak about the possibility of seeing the Prophet and the angel. It contains more accounts like it which are enough for anyone. Similar wonders and marvellous things are in other books of the People, may Allah be pleased with them.

My Lord — glory be to Him! gave me the honour of seeing him, may Allah bless him and grant him peace, at the beginning of my affair when I was young. Then we were in Fez, may Allah protect it from every harm, in 1182. At that moment, I did not see anything in myself, in anyone, or in anything, except Allah. However, we see the Prophet, may Allah bless him and grant him peace, as soon as we see Allah-ta'ala, and we see Allah-ta'ala as soon as we see the Prophet, may Allah bless him and grant him peace. Also, when I saw him, I was constantly intoxicated, constantly sober. At some moments, I was so strong in my intoxication and sobriety that my skin almost ripped apart and my essence was nearly obliterated. My Lord strengthened me with a strength of which we did not know and had not heard. No one had spoken to us about it. That was that He — glory be to Him! put my strength in my weakness, my heat in my coldness, my might in my abasement, my wealth in my poverty, my power in my incapacity, my wideness in my constriction, my expansion in my contraction, my victory in my defeat, my finding in my loss, my highness in my lowness, my arrival in my being cut off, my nearness in my distance, my love in my aversion, my rightness in my wrongness, my profit in my loss, my elevation in my humiliation, and so forth. Because of that, my feet were firm on the Path so that I could be in this difficult time without a companion, i.e. without a shaykh. There is no doubt that that time had very few charms and many ugly qualities.

Know my brothers, may Allah teach you good and shield you from evil! that whenever the people of earnestness without jest move, or we might say, fumble about in any affair, by Allah, news about that comes from all countries and is famous among the slaves and freemen, the young and old. The matter is hidden from everyone, although everyone talks about it. This confirms what the Messenger of Allah, may Allah bless him and grant him peace, said, ''Whoever conceals a secret, Allah will clothe him in its cloak.'' Understand and take note of what is said immediately. I think that great blessing and a clear secret is mentioned in it. Allah is the authority for what we say.

Peace

51

Faqir, the aim of my advice to you is that you perform

the obligatory prayer and whatever is confirmed of the sunna. Then you should be relentless about freeing yourself of your urine as is necessary, and you should persist in cleanliness, bereftness, contentment, the Istikhara of the Prophet, recitation of Qur'an, visiting (tombs), silence, wudu, the Duha prayer, greeting the mosque, and the prayer of the Prophet, may Allah bless him and grant him peace. You should be on your guard against lying, slander, calumny, forbidden and disliked things. By Allah, if you can persist in this and devote yourself as much as you can, then your lights will shine and manifest themselves, and your secrets will not be hidden. Your reality will be nothing but light and there will not be any darkness in it at all.

Peace

52

The spirit and the self are the same luminous thing from the world of light. Allah knows best, faqir, but it is not two things although it has two descriptions. They are purity and turbidity. The root is purity, and the branch is turbidity. If you say, "How is that?" faqir, I say that as long as the spirit has its purity, excellence, radiance, beauty, nobility, height, and elevation then only the name 'spirit' is true for it. When it leaves what it has of purity, excellence, radiance, honour, height, and elevation, and becomes turbid by leaving its homeland and relying on other than its loved ones, then it is true to call it 'self.' We call it according to its low ranks — commanding, reproachful, and other names. We also call it according to its high ranks. They are very numerous. It is said that it has as many imperfections as Allah has perfections.

My brother, if you wish to return to your homeland from which you came — and it is the world of purity, and to leave a foreign land behind — and it is the world of turbidity, then act! If you say, "How shall I act?" I say, "Strip yourself of the world of impurity as the sheep is stripped of its skin. Forget it, and do not remember it at all. Then, Allah willing, your luminosity will grow stronger, i.e. the meanings will come to you with their immense, powerful, forceful armies. They will carry you swiftly to your homeland. However, test it. The knowledge of the realities lies in the testing.

There is no doubt that only Allah knows the reality of the spirit since it has secrets which cannot be counted or enumerated as Allah said to His Prophet, may Allah bless him and grant him peace, when the jews asked about its reality. He did not know it, rather he could not know its reality. They said when they wanted to question him about it, "If he answers us, he is not a Prophet. If he does not answer us, he is a Prophet." Then he did not answer them until Allah taught him what to say to them. There is no doubt that incapacity is the attribute of the slave. Slaveness is nobility. Because of that, Allah praised His Prophet with it when He said in His Book, *"Glory be to the One who travelled with His slave by night."* He did not say, "His Prophet" or "His Messenger" or anything else. He chose the name 'slave' for him because nobility is slaveness. It is said that the self has a secret. That secret did not manifest itself to any of His creation except for Pharoah. He said, "I am your Lord Most High."

Peace

53
The sensory has overpowered people and seized their hearts and limbs. It has left them deaf, dumb, and blind in spite of the existence of their 'ulama, salihun, and amirs. There are very few of them indeed who are safe from it. Most of them absorb themselves in it alone. However, it has overwhelmed them with its fierce attack, and disposes of them by its force so they are absorbed only in it, and they are occu-

pied only with it. That is all they recognise. It is as if Allah ta'ala had not given them anything at all of the meanings although He — glory be to Him! has made each of them a part of the meanings as the sea has waves. By Allah, had they known this, they would not have occupied themselves with sensory things and have been distracted from the meanings. Had they known it, they would have found that in themselves are seas without any shore. Allah is the authority for what we say.

If you say, "How does that happen to people to such an extent that it seizes their hearts and limbs while they have their 'ulama, salihun, and amirs?" I say: This happens to all except the very rare exception. The very rare exception has no general principle. I heard our Master, may Allah be pleased with him, say, "This world is introduced into the knowledge of the 'ulama and the poverty of the fuqara. It strips them of the reality of what they have." The matter is as he stated, may Allah be pleased with him.

Peace

54

If you want your needs to be taken care of without working for them, then turn away from them and turn to your Lord. They will be taken care of, Allah willing. If you had left them altogether and turned to your Lord in them, He would give you what you desire of the good of this world and the good of the next world. You would have roads in heaven as you have on the earth, or even more since the Prophet, may Allah bless him and grant him peace, said in what he related from his Lord, the Mighty, the Majestic: "Whoever is distracted by My invocation from asking from Me, I will give him better than what those who ask are given."

Listen, faqir, to what I said to one of the brothers, may Allah be pleased with them, "There was nothing which I needed and turned away from, turning to my Lord, but that it was there in front of me, great or small, by the power of the Hearing, the Knowing. We think that the needs of the common people are taken care of by their working for them. The needs of the elite are taken care of by turning away from them and turning to Allah.

Peace

55

Whoever is annihilated — or we might say, drowned — in contemplating the immensity of the essence of Allah can only be exalted by all of the slaves of Allah. They do not exalt the one who is not drowned in contemplation of the immensity of Allah. They exalt whoever exalts Allah — or we can say, the command of Allah. There is no doubt that indifference to the command comes from lack of recognition of the commands. Had they exalted the command of Allah, they would have exalted Allah. Had they exalted Allah, the creatures of Allah would have exalted them.

Peace

56

Listen, faqir! There was a certain person who used to keep our company for about eight years. His state of affairs with us was that sometimes his love for us was strong, and sometimes it grew weak. This was all in the period of time which we mentioned.

One day when we were with him, we taught him a teaching of the heart which reached the very core of his heart, and Allah knows best His Unseen. Because of that, he did without something of this world and inclined to us strongly. Then suddenly the meanings came to him with all their armies. He had not had any experience of them, so they flocked to him and piled up until he supposed that no one on the face of the earth had more knowledge than him at that moment.

He hurried to us to tell what he had learned, as we lived a certain distance from each other. After he had spoken to us and we had answered him, he rejected what we said and threw his words in our face with vehemence and anger. That was all at a gathering of the brothers, may Allah be pleased with them. It had not been his habit with us before this, so we excused him. He did not excuse us. He continued to browbeat us with his knowledge very oppressively. In front of him we were like the robber in front of his band. We did not accept what he said except for a part of it which we found to be true and irrefutable. When he had finished, he left us and went to some of the brothers who had a good intention towards us and sincere love for us. However, they had a weak state, and had no other power than that of knowledge. He uprooted them from their intention and love and sincerity, and very nearly pulled them to one side after their good intention and sincere love.

May Allah be kind to him, he wanted to move us from the state of divestment to the state of means of subsistence. We told him, "If we were to return to what you wish us to return to, we would be excellent in our return since all of us have recognised this side and that side. As far as you are concerned, you should only flee from the sensory so that it does not seize you as it has seized many of your companions, some of whom had stronger states than yours. It is absolutely necessary if you wish to save yourself. Listen to what I tell you and keep to it, and do not keep to other than it. May Allah take you by the hand! My brother, the sensory is very near to you since you recognise only it. Similarly, common people, or most of them, recognise the sensory and do not recognise the meanings, nor the Path which leads to them. Now, if you desire them, then flee from the sensory as we

have fled from it. Strip it off as we have stripped it off. Fight
it as we have fought it. Travel as we have travelled. My
brother, if you desire the sensory, you do not want the
meanings and your heart is not attached to them since whatever grows smaller in it, grows larger in them. Whatever grows
weaker in the sensory, grows stronger in the meanings, and
whatever grows stronger in it, grows weaker in them." He did
not accept what we said. The sensory stripped him of the
meanings which had come to him with their armies as we
had cautioned him. It did not even leave him a scent of them.
Allah is the authority for what we say.

Peace

57

If you increase the dhikr which I told you about, Allah
will increase you in nearness to Him. Be careful not to do so
much that you become exhausted and slacken off since the
Prophet, may Allah bless him and grant him peace, said,
"Take on as much as you can do. Allah does not slacken off
so you should not slacken off."

Fear the tricks of hunger and satiety
Often an empty stomach is better than indigestion

as was said by Sayyidi al-Busayri in his Burda, may Allah
be pleased with him. If the inward — and it is the heart — is
divested in reality then the outward will be divested. If the
inward is not divested, it will not be divested. The wilaya of
any of us is not perfected unless what we have in our inward
is on our outward, and what we have on our outward is in
our inward. There is no doubt that those who are divested
outwardly and inwardly are among the people of Allah, or
we can say, among the people of the tariqa, may Allah be
pleased with them. Their reflection is stronger than the reflection of those involved with means, and their station is
higher than that station. It grows from freeing the inward

and freeing the outward. There is no doubt that the outward follows the deen of the inward, and profits or loses by it since it is the root. The Prophet, may Allah bless him and grant him peace, said, "There is a morsel of flesh in the body. If it is sound, the whole body is sound. If it is bad, the whole body is bad. It is the heart." Ibn 'Ata'Illah says in the Hikam, "Whatever is lodged in the unseen part of the secret appears in the testimony of the outward."

This is what moved us to divestment, and it is that which moved other people to it. There is no doubt that it is a great station. Sayyidi Ibn 'Ata'Illah, may Allah be pleased with him, called it "high himma." He said in his Hikam, "When Allah establishes you in means, your desire for divestment is from hidden appetite. When Allah establishes you in divestment, your desire for means is falling from high himma." We would like you to forget yourself, divestment, means and everything, for your Lord. May Allah take you by the hand. If you have firm resolution about it, then rely on Allah since your luminosity will be strengthened by your divestment from your occupations. When it is strengthened, your certainty is stengthened. When it is stengthened, your himma becomes high. You reach your Lord by high himma. Your reaching your Lord is your reaching knowledge of Him.

Peace

58

The outward state of the faqir which you see must inevitably be his inward state as Ibn 'Ata'Illah said in the Hikam, "Whatever is lodged in the unseen part of the secret appears in the testimony of the outward." Faqir, sometimes we see you inclining to the people of the outward, and sometimes to the people of the inward, sometimes you turn in both directions and sometimes you turn away from both directions. Sometimes you are energetic, and sometimes you are lazy

and slacken off. Sometimes you accept the truth and sometimes you do not accept it, and so on. We see that your
words are the words of the sufis, may Allah be pleased with
them, and at the same time your passions play with you. It is
always like that. Your state saddens me, and I want to offer
you counsel. The aim of my advice to you is that you turn
in tawba to your Lord from the passions which play with
you. You should only approach the one who calls you to
your Lord without confusion. As for your attachment to
everyone, there is no good in it for you since Allah-ta'ala said,
"If you obey most of those in the earth, they will misguide
you from the way of Allah." There is no doubt that your
safety, my safety, and the safety of everyone lies in following
the people of the Muhammadan sunna. They are the gathering about which the hadith of the Prophet, may Allah bless
him and grant him peace, has come down; "The hand of
Allah is with the gathering" since there is no doubt that it
follows the agreement with Allah. If there are few people in
it, still they are many. The gathering can consist of one man
if his foot is firm in the sunna of the Messenger of Allah, may
Allah bless him and grant him peace outwardly and inwardly.
The gathering of many people is not a gathering if it is not
based on the sunna of the Messenger of Allah, may Allah
bless him and grant him peace. One man can be a community
as well if his heart is based on the heart of the prophet of
Allah-ta'ala, Sayyiduna Ibrahim, the friend, peace be upon
him since Allah-ta'ala said in His Book: "Ibrahim was an
obedient community."

Peace

59

If the thoughts of the self and shaytan try to get the better of you and you want to banish them, we might say,
drive them away from you, then turn away from them and

turn to your Lord. Strip away your will for Him and always **be** like that. They will leave you and will never come to you.

Peace

60

If anyone wants this noble ayat to apply to him — and it is *"You see the mountains and reckon them to be solid while they are passing by like clouds"* — as it has been applied to others, he must be content with the smallest amount of this world and he must always wean his self from it and follow the Messenger of Allah, may Allah bless him and grant him peace. He should look at his shaykhs, his brothers, and all the slaves of Allah with the eye of esteem. If he acts as we have mentioned, divine waridat will come to him. They are knowledges by divine gift which flow as water flows by the clouds of mercy, the thunder of mercy, the wind of mercy, the lightning of mercy, the coolness of mercy, until the rain of mercy begins to fall on his heart every hour. Then there is new knowledge and new action. This is forgotten through sweetness and pleasure.

Peace

61

Faqir, if you have urgency in the inward, you do not have it in the outward. If you have it in the outward, you do not have it in the inward. The inward is only wide by constriction of the outward as the outward is only wide by constriction of the inward. Knowledges by divine gift do not come to you while you are occupied with traditional knowledges. The inward is not present for you as long as you are occupied with the outward since strength cannot be in two directions. Whenever it is in the inward, it is not in the outward. Then certainly, there must be inclination to one direction rather than another since Allah-ta'ala said, *"You will not be able to be just between women, even if you desire to. Do not incline completely (to one of them)."* He does not say that either of them is useless. We say that only the strong ones among the awliya of Allah, may Allah be pleased with them, can join attraction and wayfaring, the reality and the shari'at of Muhammad, intoxication and sobriety, or gatheredness and separation. As far as the others are concerned, they only have wayfaring without attraction or attraction without wayfaring, or the shari'at of Muhammad without the reality or the reality without the shari'at of Muhammad, separation without gatheredness or gatheredness without separation, or intoxication without sobriety or sobriety without intoxication. Or else he has neither wayfaring nor attraction. This type exists, even if he is with the donkeys, or near them.

Peace

62

Faqir, the great sickness is love of this world which strikes at the hearts. It is not the love which strikes the bodies since this world is a cause for our distance from our Lord. Had it not been for the love of it which fills our hearts, we would always be in the presence of our Lord. All that veils us from Him is the love of it which dwells in our hearts.

Intention is the elixir. If intention is present with anyone then good must inevitably be present with him. If it is absent, the good is absent from him. No one was greater than our Prophet, may Allah bless him and grant him peace among all creatures, but in spite of the majesty of his value and the immensity of his affair, whoever does not have a good intention towards him does not profit. Whoever does have it gains great profit.

Peace

63

Faqir, whoever has this world turn to him but does not turn away from it as our Prophet, may Allah bless him and grant him peace, turned away from it, is among the deluded − or we might say, the destroyed. How can that not be the case when he turns his back on the sunna and his face towards innovation? We seek refuge with Allah! Had he thought, may Allah bless him and grant him peace, that it would not harm us, he would not have turned away from it when it turned to him. We seek refuge with Allah from being pleased with it so that we change the lasting for the passing. Do not be deceived by something other than the opinion of the Prophet, may Allah bless him and grant him peace. Take note of the man who was seized by this world in front of him! The story is well-known in the Book of Allah-ta'ala when Allah-ta'ala said about him, *"Among them is the one who made a contract with Allah ...."* to the end of the ayat. Be moderate with it and constantly wean the self from it. Then you will be happy. Only take what is necessary of it. Do not choose your food, clothes, dwelling, mount, or any of your affairs. Advance to what you find of it and be pleased with it and content with it. Contentment is the peak of wealth. It is pleasing life according to some of the commentators. Whoever takes more than is enough for him, Allah blinds the eye of his heart. Part of the perfection of Allah's blessing to His slave is that He gives him that amount of provision that will be enough for him and forbids him that which exceeds it since Allah-ta'ala said, *"Had Allah expanded His provision to His slaves, they would have acted unjustly in the earth."*

The best hidden dhikr and the best provision is that which is enough, as has been related. It has always been related that this world is like the river of Saul. No one who drinks is saved from it except the one who scoops up a handful. How remarkable! Someone is imprisoned in the land of Islam while he grieves for one who is imprisoned in the land of kufr. He is not aware of his imprisonment in his own land. It does not make him grieve and weep for others although it is right and proper that he should grieve and weep for himself. How shameful is the state of the one who is in the hands of the enemy while he is not aware of it, and it is worse still when he is aware of it and does not ransom himself! Even more shameful is the state of the one who lives for many years and does not ransom himself. He remains in enemy hands until he dies while still in their power. The man of intellect should not grieve for the captives of the christians until he is no longer the prisoner of this world, the self, the shaytan – may Allah curse him! and passion – or we might say, illusion.

> I am afflicted by four who bombard me with arrows
>   from a taut bow.
> Iblis, this world, the self, and passion.
> Oh Lord! You have the power to deliver (me).

Faqir, if you ransom yourself from the hands of your enemies who are constantly with you, then you can grieve for the captives of the christians, and be worried and saddened because of them. You can weep for them until your eyes are red or until the whites show. There is nothing wrong in that and you will have an immense wage and great reward.

Peace

64

We only like one to divest himself after he has turned in tawba from every wrong action and does not return to it. The one who turns from wrong action is like the one who has no wrong action. He should also always flee from words which do not concern him. When someone is like that, there is no harm for him if he divests himself of his means and clothes since he is adorned with the meanings when he relinquishes that which we mentioned. He must often make his self despair of its passion as we said. Opposition to passion truly results in knowledge, by divine gift. Knowledge by divine gift results in great certainty. Great certainty banishes doubts and illusions altogether. Then it pushes him into the divine presence of the Lord. If he is adorned with the meanings which come to him from the presence of his Lord, we do not fear that he will return to what he left. That is like a tree which one wishes to graft on to another. Its owner must cut its branches as much as Allah wills so the water can return to it and it can become strong. Then it will live, or we might say, it will do well and be useful.

Divestment is present in four things: in fleeing from this world, fleeing from people, disregarding the body and disregard for the outward. The divested is not concerned with them like most people. He disregards them. There is no doubt that true sincerity will lead one to show other people what they dislike in him, like eating radishes in the market, or turnips, carrots, onions, kebabs, salt and beans, sfinges (doughnuts), grilled meat, or Bashshaq 'Ayn. The true sincere person wants to be like this in the presence of the people of manliness. They look at him and feel sorry for him. When the people of manliness are not there, he does not eat that or when he is with people who are fallen-down like himself since that would be easy for him. He does not want to be easy on himself. He wants to be like a dog or less than a dog. He likes to bare his head in the presence of those we have mentioned and other people like his companions, tribe, and loved ones. He begs from people like someone who is in great need of their money or whatever Allah wills. He exaggerates the morsel of food when he eats and opens his mouth wide for it. He wears the short-sleeved hooded jelaba. When he sits, he stretches out his legs and puts them apart and does not put them together. He uncovers near to his backside, not his backside itself. He leaves his private parts covered in order to guard the shari'at of Muhammad and to inform whoever sees him that he has his intellect and to stop him from trying to have power over him. This is in the presence of someone who dislikes his presence and he does not give him anything to gratify his desire to blame and abuse him. He wears a clean old straw narrow hat since nothing is dearer to the people of true sincerity than means which will make them fall low in the eyes of the people. This is their habit and their state. There is no doubt that all the states which we have mentioned are practices with us. They are bad actions with other people.

Peace

65

Faqir, listen! When one of you possesses miracles (breaking norms), then I want him to be on his guard against falling into forbidden and disliked things in case his luminous reality is transformed into a dark reality as has occured with many of the people of the Path. I saw one of them gliding over the shari'at of Muhammad without concern. I told him, "Fear your Lord!" He said, "He is only He." However, his self was like that of Pharoah and Nimrod. There is no power nor strength except by Allah, the High, the Great. It is not permitted for a faqir or for anyone to be like that unless he has been overpowered by intoxication so that he has withdrawn from his senses in such a way that he is not aware at all, like the famous wali Abu'l-Hasan Sayyidi 'Ali b. Hamdush at Zarhun or like the famous wali, the sharif Abu'Abdillah Sayyidi Muhammad b. 'Ali b. Raysun al-'Alami at Tazrun, and their likes, may Allah be pleased with them. Whoever withdraws from his senses into the contemplation of the immensity of his Lord is like these people, and so he is excused and not taken to task since the killer must pay the blood money. Whoever has a self like Pharoah and Nimrod is not excused in the shari'at of Muhammad. He is taken to task with strong censure unless there is no one present to limit him. Then the affair belongs to Allah. If he acts like that without the shari'at of Muhammad, he is like Pharoah, Nimrod, and Abu Jahl. It is the same. None of them is any better than the others. May Allah rescue our inward and outward from every error!

Peace

66

Whoever wants freedom to show its face to him, should show it the face of slaveness. It is good intention, true love, good opinion, noble character, and staying with the command and prohibition without alteration or change. It will show its face to him and not veil itself from him.

Peace

67

Shaykh, do not oblige the one who comes to you to say "Allah, Allah, Allah" constantly, to pray constantly, to fast constantly, or to recite constantly when his state is intense thirst for this world and devotion to idle talk. You should oblige him to do the obligatory prayer and confirmed sunna. He should leave whatever does not concern him and take on noble character. If he mentions Allah once, prays one prayer, or recites one sura, or the like of that, with the state of the shari'at of Muhammad, it is better for him than doing it a thousand times with the blameworthy state which is intense thirst for this world and devotion to idle talk, and absorbtion in misguidance. May Allah save us!

Peace

When I had reached my master, may Allah be pleased with him! in 1188, he gave me permission to take by the hand one of the masters who had been one of my shaykhs in learning the Noble Qur'an. He wanted to take my master as a shaykh as he had taken me. He wanted permission from the shaykh and kept on at me about that. When I informed my master about it, he told me, may Allah be pleased with him, "You take him by the hand since you have informed him about it." I told him what he had told me, may Allah be pleased with him, and the remainder profited him by the baraka of the permission of my noble master, may Allah be pleased with him. However, we were parted when I moved from him in Fez to the tribe of the Banu Zarwal where we had left our ancestors — may Allah bless it!

The master remained near Fez al-Bali. When I had resolved to travel to this tribe, I said to my master, "I have no one there with whom to discuss the business of the Path and the business is only established by that." He told me, "Beget him" as if he, may Allah be pleased with him, intended that the birth of meaning would be by my hand or that he already saw it. I repeated that to him again. He told me, "Beget him!" By the baraka of his permission and his secret, a man came to me — may Allah make many like him in Islam! As soon as I saw him and he saw me, Allah finished his business, i.e. he obtained the station of annihilation and going-on at first glance. Allah is the authority for what we say. The excellence of permission and its secret was clear to me, and that banished all doubts and illusions from me. Praise and thanks be to Allah!

Then my self yearned for permission from Allah and His Messenger, may Allah bless him and grant him peace. I had a very strong need for this. One day, when I was in a deserted place in the middle of a forest, I was intoxicated/sober, utterly absorbed in my intoxication and utterly absorbed in

105

my sobriety. I joined both of them and was very strong in them. Then I heard myself addressed from my entire essence: "Remind. The Reminder profits the believers." My heart was reassured and at peace. I was certain that I had been spoken to by Allah and His Messenger, may Allah bless him and grant him peace, since I was in the two noble presences of the Prophet. By Allah, that was a breaking of norms which came from my entire essence. There is no "how" by which it is recognised. It is recognised by whoever Allah causes to recognise it. Sometimes Allah — glory be to Him! addresses His slave from himself as happened to me and others. The lofty shaykh, the wali of Allah-ta'ala, Sayyidi abu'l-Hasan ash-Shushtari, may Allah be pleased with him, said:

> I heard words from my essence from a near place,
> My life! You are present in my essence, not absent.

Sometimes He speaks to him from his fellow men. Sometimes it is from inanimate things, sometimes from animals, sometimes from the air, sometimes from one direction, and sometimes from all directions. That is only recognised by the one whom Allah causes to recognise it. Only the one strengthened by Allah can bear it. The noble ayat with which I had been addressed from my entire essence remained mixed with flesh and blood for about ten days or more. Allah is the authority for what we say.

When this permission had come to me, the believers came immediately. As soon as they saw me and I saw them, they remembered and we remembered, we benefited from them and they benefited from us, they profited from us and we from them. There was whatever there was of good, the secret, excellence, baraka, and concern. That was among the tribe of Zarwal. Praise and thanks belong to Allah!

Peace

69

As far as the faqir who does not learn from the teacher is
concerned, the reason for that is that he has not travelled
from the sensory world to the world of meanings. Had he
been in the world of meanings, he would have learned since
none learns except the one who exists. He is the one who is
created in the meanings. As for the non-existent, how can
one conceive of him learning while he is in non-existence?
People have said: When it is created, we give it a name.

Faqir, if you want to teach whomever you like, then be
instrumental in his birth in the meanings until he obtains
them. When he obtains them, then teach him, and he will
teach you. I searched very hard among my brothers, the
fuqara and did not find any among them who had left the
sensory world for the world of meaning except for the rare
exception. The rare exception has no general principle. By
Allah, their state grieved me deeply. Then I searched to see
what was the reason which stopped the meanings from
coming to them in spite of the existence of their divestment
from means, clothes, loved ones, and companions. I dis-
covered that it was their love for this world and their reliance on it. They – may Allah be kind to them – after they
had been divested as we mentioned, were extravagant in
begging! Had it not been for their love of this world and their
reliance on it, they would not have been extravagant in it.
The truthful might be extravagant while he has no need of it
since there is no need for extravagance in the one whose
love of this world has departed from his heart.

Faqir, take note! You can tell whomever you like from
me that if you want the meanings to come to you as they
have come to others of the people of true sincerity or even
more than them, then put aside this world and all your appetites. Then they will come to you with their immense,
powerful, forceful armies. They will take you to them by

force in spite of yourself. There is no doubt that Allah has made you and everyone part of the meanings as He gave the sea waves. Had they known that, nothing would have distracted them from the meanings. Had they known them, they would have found within themselves seas without any shore. Allah is the authority for what we say.

Peace

70

Faqir, always have high himma and you will see wonders. If you say, "How is that?" I say that the Sa'di Sultan, Mawlay Ahmad adh-Dhahabi, said to the famous wali, Sayyidi Abu'sh-Shita' al-Khammar, may Allah profit us by him, "Shall I give you a sanctuary which stretches from Wadi Asbu to Wadi Wargha?" He told him, "Allah-ta'ala has given me a sanctuary which extends from the Throne to the earth itself." The wali of Allah-ta'ala, Sayyidi 'Abdu's-Salam al-Aghzawi, may Allah be pleased with him, when Sayyiduna al-Khidr, peace be upon him, greeted him, returned the greeting to him and went on about his business. He only turned to him to return the greeting. Then he said to him, "Do you recognise me?" He said, "Who are you?" He told him, "I am al-Khidr." He said to him, "What do you want?" Such is high himma. If it is not like that, it is not high.

Peace

71

I said to one of the pretenders whose hearts are filled with rancour, envy, pride, showing-off, vanity, miserliness, greed, and other bad qualities: Have a sound heart and decrease the amount of your prayers and all your actions. Only perform the obligatory and confirmed sunna. Then you will be increased in something. A lot of your actions have no profit for you when your heart is malignant, no matter what you do. You will have profit from a sound breast along with what Allah has obliged you to do. If you have that, then a little bit of action is enough for you. Fasting all day, praying all night, and constant 'ibada will have no profit for you if your heart is sick and you are absorbed in what Allah dislikes in you. We seek refuge with Allah from your state and the state of those like you!

Peace

72

I have seen many fuqara, many of the people of knowledge, and many people who were engaged in a lot of 'ibada. In spite of this, they did not have anything of the secret appear to them as it appears to the one who does only a little since only the ignorant and disappointed lack any of the secret. It was clear to me that that came from their hesitation in turning to their Lord since, may Allah be kind to them! after they had turned away from passion and turned to their Lord with their bodies, their hearts remained with the same heedlessness. It is a miserable state. We seek refuge with Allah! Had their hearts been in harmony with their limbs, they would have seen secrets, benefits, and the breaking of norms.

Peace

73

Know, faqir, that I wrote to some of the fuqaha who rejected what we had of the state of poverty: "Peace be upon you. May Allah be kind to you, and may Allah rescue you and us from every misguidance! It has reached us that you have abandoned your faults and occupied yourselves with the faults of others. Do you not know that it says in the Book of

Allah-ta'ala: *'Do you command people to dutiful obedience'* ...... to the end of the ayat. Or perhaps you have no faults? Far be it from the one who is free of faults that he should see other than the Beloved! Only the defective sees the fault. What fault is greater than seeing others who you only see day and night? There is no doubt that both the comely person and the ugly one only see their own face among people. Be comely, you will see comeliness. Be ugly, you will see ugliness. Shaykh al-Busayri said in his Burda, may Allah be pleased with him:

> The eye may reject the light of the sun because of
> ophthalmia,
>> And the mouth may reject the taste of water because
>> of illness.

"This is a valid measure. By Allah, if we were ill, water would be bitter in our mouths. If the faces of our meanings were good, then our sensory faces could only be good. People are like a mirror for those who look at them. Whoever has a comely face sees a comely face in them. Whoever has an ugly face sees an ugly face in them. It is not possible for the comely to see who is ugly as it is not possible for the ugly to see one who is comely. Because of this, Shaykh Abu'l-Hasan 'Ali al-Kharrubi, may Allah be pleased with him, said, "Say to those who see what they reject in us, 'Because of the purity of our drink, you see your faces in us.' "

"Fuqaha, we were like you, or worse than you, when we found the states of people ugly and our states excellent. A lot of people were like us — like Shaykh 'Izzu'd-din b. 'Abdi's-Salam, Shaykh al-Ghazali, Shaykh Ibn 'Ata'Illah, Shaykh Ibn al-'Arabi al-Hatimi, Shaykh Abu'l-Hasan ash-Shadhili, and their likes, may Allah be pleased with them. Then Allah opened their inner eyes and illuminated their secrets and removed the veil of illusion from them. They looked for ugliness and did not find any report of it. Listen, fuqaha, to what one of them said,

Had I been obliged to see other-than-Him, I would not
have been able to do it since there is nothing else with
Him, so how can I see it with Him!

They said:

Since I have recognised the divinity, I do not see other-
than-Him. Similarly, other is forbidden with us.

Since I have gathered together what I feared would
separate, today I have arrived gathered.

They said:

Those who are realised refuse to see other-than-Allah.

They said:

Say: 'Allah!' and leave existence and what it contains if
you have any doubts about reaching perfection

If you are exact, all except Allah is non-existence in detail
and in sum.

Know that had it not been for Him, you and all the worlds
would have been obliteration and extinction.

Had it not been for Him, the existence of one whose existence is not by his own essence would have been the impossible itself.

The gnostics are annihilated and do not see anything
except the Great, the Exalted.

They see that other-than-Him in reality is perishing in the
present, past, and future.

"The matter of dhikr is vast, and the overflowing favour
of Allah, His generosity, openhandedness, and mercy is vaster
and vaster still. What is it that you find that you reject, dislike,
abhor, and find heavy except the dhikr of Allah-ta'ala in the
houses of Allah which Allah, glory be to Him! has commanded in His Book? He said, may He be exalted! *'In houses
Allah has allowed to be raised up ....'* to the end of the ayat.
Or are you worshipping your Lord while the one you reject
tempts you? If this is the case, then do not accept it from the

one who does it. Turn him aside and strike him in the face. Only the ignorant and the one who is pleased with himself think well of him. We do not see anyone in your area worshipping Allah as you claim. Rather we see that some of the students who recite Qur'an do not pray most of the time. As for the use of tobacco, hashish, sodomy, slander, calumny, and the like of that which our Lord has forbidden us, we will not say anything to you or them about that. We do not see you hastening to anything like you hasten to talking about the people of the tariqa, may Allah be pleased with them. It has become a general necessity for you in all lands. The people who are affiliated with Allah are those who turn in tawba from that to Allah. Do not be occupied with them and their faults as if Allah-ta'ala had made you secure from faults. It is far from that! Only the people who are losers feel secure from the device of Allah.

"The upshot is that if you desire counsel and safety from disgrace, then turn to Allah, your Lord in tawba from your wrong action since Allah-ta'ala said, *'Turn in tawba to Allah altogether....'* to the end of the ayat. The Prophet, may Allah bless him and grant him peace, said, 'Turn in tawba. I turn in tawba every day 70 times.' Another hadith has 100 times. This was in spite of the fact that Allah-ta'ala had forgiven him his wrong actions, past and future. We see that he, peace be upon him, was rising through the s tions. Whenever he reached a station, he found one higher than the one before it, even if that station was high, i.e. a station of security. Would that we could reach a station such as he, may Allah bless him and grant him peace, had left. The good deeds of the dutifully obedient are the bad deeds of the best. The good deeds of the best are the bad deeds of the near. You must absolutely turn in tawba to Allah and return misdeeds to their people. You should avoid lying, slander, calumny, and all forbidden and disliked things. You must be aware of the repulsive things which are in your hearts and which Allah has forbidden you, inwardly and outwardly. Heedless students, what you have outwardly is what we have mentioned and clarified.

"We will now mention the inward — pride, showing-off, envy, vanity, slander, calumny, deviation from the right way, stupidity, greed, miserliness, and other repulsive qualities with which it is not permitted for the believer to fill his heart. It is permitted for him to purify his heart of them by night before day, and while sitting before standing if he can do that. If not, he must search for a doctor throughout all of North Africa, in the cities and the deserts. If he finds him, he should not leave him and should cling to him until he purifies his heart for him of the foulness which has afflicted it and of all his faults. If he does not find him in North Africa, he should set out for the East — may Allah guard it! Immediately. Do not dally until you can go with the hajjis. Go quickly there so that tawba will not be delayed. Then you would need yet another tawba since delaying tawba is a wrong action demanding tawba. The one who turns in tawba from wrong actions is like the one who has no wrong actions. It is as the Prophet, may Allah bless him and grant him peace, said in the Book of Allah, *'Your Lord has prescribed mercy for Himself....'* to the end of the ayat. *'He is the One who accepts tawba from His slaves....'* to the end of the ayat."

Peace

74

For the people of the station of annihilation, may Allah be pleased with them, the essence of Allah is the source of the attributes because when they are annihilated, they only see the essence. When they witness it, they do not see anything except it. For that reason, they are called dhatiyyun (essential). The essence of Allah has such perfection, excellence, and beauty that all intellects among the elite are bewildered in it, let alone that of common people. This is because it becomes progressively finer and more subtle until it disappears through the sheer intensity of its subtletly and fineness. When it disappears, it says to itself, "My perfection excellence, beauty, radiance, nobility, height and elevation have no end. It has disappeared and is not manifested. Perfection is not perfection being perfect unless it is present and absent, subtle and dense, near and far, beautiful and majestic, and so forth." It desired to manifest this and said, "How shall I manifest it?" while it already knew that. It said, "I shall become dense and variegated." It did that. These are the essences, or we might say, the forms which are present as such and absent as such, dense and subtle, high and low, near and far, meaning and sensory, beautiful and majestic. They are all essence. If you like, you can say, they are its form in which it manifests its beauty. It only manifests it in itself since there is only it, the Essence, and there is nothing except it. One of the shaykhs of the tariqa from our brothers in the East, may Allah be pleased with them, said:

All is beauty, the beauty of Allah. There is no doubt about it.
Doubt overcomes the blotches of the intellect
Oh you who come to the source, doubt vanishes after realisation
The essence is the source of the attributes. There is no doubt about the meanings.

More has been said in this meaning by the shaykhs of the Path in the East and West, may Allah be pleased with them.

Faqir, if you understand our indication and allusion, blessed is Allah! If not, then examine your attribute, and Allah will help you with His attribute. May Allah have mercy on you! Know that majesty is the essence and beauty is the attributes. The essence is the source of the attributes as it is with all of the people of the station of annihilation, may Allah be pleased with them, as we have said. It is not the case with others, our masters, the people of outward knowledge, may Allah be pleased with them. There is no doubt that the outward is pure majesty and the inward is pure beauty. However, the outward lends some of its majesty to the inward as the inward lends some of its beauty to the outward. The outward becomes majestic-beautiful, and the inward becomes beautiful-majestic. However, the majesty of the outward is real and its beauty is borrowed, and the beauty of the inward is real and its majesty is borrowed. This is only recognised by the one who has plunged into the knowledge of the people as we have plunged, and who has immersed himself in it as we have immersed ourselves, and been annihilated in it as we have been annihilated in it, may Allah be pleased with us.

Faqir, listen to what the Shaykh Muhammad b. Ahmad al-Ansari as-Sahili said in his book, Bughyat as-Saliki fi ashraf al-Masalik (The goal of the Wayfarer in the noblest paths): "Know, may Allah illuminate our hearts with the lights of gnoses and carry us on the road of every gnostic wali!, that gnosis is the end of the station of ihsan and the last of its stages. Allah-ta'ala said. 'They have not valued Allah with His proper value,'' i.e. recognised Him as He should be recognised. He, may He be exalted! said, 'You see their eyes overflowing with tears by what they recognise of the Truth.' The Prophet, may Allah bless him and grant him peace, said, 'The support of the house is its foundation. The support of the deen is recognition of Allah.' By recognition/gnosis here, we mean making the state of the contemplator firm while it is accompanied by the administration of justice and following wisdom. This is not the usage of the people of fiqh. They think that recognition is knowledge of rules. As a whole, recognition can be validly applied to knowledge such as it is, its most particular requirement is gnosis of Allah–ta'ala by the meanings of the names and the attributes without separation between the attributes and the essence. It is gnosis which issues from the source of gatheredness, is taken from complete pure sincerity, and is given expression from the secret being constantly with Allah, the Mighty, the Majestic."

He says, may Allah be pleased with him, "If this is established, then the gnosis which is indicated is the goal of the
wayfarers and the end of those who travel to Allah-ta'ala,
and it is the attribute for which they exchange themselves for
Allah, the Majestic, the Mighty as a price. If today nothing is
left of them except their name alone and not the named, we
still certainly continue to mention their states and exercises
so that by them you will know how much we have missed
from Allah-ta'ala and you will be acquainted with some of it
according to what the near have gone ahead to, what the
gnostics have obtained, and what the incapable and students
have denied. *We belong to Allah, and to Him we return.'*"

Peace

75

Faqir, listen! I want whoever follows my example to per-
form the obligatory prayer and confirmed sunna, and to visit
the shaykhs of the tariqa like Imam al-Ghazzali Najziratu'l-
Andalus, Sayyidi Ibn al-'Arabi al-Ma'afiri, Sayyidi 'Ali b.
Harazim, Sayyidi 'Abdullah at-Tawdi, our master Sayyidi
'Ali al-Jamal and his shaykhs, the sons of Ibn 'Abdillah, and
their shaykhs, the masters of Fez. All of these last are in Fez.
Similarly, one should visit Shaykh Abu Ya'za al-Maghribi at
Taghiya, Abu Madyan al-Ghawth at Tlemcen, Mawlana
'Abdu's-Salam b. Mashish at Jabal al-'Alam, and their likes
among the people in the West and others. They are many,
may Allah be pleased with them. They are only recognised
by the one who has reached their station or who finds their
track and it guides him to them. The track is a pointer to the
one who left it. However, this is only recognised by the sincere one who has inner core among the people of knowledge
and taqwa, may Allah be pleased with them. None except
them recognise it.

There is no doubt that the common people make the
people of their time into shaykhs. Then they leave them in

their treachery, i.e. in the appetites of their selves. Yet they think that tneir shaykhs are tne shaykhs of the tariqa. They do not recognise them at all. They are part of the common people who are the people of practices. Generally they put their station above their station, and they consider them to have the office of qutb. They will not accept anyone else at all having the office of the qutb, no matter what you say to them. Do not concern yourself with talking to them about that. No, by Allah, the matter is not as they believe. It is the opposite of what they believe. There is no doubt that gold is only recognised by its people. As far as others are concerned, sometimes they find it lying on the ground and do not pick it up and pay no attention to it because they suppose that it is brass, copper, or fools-gold. Sometimes they find brass, copper, or fools-gold and suppose that it is gold. They take it away and consider it dearer than their own treasure. This is generally their state at all times. How far it is from the real business! This is because the shaykhs of the tariqa, as we mentioned in our teaching, are such that they, may Allah be pleased with them, are practically prophets, blessings and peace be upon our Prophet and them! because they have inherited their attribute from the attribute of the prophets and their quality from the Prophet's quality. Their outward is human, and their inward is lordlike. Their outward is wayfaring and their inward is ecstasy. Their outward is sobriety and their inward is intoxication. Their outward is separation and their inward is gatheredness, and so on. How can one attribute resemble the other when there is an incredible distance between the two attributes — or we can say, the two matters, or the two directions.

Faqir, do not describe any shaykh, except by that with which Allah has described him. Never describe him with what Allah has not described him. If he is outwardly knowing, then describe him as such. If he is inwardly knowing, then describe him like that. We could say, when he is one of the people of proof and exposition, then describe him as such. If he is one of the people of eye-witness and contemplation, then describe him like that, and so forth. Do not call the horseman a faqih or the faqih a horseman. Do not say the chief is not a chief, or the one who is not a chief is a chief. This is what a lot of ignorant students do in their letters. There is no doubt that visiting the shaykhs, may Allah be pleased with them has great virtue and a clear secret as the Shaykh Ibrahim at-Tazi who is buried at Wahran said, may Allah be pleased with him!:

> Visiting the lords of taqwa. Go to them — it heals and it is the key of the doors of guidance and good.

And so on to the end of his precious song.

Faqir, we strongly urge you and whoever follows us always to do it if that is possible. He should also visit its people as long as they are alive. He should do what will lower the position of his self for that is a condition in the Path. He should not do what will affirm its elevation as most people do except for the rare exception. The rare exception has no general principle.

Peace

76

Faqir, be on your guard against letting your heart incline to your self since that is part of the hypocrisy of the heart. Inclining to it is letting it follow what is light for it rather than what is heavier for it. The people, may Allah be pleased with them, follow the heavier. I also advise you to have what is heavy for your self constantly. Do not have what is light for it until it is annihilated. We have said many times to oppose passion and it will result in knowledge by divine gift. Knowledge by divine gift results in great certainty. Great certainty banishes doubts and illusions and pushes one into the presence of the King, the Knowing.

Peace

77

The common people have capital and profit. We think that the elite only have profit. The one who follows them should not store up anything. He should always keep his hand open and take on the character of his Master since Allah–ta'ala said, *"His hands are open, outspread. He spends however He wills."* The hand of Allah is filled, and it has no fear of poverty. It says in the noble hadith: "The only one who fears poverty is one who is far from his Lord." How can he fear it when he has profit without capital? We seek refuge with Allah from being without capital from Allah, our Lord, and Muhammad, our Prophet, may Allah bless him and grant him peace. The wali of Allah–ta'ala, Sayyidi Abu'l-'Abbas al-Mursi, may Allah be pleased with him, said, "People have means of subsistence, and our means is Allah." Another time, he said, "People have means of subsistence and our means are iman and taqwa." Allah–ta'ala said, *"Had the people of the cities believed and had taqwa...."* to the end of the ayat.

One day, we spoke with one of the fuqara from our brothers, the people of Fez, about this meaning. He preferred the people of means over the people of divestment. As a proof, he used the noble hadith: "Allah loves the slave with gainful employ." I told him, "Yes, Allah loves the slave with gainful employ. However, the great profession is leaving professions." Allah-ta'ala said, *"Whoever fears Allah, He will make a way out for him..."* to the end of the ayat, and *"Whoever relies on Allah, He is enough for him..."* to the end of the ayat. He did not know, may Allah be kind to him! that the best one engaged in means is the one who has acquired reliance on Allah. Then he comes down to means after having obtained freedom, like our master, may Allah be pleased with him! who always used to beg for money from shop to shop in spite of his lofty value and high position, may Allah be pleased with him. This is also like Abu Silham who turned to the sea and fish came to him immediately. In spite of his high station and immense affair, he was veiled by the weakest of means — fishing with the hook!

Peace

78

Faqir! Listen! I said to one of the sharifs, who had behaved badly towards a certain person who claimed that if he was a sharif and had bad character, he was a liar: "The sharif is truly the one with noble character." How can he have bad character? His root is the Messenger of Allah, may Allah bless him and grant him peace, about whom Allah–ta'ala said, *"You are on an immense character."* My brother, if your attribute is not from his attribute and your quality is not from his quality, then what direction are you from? What door are you near to since the Messenger of Allah, may Allah bless him and grant him peace, only had noble qualities and tremendous good character. He did not have any other qualities at all. Allah is the authority for what we say. The lofty Shaykh Sayyidi al-Busayri, may Allah be pleased with him said in his Burda:

> Leave what the Christians claim about their prophet.
>> Express whatever praise you wish about him and proceed in it.
> Ascribe whatever you like of nobility to his essence.
>> Ascribe whatever you like of greatness to his value.
> The excellence of the Messenger of Allah has no limit that a speaker can express.
> The extent of knowledge about him is that he was human, and he was the best of all of Allah's creation.

Similarly, I said to one of the fuqara who was famous at al-Marabit with all the people of his city: "My brother, you are famous at Marabit more than all of the fuqara. Be famous with good qualities more than them. I have a relationship to your name."

Peace

79

Faqir, be on your guard against your self leading you to what your Lord has forbidden you, and then leaving what He has commanded you to do. Be on your guard against it. Be content with a little of this world and wean your self from it always. What we have said to you seems great since it is close. Illusion distances it, and illusion is baseless so do not pay any heed to it. Weaning your self from its appetites is not too great for you from the first to the last. We see that you rely on certain matters that man cannot conceive of being parted from although leaving them is very near. The self is like a child. If you neglect it, it will grow up loving to suckle. If you wean it, it is weaned as Shaykh al-Busayri said in his Burda, may Allah be pleased with him. It is valid to test time after time what he said, may Allah be pleased with him. By Allah, we do not say that we leave certain matters if we have not left them and forgotten them when these are impossible with us. There are matters which cannot be conceived of leaving – like sleep, food, speech, mixing with people, and being friendly with them. If we wanted not to eat, sleep, speak or mix with people, we could have done that without fatigue or trouble. Allah is the authority for what we say.

Peace

80

Sayyidi Ahmad Aka'rir az-Zayati, be on your guard against pursuing outward knowledge! Caution the lofty scholar, Sayyidi Ahmad b. 'Ajiba al-Manjari, the sharif, may Allah have mercy on him and be pleased with him! Shaykh Abu Hafs Sayyidi 'Umar b. al-Farid, said in his poem in Ta', may Allah be pleased with him!:

Do not be among those with aimless studies since these undervalue the intellect and unsettle it.

There is a knowledge beyond written transmission
which is finer than the ultimate perception of sound
intellects.

I learned it from me and I took it from me. My self
profited from my gift.

Shaykh al-Majdhoub said, may Allah be pleased with him:

If it is the knowledge of pages, then the sweetness of
tongues is limited.

If it is the knowledge of tastes, you see him intoxicated
in gardens.

Shaykh ash-Shadhili, may Allah be pleased with him! said
"Whoever does not become embedded in this knowledge of
ours, dies persisting in great wrong actions while he is not
aware of it." Shaykh Ibrahim b. Adham, may Allah be
pleased with him! said, "By Allah, had I known a knowledge
nobler than this one on the surface of the earth, I would have
gone to it." Shaykh al-Mursi, may Allah be pleased with him,
said, "If you see someone who has been given knowledge and the
treasures of understanding have been opened for him, then
do not bicker with him about written texts. Do not argue
with him from the jealousy of the self because gifts are
above acquisitions." It was said to Shaykh Abu'l-Hasan 'Ali
b. Maymun, may Allah be pleased with him! at the beginning
of his affair: "Throw away your book and bury your self in
the ground. Then a spring will emerge for you. If not, then
leave me." The shaykh, our Master Abu'l-Hasan 'Ali al-
Jamal, may Allah be pleased with him, said, "Books are
derived from the hearts. They are what support the books
from the beginning of this world to the end of it since the
hearts are the root." Shaykh ash-Shadhili, may Allah be
pleased with him, said when he found his shaykh, the qutb,
Mawlay 'Abdu's-Salam b. Mashish, may Allah be pleased with
him!: "Allah! I have washed myself of my knowledge and
my action so that I will not recognise any knowledge or
action except what comes to me by the hand of this shaykh,"

i.e. Ibn Mashish. Then he washed himself at the famous spring at al-Hasan. It is near to that shaykh at the foot of the mountain on the qibla side, may Allah honour it! That became a sunna for whoever came after him since that is the only way to obtain knowledge of the reality. Because of that, we have mentioned here what I know of the words of the shaykhs of the tariqa, may Allah be pleased with them! about this meaning. Shaykh Mawlay Abdu'l-Qadir al-Jilani, may Allah be pleased with him, said in his song in 'Ayn:

> If the decreed is helpful in carrying your baggage of
> fate to a real shaykh who is skilled in the reality,
> Then concern yourself with his pleasure and follow
> what he wants. Leave all that you were doing before.
> With him, you should be like the corpse in the hands of
> the washer. The washer turns him about as he likes
> and he is completely pliable.
> Do not object to that of which you are ignorant. Objection is struggle.
> Surrender to him in whatever you see. If it is contrary
> to the shari'at of Muhammad, there is deception.
> There is enough in the story of al-Khidr about the killing of the boy when Musa objected.

It continues until he says, "Such is the knowledge of the people. There are marvels in it."

Sayyidi Ahmad, be careful that you do not understand me to say that you should neglect outward knowledge for the love of inward knowledge. No, by Allah! again no, by Allah, no! I have this although I recognise that the only way to the reality is by the door of the shari'at of Muhammad. The only way to freedom is by the door of slaveness. What moved me to quote the words of the shaykhs of the tariqa, may Allah be pleased with them! on this meaning? It was only because I saw that most of the fuqaha of outward knowledge did not think badly about the people of error as much as they thought badly about the people of the tariqa. They are the people of inward knowledge, may Allah be pleased with them. They did not rush to reject any of the rebels like they rush to reject them. They claim that they act correctly in their occupation with outward knowledge, and that they, may Allah be kind to them! are occupied with the knowledge by which our Lord is worshipped. It is as if Allah-ta'ala did not command them to oppose their passions. This is great ignorance on their part and well-known error. We seek refuge with Allah!

We think that they should turn in tawba from what they are doing without delay. If not they will destroy themselves and they will destroy the ignorant common people who follow them since they have closed the door of tawba in their faces and in the faces of their followers. That door will remain open until the sun rises in the West as Allah-ta'ala said, *"A day when some of the signs of your Lord come."* What is meant is the sun rising from the West, and Allah knows best. How remarkable! How often they are harsh to people, and how often they distance them, make things difficult, and make the paths narrow for people and turn them to perilous places! In spite of that, the people of true sincerity always turn in tawba, always return, always travel, and always arrive. The door of generosity is the door. How many there are who do not recognise error from right conduct! How remarkable! The one who arrives is not harsh nor does he constrict when he is near. The one who is cut off is harsh and constricts when he is distant.

Our master, may Allah be pleased with him, always used to say to us, "We have only the overflowing favour of Allah, and the favour of our masters, the outward 'ulama who put in our possession the waymarks of the Prophet, may Allah bless him and grant him peace. Then, when one of us is drowning in the sea of the reality, he looks at the waymarks of the Prophet, may Allah bless him and grant him peace, which are in the hands of our masters, the outward 'ulama, may Allah be pleased with them. He returns to him and is saved from drowning. The words of the perfected ones among the people of knowledge are always repeated to us. They are the ones who join the knowledge of the shari'at of Muhammad and the knowledge of the reality, may Allah be pleased with him:

Whoever has the shari'at without the reality has left
  the right way,
Whoever has the reality without the shari'at is a
  heretic.
Whoever joins the two of them has realisation.

They also repeat their statement to us: "Some people are veiled by the reality from the shari'at of Muhammad. Some people make the shari'at of Muhammad a door and the reality a pavilion. Those are the party of Allah. The party of Allah, they are the successful."

Sayyidi Ahmad, among the shayks of the tariqa, may Allah be pleased with them! we met and perceived our master, Abu'l-Hasan 'Ali al-Jamal, may Allah be pleased with him. He met a noble man of advanced age and a beautiful face, a collected state, high himma, and noble charac-character. He was from the East, and his name was 'Abdullah. He found him in the city of Tetuan. He was with some people in a house which he neither left nor entered. No one recognised him. The wali of Allah, may Allah be pleased with him!, said: "I have not seen any noble nature which was greater than the one Allah honoured, may Allah be pleased with him! since he had taken on the quality of the name of Allah, the Noble (al-Karim)." He said to me, "The cause that precipitated our meeting with him was the baraka of visiting Mawlay 'Abdu's-Salam b. Mashish, may Allah give us the benefit of his baraka." I heard him say that he was his companion for two years at Tetuan.

He also met the Shaykh Sayyidi al-'Arabi b. 'Abdillah

al-Fasi, may Allah be pleased with him, at the al-Makhfiyya district. He had recognised him before my master recognised him, but it was not valid for him to put out anything on his part since he had the quality of the name of Allah-ta'ala, the Restrainer (al-Mani'). For that reason, he searched for what he needed until he found it with that sharif, and Allah gave him opening through him. When the sharif died, then he returned to Fez, having been opened as we have stated. Then he kept the company of Sayyidi al-'Arabi b. 'Abdillah for 16 years. The secrets which he saw from him are almost too many to count. I did not hear him mention him and he did not weep for him. Allah is the authority for what we say. He, may Allah be pleased with him, was very old and undistinguished among his fellow men. No one recognised him nor was he acknowledged by overflowing favour since he had an inclination toward ruins. People are averse to the state of ruin, and flee from it. He was silent a lot.

He met his father, Abu'l-'Abbas Sayyidi Ahmad b. 'Abdillah who was very famous with all of the people of North Africa. He, in turn, had met Shaykh Sayyidi Qasim al-Khassasi, may Allah be pleased with him. I heard that he advised one of the brothers in Allah: "Do not be occupied at all with the one who abuses you. Be occupied with Allah and He will drive him away from you. He is the One who makes him move against you in order to test your claim to true sincerity. Many people have erred in this matter. They are occupied with the one who abuses them, so the abuse will continue along with wrong action. Had they returned to Allah, he would have driven them away from them, and their proper business would have been enough for them." When he died he appointed Shaykh Abu'l-'Abbas Sayyidi Ahmad al-Yamani as the qutb of the circle. He was a Qadiri sharif, and Allah knows best. He took it from him, and his child was Shaykh Sayyidi al-'Arabi who was the shaykh of our noble master. He was young then. We have mentioned their chain, above, may Allah give us profit by them!

Sayyidi Ahmad Aka'rir, you told me that the scholar with lordly knowledge, the sharif Abu'l-'Abbas Sayyidi Ahmad b. 'Ajiba, may Allah be pleased with him, met a group of the salihun of the inward at the city of Fez. I find your statement unlikely and very odd indeed, may Allah be pleased with you! This is because I was there, and there was nothing of what you speak about except for our master, may Allah be pleased with him. Now there are only some pretenders or some of the brothers among his companions, may Allah be pleased with him. There is no doubt that this business is very uncommon as our master stated and as Shaykh Sayyidi Abu Madyan, may Allah be pleased with him, said:

When will I see them and how will I see them? When will my ear hear some news of them?

There is no doubt that the predominant state of the awliya, may Allah be pleased with them! is lowness. People only look at the state of highness, so how could they recognise them? How far they are from some of them unless Allah takes them by the hand! The lofty shaykh, the wali of Allah ta'ala, Sayyidi Ibn 'Ata'Illah said in his Hikam, may Allah be pleased with him!: "Glory be to the One who only directs people to His awliya in order to direct them to Himself, and who only leads one to them when He wants to bring him to Himself." If it is said to me, "How did it happen that you recognised them and took from them?" I would say, "I looked at the state of lowness, and did not look at the state of highness so I found what I needed there. Praise and thanks be to Allah!" Most people look only at this world and whoever is with them. They do not look at poverty and whoever is poor. When some of them see a faqir-wali who has nothing of this world, they flee from him and do not go near him. They say, "Had he been a wali, he would have been rich and not poor." He does not behave well inside his own head, so how can he behave well with other people? He does not know that the wali is the one who is faqir, poor in this world, rich with Allah, satisfied with Him.

As for the zawiyya which you told me about, I knew it when I was a young boy. However, incapacity and laziness dominated me. Ask Allah for success for me, and may Allah be enough for you! The actions of our master, may Allah be pleased with him, reminded us. Very few people have it although actions are based on it. It is realisation of the attributes as Shaykh Ibn 'Ata'Illah said in his Hikam,

"Be attached to the attributes of His lordliness and realise the attributes of your slaveness."

The people, may Allah be pleased with them, said, "Whenever you bury your self earth under earth, your heart rises through heaven after heaven." Sayyidi Ahmad, one of the fuqaha of Fez, told me the same thing that you have told me. I answered him at some length, and we will mention some of what I said to you out of love for you, not in order to confront you.

Part of it is the statement of one of the Companions, may Allah be pleased with them! "We pursued all actions, and we did not see any more direct matter for the Next World than doing-without in this world." We have tasted some of that. Because of that, your words leave us lukewarm as you can see. Also, whenever there is urgency in outward actions, there is none in inward actions since there cannot be strength in two directions as we have stated numerous times, and as others have stated.

Sayyidi Ahmad, I told him that no one perceives our superogatory actions except the people of unadulterated taste. They put a person far from creation and near to Allah. The thing you dislike from me is what my heart desires as has been said. Very few of the people of the Path have this. Some of the strong awliya, have this like Shaykh Abu Hafs 'Umar b. al-Farid, may Allah be pleased with him! when he said:

Hold on to the coat tails of passion and cast off modesty. Leave the path of those with pious practices, even if it is earnest.

It is as the Shaykh Abu'l-Hasan 'Ali ash-Shushtari said, may Allah be pleased with him:

> We want to go stripped,
> And the most splendid thing,
> As it goes before me,
> Is in need of me.

Shaykh 'Izzu'd-din b. 'Abdi's-Salam, may Allah be pleased with him, used to say, "Is there a path other than the one we understand from the Book and sunna?" He rejected the Path of the People. When he met ash-Shadhili and learned from him, he began to say, "By Allah, no one abides by the undestroyed laws of the shari'at of Muhammad except the sufis." Imam al-Ghazali, may Allah be pleased with him, used to speak like this before he met his Shaykh al-Bazghani.

Sayyidi Ahmad, I told him that a great number of awliya, may Allah be pleased with them, have travelled the path of the inward, and no one turned them aside from it, no one of great importance and no one of small importance. Allah-ta'ala said in His Book, *"If these reject it, we will entrust it to a people who do not reject."* That is it, and Allah knows best! The outward and the inward are two opposites, and opposites are only joined by a man whose foot is on the foot of the Messenger of Allah, may Allah bless him and grant him peace, like Imam Abu Bakr as-Siddiq, may Allah be pleased with him, Imam Sayyiduna 'Umar b. al-Khattab, Imam Sayyiduna 'Uthman b. 'Affan, and Imam Sayyiduna 'Ali b. Talib, may Allah honour his face!, and his sons al-Hasan and al-Husayn, may Allah be pleased with them all, and like the great wali, Sayyidi al-Hasan al-Basri, the great wali, Sayyidi Dhu'n-Nun al-Misri, the great wali, Sayyidi Ibrahim b. Adham, the great wali, Sayyidi Sufyan ath-Thawri, the great wali, Sayyidi Ma'ruf al-Karkhi, the great wali, Sayyidi Abu Yazid al-Bistami, and their likes among the shaykhs of the East and the shaykhs of the West. They are numerous as we have stated, may Allah be pleased with them and us. They are only recognised by the one who reaches their station or comes upon their tracks which guide him to them. As far as others are concerned, they are only among the people of the outward without the inward, or the people of the inward without the outward, or they have neither outward nor inward. This is because the two opposites are only joined by the man whose foot is on the foot of the Messenger of Allah, may Allah bless him and grant him peace, as we said. It is very difficult indeed. It is said that one of the angels, blessings and peace be upon them, glorifies Allah-ta'ala constantly and says in his glorification, "Glory be to the One who combines ice and fire!"

Shaykh Abu'l-'Abbas Sayyidi Ahmad al-Yamani, and those of our shaykhs in Fez and our shaykhs in 'Abdalawa, who were with him, may Allah be pleased with them, objected to Shaykh Sayyidi Ahmad al-Yusi when he said, "The outward is adorned by striving, and the inward is put right by contemplation." They told him that there cannot be strength in two directions. When the outward becomes strong in striving, the inward becomes weak in contemplation. When the inward becomes strong in contemplation, the outward grows weak in striving. One of the masters said, "When you see someone concerned about his outward, know that his inward is in ruins." I said: There are very few who join the outward and the inward, the shari'at of Muhammad and the reality, sobriety and intoxication, separation and gatheredness, and so on. We have mentioned this many times in our teaching. We do not need to pursue it further.

As for the interpretation of the vision which appeared to the man of knowledge, the sharif Abu'l-'Abbas b. 'Ajiba al-Manjari, it is wonderful ('ajib), related to his name, Ibn

'Ajiba! Allah knows best. Sayyidi Ahmad, rejoice at what your Prophet, may Allah bless him and grant him peace! gave you when you saw him in your dream. Know that it comes to you as a divine gift just as seeing him is a divine gift. We saw him, may Allah bless him and grant him peace, before we were with you, in the city of Fez. We were there – and Allah knows best – at the time the muslims entered al-Barija. (The Sultan Muhammad b. 'Abdillah b. Isma'il entered it in 1182). I wanted to go to him from my recumbent position, but he motioned to me with his noble hand two or three times to remain where I was. I told that to my master when I recognised him, may Allah be pleased with him. He told me, "He has given you security, may Allah bless him and grant him peace." By Allah, the face of security appeared to me and I saw it with my eyes. Praise and thanks be to Allah. After this vision of him at that time, I saw his daughter, our lady Fatima az-Zahra', may Allah be pleased with her. Through that vision, my heart left its habits and all its appetites and would never accept going back to them from that moment, and we gained great good. Praise and thanks be to Allah!

That is the secret of the true vision. My master, may Allah be pleased with him was at some moments immersed in seeing him, may Allah bless him and grant him peace, both awake and asleep. It appears likely to me, and Allah knows best that he was stronger than Sayyidi al-Mursi because of the immersion that I saw that he had in the Messenger of Allah, may Allah bless him and grant him peace, and his conversation with him. I kept his company for many years, and I also saw him describe what tasting he had taken from the Messenger of Allah, may Allah bless him and grant him peace. There was a great difference between him and Sayyidi al-Mursi. Whoever wants to recognise this one from that one should look at what Sayyidi Ibn 'Ata'Illah said about his master in his book, Lata'if al-Minan, and what our master says in his book. Allah willing, he will see which of them is strong and which is weak in seeing the Prophet, may Allah bless him and grant him peace. Allah — glory be to Him! has firm power, and Allah is our Reckoner.

If we consider him superior by reason of the appetite of our self, we consider him superior as his Lord considered him superior. We are content with the knowledge of our Lord which moved us to say what we have said about our shaykh. It was not through lack of contentment with the knowledge of our Lord. Even had we been silent about what we know about the strength of our master in seeing the Prophet due to fear of someone saying that we did it from lack of contentment with knowledge of Allah, the matter would still have been the same. This is not the case, and we have said what we know about our master, whether or not it is said about us that we are content with the knowledge of our Lord.

Something else moves us to specify the strength of our master. That is what we see of the states of the people. They do not see that the one present with them has any excellence. They think that the one who is absent has it. This is the case even if he is one of the greatest of the people of virtue. This is the state of most of them. We seek refuge with Allah!

Peace

81

Faqir, intention is certainly the real elixir. It was present with us when we were searching for someone who would take us by the hand. We found him in front of us with hardly any distance at all between us. It was almost as if he were with us in the same house. Allah is the authority for what we say.

He was, may Allah be pleased with him, outwardly majesty and inwardly beauty, i.e. his outward was abasement-slaveness and his inward was might-freedom. How ugly the opposite is! That is outward might-freedom and inward abasement-slaveness. Or else it can be outwardly sunna, inwardly innovation, or outwardly permitted, inwardly forbidden, or outwardly lordlike, inwardly shaytan, and so forth. They are deprived of arrival because they let the foundations go to ruin. There is no doubt that when the elite, like our master and his likes, abase their outward by choice, Allah elevates their outward and inward. They are constantly full of joy and happiness. The common people do the opposite. When they elevate their outward by choice, Allah abases their outward and inward. They are always in turbidity.

My master, may Allah be pleased with him! was also content with the knowledge of Allah. He did not turn to the manifested or the hidden. He only looked at what was between him and his Lord. He did not turn to regard the praise of the praiser or the blame of the blamer. He often mentioned these verses:

Would that you were sweet while this life is bitter.
    Would that You were pleased while people were
        angry.
Would that what is between You and me were filled
    and flourishing, and that what is between me and
        the world were a ruin.
If your love proves true, then all is easy, and all which
    is on the earth is earth.

The tongue of his state said: Oh Allah! Disgrace with creation and veiling faults with Allah! Not the reverse! That is veiling faults with creation and disgrace with Allah. Allah-ta'ala said, "They will not free or protect you at all from Allah."

Faqir, listen to some of his words, may Allah be pleased with him. "When people are occupied with 'ibada, then you should be occupied with the Worshipped. When they are occupied with love, be occupied with the Beloved. When they are occupied with seeking for miracles, then be occupied with the pleasure of intimate conversation. When they are occupied with repeating the wird, be occupied with the King, the Generous," and so on. He also said, after some discussion which preceded it, "Had you seen Him in everything, you would be veiled from everything by contemplation. How can anything appear to you while He is Manifest? He is the Existent by which everything exists. How can anything else appear to you when He is Manifest? He is the One with whom there is nothing. Had you joined the in-time to the beyond-endless-time, the in-time would have been crushed to nothing and the beyond-endless-time would remain. Had the attributes of the Beloved appeared, the veil and the veiled would have been annihilated. Had the lights of contemplation appeared in tajalli-manifestation, the one doing-without and that which he does without would have been annihilated. When you do without things, you elevate them above their value. That is because you are veiled from Him. Had you seen Him in them, or before or after them, you would not have been veiled by them from Him. Your preoccupation with them is what veils you from Him. Had you seen their existence as being from Him, you would not have been veiled by them from Him. All that comes between you and the Worshipped is your joy with what you have and your sorrow for what you do not have. All that veils you from bliss is this deformed quality. Had it not been for the informer and the spy, your joy with the Beloved would not be perfect. Were it not for the fire and the bee-sting, the pleasure of the honeycomb and the honey would not be perfect," and so forth.

He said, may Allah be pleased with him, "Whoever claims that he has drunk the drink of the people, or has understood their meanings, and yet has not done without in this world, is a liar. As the Garden is forbidden to the one who has not died and has been raised up, so the Garden of gnoses is forbidden to the one whose self has not died to this world, to its management and choice, to its will and appetite, and to everything except Allah."

He said, may Allah be pleased with him, "By Allah, do not say "I" before obtaining annihilation. You can only obtain life after death. Suns will only shine for you after the death of the self. You will not reach the desired goal as long as people have praise for you. You will not taste the food of iman until after you leave created beings. You will only obtain well-being after annihilation to the people of annihilation. Had the veils been rent apart for you, you would have seen the Beloved in your essence. Had the veils of illusions departed from you, you would have always seen the Enduring. Had the distance of your self been quickly traversed, you would not have seen anything in existence except for your Lord. Had your self been sound and free of vices, the Truth would have come and the false would have vanished," and so on. Among his benefits was the breaking of norms, may Allah be pleased with him.

Peace

82

Do not be deceived by knowledge from one who claims to be a sufi before he has become a sufi. The one who claims to be a sufi before he is a sufi is the one who has not realised his attribute. By Allah, no one should accept any of the knowledge of the sufis, may Allah be pleased with them, unless it springs from realisiation of an attribute, and that is not hidden — and Allah knows best. The people said, may Allah be pleased with them, "They speak and are recognised." Ibn 'Ata'Illah says in the Hikam, "All the words come forth and they wear the garment of the heart from which they emerged."

Peace

83

My brother, we do not like you to divest yourself of means of subsistence and its known garments until you intend to divest yourself of the state of the people of heedlessness and to put on the state of the people of wakefulness, or to divest yourself of the garments of the people of this world and to put on the garments of the people of the Next World, or to divest yourself of the garments of the people of habits/norms, and to put on the garment of the people of breaking habits/norms, or to divest yourself of the garments of the people of distance and to put on the garments of the people of nearness, or to divest yourself of the garments of the dead and to put on the garments of the living, or to divest yourself of the garments of abasement and to put on the garments of elevation, or to divest yourself of the garments of the poor without Allah and to put on the garments of the rich by Allah, or to divest yourself of the clothes of the rabble and to put on the clothes of the elite, or to divest yourself of the clothes of children and put on the clothes of men, or to divest yourself of the clothes of the rabble and to put on the clothes of the sultans of the presence of lordship.

Peace

84

Be always on your guard against the people of wordly desires. There is distance from Allah in nearness to them. There is no doubt that when there is withdrawal with its proper conditions, sincere action results. Sincere action results in a sincere state. The results of good actions are good states in one who realises the stations of descent, as the wali Shaykh Ibn 'Ata'Illah, may Allah be pleased with him! said in his Hikam.

Peace

85

It is not possible that our Lord be seen, may His majesty
be exalted! while other-than-Him is seen with Him. It also is
not possible that anyone think that his Lord has bad nature.

Peace

86

I want you to respect and exalt the presence of your Lord
because respect is the cause of profit. Whatever election and
baraka is obtained at the hand of any of the people of Allah
is only through respecting and exalting them. Had it not been
for that, no one would have obtained any of it. My brother,
you did very well in recording our words, may Allah repay
you with good from us! Knowledge is the quarry, and writing
is its tether. Tether your quarry to the firm mountains.

As for your statement, "The tongue and pen are with me,"
we do not know whether you have them or not. Test yourself at the moment of your neediness, the moment when
people blame you and the moment when you do not have
your appetites. If your breast is expanded, then there is no
doubt that you have the heart. Our witness is from the Book
of Allah-ta'ala, *"The one whose breast Allah has opened to
Islam, he has a light from his Lord. Woe to those who are
hardhearted to the remembrance of Allah...."* We think that
this is a very great and appropriate witness.

The high Islam is the Islam of Ibrahim which the sufis
have. They, may Allah be pleased with them, are such that
their hearts find the moment of hardship the same as in the
moment of ease. They find the moment of illness the same as
the moment of health. They find the moment of affliction
the same as the moment of well-being. They find the moment of poverty the same as the moment of wealth. They
find the moment of abasement the same as the moment of
elevation. They find the moment of constriction the same as

the moment of wideness, and so on. It is like Sayyiduna Ibrahim, peace be upon him, whose heart was ecstatic in the strongest possible constriction — or we could say affliction or trial. Oh Allah! Make us and all those connected to us belong to the system of Ibrahim by the rank of the best of creation, our lord, master, and beloved, Muhammad, may Allah bless him and grant him peace.

My brother, be on your guard against interpreting any ayat of Qur'an with an insufficient interpretation. Go to the utmost in its commentary, then you will be right. If you do not go to the utmost in its commentary, then you must necessarily err since it is the Immense Qur'an. The meanings of the immense are only immense. None knows its interpretation except Allah. When those masters, the 'ulama, the people of outward knowledge, were interpreting it, would that their recitation could distract them from its commentary so that Allah could give them opening to its inward meanings. Then they would join the knowledge of the outward and the knowledge of the inward, or the knowledge of the sharia'at of Muhammad and the knowledge of the reality. Then they would give commentary on it as many of the perfect have given commentary, may Allah be pleased with them and may He give us the profit of their baraka. Amin.

If you say, "The Qur'an testifies to other ways as well as that of Ibrahim, " I say "Are they equal? — the one whose breast is only expanded by the existence of his appetites and desires and the one who has withdrawn from his appetites and desires into the contemplation of the immensity of his Lord?" No, by Allah, by Allah, by Allah!

Also test your heart again. Does it seek help from the Immense Qur'an, the hadith of the noble Prophet, may Allah bless him and grant him peace, from the shaykhs of the people of the outward and the people of the inward, from the brothers, from Allah, and from His Messenger, may Allah bless him and grant him peace? If you find that it seeks help

from all, then it is a great heart. If not, then it is lower than
the one who has this state. Therefore, you should not leave
him until you are like him — your dye is his dye and his dye
is your dye. As for the one who takes from Allah and His
Messenger, may Allah bless him and grant him peace, all
creatures seek help from him, high and low, absent and present, near and far, dense and subtle. Whenever his support is
strong, their support is strong. Whenever his support is weak,
their support is weak. However, we think that if he is perfect,
whenever his help in one direction is strong, he turns to the
other direction so that there will be balance between the two
directions which seek help from him so that neither of them
will be obliterated. Such is the one who possesses this heart,
or we can say, possesses this immense station, until the extinction of this world. Allah is the authority for what we
say.

Peace

87

I think that knowledge is based on two things. One of
them is true sincerity in word and deed constantly, without
change or alteration. The second is the aptness of words to
answer words. That is only given to the one who has taqwa of
Allah. "Have taqwa of Allah and Allah will teach you." "You
who believe, if you have taqwa of Allah, Allah will make a
Discrimination for you."

Peace

88

If you want always to be strong, you must always be weak,
and make do with a little food, few words, and not much
socializing with people. If you want always to be rich, always
be poor. If you want always to be mighty, always be abased.
If you want always to be high, always be low. If you want al-

ways to be free, always be a slave. If you want always to see what you love and what pleases you, then always put your self with what it does not love and what does not please it. If you want creation to recognise you always, then always be content with the knowledge of Allah. If you always want benefits, always break the habits of your self, and always fear impediments, and always leave attachments.

Peace

89

"May Allah give you the proof of good actions which annihilate the self and give life to the hearts! Listen to what our beloved Sayyidi al-Buzidi said, may Allah be pleased with him, ' The self will not die as long as it is a neighbour and intimate of people with self. It will die by being a neighbour to the people of dead self.' May Allah make you an invincible fortress, so that whoever attaches himself to you is rescued and finds happiness by the rank of Sayyiduna Muhammad, may Allah bless him and grant him peace."

We wrote this teaching to our brother in Allah, Abu 'Abdillah Sayyidi Muhammad b. 'Abdillah al-Makudi at Taza, since he wrote for our father Ahmad, may Allah have mercy on him! "The Proof of Good Actions and the Fortress of the Invincible."

Peace

90

Be on your guard against being greedy for anyone's teaching unless he is in need of giving it. The sign of his being in need of you is that he makes easy for you what is offered of the gifts of the presence of lordship which are knowledges by divine gift, and which come to hearts which are free of love of this world and purified of every misshapen attribute.

140

You must also be content with your Lord. The only one who is content with Him is the one who recognises Him — glory be to Him! It is impossible to recognise Him with the gnosis of eye-witnessing and then to turn to the bliss of the gardens. Whoever claims to have recognised his Lord — or we could say, have seen Him, while turning to something other-than-Him, great or small, is a liar. When someone sees the One "who there is nothing like," how can he be other than withdrawn from everything else? What beauty is like His beauty? What is desired in the two worlds like the vision of the face of his Lord? His vision — glory be to Him is not perceived nor can anyone hope for it except after the annihilation of the self, its obliteration, departure, and extinction as we have related from our shaykhs, their shaykhs, and all the shaykhs of the Path, may Allah be pleased with them.

Our Lord is not seen by forms which are the stuff of annihilation. He is seen by spirits which are the stuff of going-on, so understand!

Peace

91

Teaching by mutual reminding among the people, may Allah be pleased with them! is one of the most important matters. No one can do without it except for the one who is ignorant about its value. The shaykh of our master, Sayyidi al-'Arabi b. 'Abdillah, may Allah be pleased with him! used to say, "People's wine is in the hadra (sufic dance). Our wine is the hadra (words or teaching by mutual reminding)." Also "The mutual teaching of two is better than carrying two heavy loads" as the people do and have. We do not like any of the brothers to be silent at the time of mutual teaching. We dislike it intensely since there is absolutely no benefit in silence at that time. Benefit is through lack of silence in it because the meanings move by means of words until they move the one who has them to the divine presence of the Lord.

It is quite obvious that the chicken is only born after the hen lays her egg. It is like that with the shaykhs of the tariqa, may Allah be pleased with them. The knowledges which they give out to their followers only come to them through the existence of their search and their scraping and testing with the touchstone. The question calls for the answer, and the answer calls for the question. It is like that until one obtains arrival.

One day we were engaged in teaching by mutual reminding in Fez al-Bali, some of the brothers with us were silent and did not speak. I said to them, "Speak with us or leave us!" Our master disliked that any of the fuqara be silent at the time of mutual teaching. He found it heavy and disgraceful to such an extent that the effects of that showed in his face, may Allah be pleased with him. He would recite the word of Allah, the Majestic, the Great, *"The word has fallen upon them because of the wrong they were doing and they do not speak."* He used to say, "The only one who does not speak at the time of mutual teaching is the one whose heart is like a dark house filled with bats. As for the one whose heart is free of bats, he is not silent. He speaks and brings out what is inside him into the middle of the circle, putting it down, beautiful or ugly. As for the one who does not bring out the beautiful and the ugly, he stores it up inside of him and is too shy to bring it out. This one will not be healed of his sicknesses. He has deceived himself while he is in front of the doctor. Allah can heal every sick person out of pure generosity by the rank of the beloved Prophet, may Allah bless him and grant him peace, and his family and Companions.

Peace

92

If you want to be purified of doubts and illusions, then always be strengthened by the sunna of the Prophet, peace be upon him. One of the most important things is to remove all traces of urine. Do not do wudu' until you have no doubts about having removed your urine. If you wish to be certain about that, as is necessary, then the sunna is enough to make the matter easier for you. If you have your fill of innovation, it will lead to your self being too constricted to rise or descend as is our business and the business of most people. You will not be able to do it because you will have too much urine and faeces. Since they will be too much for you, you will find it difficult to free yourself of urine and to do wudu' every time. If you find it difficult to free yourself of urine, you find wudu' difficult. If you find wudu' difficult, you find the prayer difficult. If you find the prayer difficult, you find the deen difficult. Our wages and your wages are up to Allah, the Lord of the worlds.

If you wish to be freed of your self, then put an end to its conversation when it whispers to you, and do not turn to it. It tries to get the better of you and will not leave you alone. It says to you, for example, "You are one of the losers!" Do not let its words disturb you or alarm you. No matter what it says. Remain seated if you were sitting, standing if you were standing, reclining if you were reclining, eating if you were eating, drinking if you were drinking, laughing if you were laughing, praying if you were praying, reciting if you were reciting, and so forth. Do not listen to it unless it tells you, "You are of the believers, or one of the gnostics, or in the hand of Allah, and His favour and generosity is great." It will not stop whispering to you until you are always steady in the above-mentioned state and take your strength from the sunna of Muhammad, Allah's blessing and peace be upon him. If you listen to what it says, it will tell you, "You are one of the losers," then one of the evil doers, then one who leaves the right way, and had it not been that kufr is the very limit of affliction, it would have said that you are one of the kafirun or worse.

We had a brother, may Allah have mercy on him, who used to listen to what it said. He believed it and was very worried and sad because of that. One day he said to our father, may Allah have mercy on him, while he and I were with him, "By Allah, my father, we only see our ship smashed to pieces." He said, "How dare you say such a thing! By Allah, it is not smashed to pieces! It is whole as it was. You are smashing it to pieces with your mouth!" These words made him extremely happy and because of those words he set out for Allah with a great energy.

We see many people with complete and total blessings — iman, health, food, drink, clothes, mounts, wives, abundant well-being and others of the blessings of Allah. Yet they are always full of worry, sorrow, and constriction. That is because they are heedless of their Lord and remain with their own portions. Had they left their portions and turned to their Lord as He has commanded them, every harm would have left them since only the people of heedlessness have it. As for the people of dhikr, it has come down to us that "the bolt of lightning does not strike the person doing dhikr."

My brother, be steady in this teaching and cling firmly to it if you want the Path to act on all of created being. If not, then created being will make it act on you as it has made it act on your companions. If you do not make it act on created being, created being will make it act on you. Our master, may Allah be pleased with him! used to say to us, "Created being always says by the tongue of the state: 'Strike!' If not, then stretch out your neck to eat and watch out!" The matter is as he said. Allah is the authority for what we say.

Peace

93

May Allah have mercy on you! Know that we see many of the fuqara' and others doing good actions while they do not know that they are doing them. They also do bad actions while they do not know that they are doing them. They do not distinguish between obedience and rebellion, or we might say, the spiritual and the human. We seek refuge with Allah! The one who knows what he does is not like the one who does not know. *"Say: Are they equal, those who know and those who do not know?" "Are darkness and light the same?"*

There is no doubt that the reality of the one who cannot recognise obedience from rebellion and the spiritual from the human is dark. His reality is not light. May Allah take us by the hand!

Peace

94

There is nothing more likely to lead to gathering the heart to concentrate on Allah than silence and hunger. There is nothing more likely to lead to dispersal than a lot of food and talk even about what concerns us. There is no doubt that the believer has few words and a lot of action. He will certainly have few words and much action since silence results in reflection. Reflection is an action of the heart. An atom's worth of the action of the heart is better than mountains of the actions of the limbs. It has come in tradition, "An hour of reflection is better than seventy years of 'ibada."

Peace

95

Sayyidi Ahmad Aka'rir az-Ziyati, may Allah be pleased

with you and may He have mercy on you! Know that I looked at one of your letters and you said that the scholar Sayyidi Ahmad b. 'Ajiba al-Manjari, may Allah have mercy on him! is involved in reading the books of sufism, especially the Hikam of Ibn 'Ata'Illah, and that he had a commentary on the prayer of Ibn Mashish. It was clear to me that you were like him in that respect. Because of that, I warn you about halting with them in what happens. If they are incredibly beautiful, they can also be incredibly ugly if one halts at them because the secrets are not received from books. They are received from breasts as it says in the Immense Qur'an. What is in the breasts is obtained. It is clear to me that the divine waridat which came to Sayyidi al-Junayd, Sayyidi al-Jilani, Sayyidi al-Ghazali, Sayyidi ash-Shadhili, and Sayyidi 'Ali, our master, and their likes, may Allah be pleased with them will come, Allah willing, to Sayyidi Ahmad Aka'rir and Sayyidi Ahmad b. 'Ajiba, and us, and others if they act by what they know. It has come in tradition. Whoever acts by what he knows, Allah will bequeath him a knowledge which he did not know. Do not be veiled by the meanings other people have from what you have. You have meanings as the sea has waves. You know that whoever acts by what he knows, Allah will bequeath him a knowledge which he did not know. It was related from Ibn Abi Al-Khawwari from his Shaykh ad-Darani, may Allah be pleased with both of them! "If the self is firm in leaving wrong action, it moves freely in the malakut, and returns to you with modes of wisdom without the knower directing knowledge to it. This is the business of the masters:

Tongues whisper secrets which are hidden from the Noble Scribes.
Wings fly without feathers to the malakut of the Lord of the worlds.

Sayyidi Ahmad al-Haddad al-Khumsi warned Sayyidi Ibn 'Askar, when they were talking about sufism, may Allah be pleased with them, because Ibn 'Askar was mentioning a lot of quotations from the words of the masters. Sayyidi Ahmad al-Haddad said to him, "How long will you say so-and-so said, and so-and-so related. What do you yourself say? And me?" Similarly, Sayyidi 'Ali b. Maymun was warned by his shaykh, ad-Dabbas. We do not caution you against knowledges of the deen as you imagine, Sayyidi Ahmad Aka'rir, since our Lord is only worshipped by means of knowledge. We warn you about stopping there as we told you. How could we warn you against them when there was none greater than the Messenger of Allah, may Allah bless him and grant him peace, and Allah ta'ala commaded him to say every day, "My Lord, increase me in knowledge." He said, peace be upon him, "Whatever day contains no increase in knowledge that will bring me closer to Allah-ta'ala, there is no baraka in the sunrise that day."

We do not dislike reading the books of sufism. Among their benefits is the breaking of norms. They said: "Beware of the company of three types of people: heedless tyrants, hypocritical Qur'an recitors, and ignorant sufis."

Also, Sayyidi Ahmad, had it not been for knowledge, none of us would have been good for anything. If we are in need of our Lord, knowledges of divine gift will come to us from Him as they have come to whoever has freed his heart of preoccupations. Shaykh Ibn 'Ata'Illah, may Allah be pleased with him, said in his Hikam: "Lights may come to you and find the heart filled with the forms of effects. They will return to the place from which they came. Free your heart of others! They will fill it with gnoses and secrets."

I say: By Allah, Sayyidi Ahmad Aka'rir, nothing stops us except the lack of our need for our Lord. Had we needed Him, He would have made us rich as He has made our companions rich since Allah-ta'ala said, 'If they are poor, Allah will enrich them from His overflowing favour. Sadaqa is for the poor.' Abasement and poverty are two of our necessary attributes.

In spite of that, it is heavy for us to be poor, abased. The only way to freedom is by the door of abasement and poverty. You must have that if you want to win.

> Abase yourself to the One you love — you will obtain might. How many men have obtained might by abasement!
> If the One you love is Mighty and you are not abased to Him, then say goodbye to arrival.

Another said:

> Abase yourself to the One you love. Love is not easy. If the Beloved is pleased, then arrival is permitted to you.

Another said:

> If you are not steadfast in abasement in passion, you will be parted from the One you love in spite of yourself.

Another said:

> Had abasement been exalted in it, how sweet passion would be for me!
> Had it not been for abasement in love, I would have no might at all.

Shaykh ash-Shadhili, may Allah be pleased with him! said, "By Allah, we have only seen might in abasement." We say, May Allah be pleased with us, "By Allah, we have only seen abasement in poverty." Whoever wants to abase his self should make it poor in this world and among people except for the one who uplifts his state. His words should guide one to Allah since there is nothing more weighty than that. Rise for him, Sayyidi Ahmad, do not rise for others, and you will see wonders.

Beware of saying, "Later, later." Then the leader comes and the others rise for him and leave you with yourself, plunging into yourself. Death comes to you and finds you in emptiness alone, neither compassionate, merciful, nor tender. It hangs you and withdraws you from existence and takes you to your Lord in spite of yourself. Only He knows your state since you do not know what He will do with you. However, in general what dominates you is fear and conflict. Conflict is worse than killing!

The secret of poverty which we mentioned is only recognised by the one who has expelled love of this world from his heart. Listen to some of it, Sayyidi Ahmad Ibn 'Askar said in his Dawha, "More than one of the distinguished people of Meknes told me that they were in great despair and went to Shaykh Abu'r-Rawa'il al-Mahjub, may Allah be pleased with him! to ask him to do the rain-prayer with them. He said, "Wait for me a bit until I come back to you." He went into his house and gave away all that he had in it as sadaqa. He did not leave anything. Then he got dressed and went out to them. He said, "Let's begin. The request is valid and the supplication is true." When they came back, there was practically a flood from the intensity of the rain. This is something of the secret of poverty. There are wonders and marvellous things among its secrets. The word of Allah is enough for us concerning its secret, "Sadaqa is for the poor." Shaykh Abu'r-Rawa'il al-Madjub, may Allah be pleased with him, was one of the shaykhs of Shaykh 'Abdu'r-Rahman al-Majdhoub, may Allah be pleased with him.

Sayyidi Ahmad, as far as the practices which you do are concerned, they are not hidden. However, we would like you to recognise what we say to you. It is: When you have urgency in the outward, you do not have it in the inward. When you have it in the inward, you do not have it in the outward since strength cannot be in two directions as we have told you. We have repeated our words many times. Perhaps someone will hear them. We said in a certain teaching we do not like one to say "Allah, Allah" always while his state is intense thirst for this world and devotion to idle talk.

We like him to perform the obligatory prayer and the confirmed sunna, leave what does not concern him, and always to take on noble character. If he says, "Allah" once, prays once, or recites one sura, that is better for him than 1000 times with a blameworthy state. Allah knows best.

Sayyidi Ahmad, if you understand this and pursue it, you will lighten the burden of your self and bring it to your Lord. There is no doubt that it is nearer to taqwa. Allah knows best. Similarly this secret of abasement is only recognised by the one who has left his self like the one who said, "This path of ours is only useful for people who sweep the rubbish heaps with their spirits." There must be a shaykh in this discipline and in other disciplines, and Allah knows best since they said, "Whoever has no shaykh, shaytan is his shaykh." They said, "Whoever has no shaykh, has no qibla." Ibn Shayban, may Allah be pleased with him said, "Whoever has no matter is idle. Dropping off the means (of arrival) is lack of proper balance. Basing action on them is misguidance." We think, and Allah knows best, that whoever has opening in the knowledge of the reality without proper means, must take on the shari'at of its people, may Allah be pleased with them. He must take one of their shaykhs, i.e. the shaykhs of the knowledge of reality if he finds him. None misses him except the one who makes himself independent by his own opinion and thinks he knows more. As far as the one who needs him is concerned, I think that he will find him whereever he is, near or far, in the land of Islam or in the land of the Christians. His need of him will join him to him wherever he is. Either the shaykh will come to the murid or the murid will come to the shaykh. Capacity will carry the shaykh to the murid or the murid to the shaykh. Allah is the authority for what we say.

As for travelling the Path without the shaykh and by his own opinion, by Allah, he is as Sayyidi Abu Hamid al-Gahzali. may Allah be pleased with him, said in the Bidayau'l-Hidaya

(Beginning of Guidance): "When the murid has no shaykh, nothing comes from him. He is like a tree growing in the deserts. It grows but its fruits never come to fruition." As for the one who says that there is no shaykh today, he is wrong and has not hit the mark. Listen Sayyidi Ahmad, to what happened to one of the people of the East when he came to Morocco to ask about the qutb. He met Shaykh 'Abdu'l-Warith al-Yalsuti who was among the Banu Zarwal. He asked him about the qutb, and he told him. "Had Allah opened your eye, you would have found him in front of you."

As far as the statement of Shaykh Ahmad Zarruq is concerned which he related from his Shaykh, al-Hadrami, may Allah be pleased with both of them, we have not heard it. Had we heard it, we still would not accept it. We do not recognise that from our Lord. We recognise baraka from Him, or we could say that wisdom is not cut off as long as the Kingdom of Allah lasts. Allah—ta'ala said, *"We do not abrogate any ayat or cause it to be forgotten, but that We bring one better than it or equal to it. Do you not know that Allah has power over everything? Do you not know that Allah has the kingdom of the heavens and the earth. You do not have any protector or helper apart from Allah."*

Many fuqaha' and others have opposed us in this. Our intellects did not accept it and our breasts were not expanded by it when were young as a favour and blessing from Allah. The paths which follow al-Hadrami, may Allah be pleased with him, are branches, not the root. The root is truly the pure Shadhiliyya tariqa. No one will change it or alter it until the last day. It is as Shaykh al-Kharrubi at-Tarabulusi said to Shaykh 'Umar b. 'Abdu'l-Wahhab al-Hasani al-'Alami who was among the descendants of the great qutb, Mawlana 'Abdu's-Salam b. Mashish, may Allah be pleased with all of them, "This Path has guardians who protect it and guards who guard it until the Day of Rising. They are the people of Allah—ta'ala and the helpers of his deen. Allah has given them outward and inward knowledge. He has helped them with His name the Helper (an-Nasir) and His name, the Protector (al-Hafidh)...." until the end of his words.

I think that you will recognise this in the answer that al-Kharrubi gave to the sharif about the states of the office of qutb. I saw something of it in your handwriting at the end of our letters which you have in your possession. One day, we spoke about the states of the office of the qutb and taking on the character of mercy. We were deeply immersed in that, and Allah helped us with it since we had no proof of what we thought about the states of the office of the qutb and we had absolutely no knowledge of it. Our Lord brought it to us from the unseen and from nearness, not from distance, and from gnoses, nor from anything else. This only happens to the people of great true sincerity. It happened to us. Praise and thanks be to Allah.

We do not like the one who shuts the door of Allah in the faces of Allah's slaves. It is always open. We dislike that intensely. Allah is the authority for what we say. We only see virtue in the one who expands and makes things easy for Allah's slaves by ayat and hadith. We also think that Allah will constrict the one who constricts them, and Allah will expand the one who expands them. Allah will be harsh to the one who is harsh to them. Allah will make things easy for the one who makes things easy for them.

There is no doubt that nothing cuts off the people of intention, love, true sincerity, and good opinion from their Lord. Nothing blocks their way to Him. They are always from them to Him and from Him to them. Nothing comes between them and Him — glory be to Him! The barrier is impossible in respect to Him, may His Majesty be exalted! Shaykh al-Busayri said in his Burda:

You offered me sincere advice, but I did not hear it.
The lover is deaf to critics.

May Allah bless them! They and us turn in tawba, and always return, always travel, and always pray. The door of generosity is the door. How many do not recognise the correct way! As for the one who wants to enter by other than this door, he will never enter since Allah–ta'ala said, *"Had it not been for the favour of Allah to you and His mercy, you would have been among the losers."* Had it not been for the favour of Allah to you and His mercy, you would have followed shaytan except for a few. Had it not been for the favour of Allah to you and His mercy, none of you would have ever been purified, etc. He – glory be to Him! brings near the one He brings near without reason, and He makes distant the One He makes distant without reason. Allah-ta'ala said, *"Whoever has not been given a light by Allah, he has no light."*

Peace

96

Our masters, may Allah preserve their existence! told us that they always set aside a moment for Allah alone without any portion for anything else, whether it was at night or in the daytime. They would recite the word of Allah in it, or do dhikr of "La ilaha illa'llah" or the divine name alone, or pray as much as Allah willed, or do the prayer on the Messenger of Allah, may Allah bless him and grant him peace. By Allah, if you do as I have told you, Allah will give you an opening which He has not yet opened to you. It will be greater than the one which you have. His overflowing favour will appear on you as it has appeared on your like among the people of knowledge and others. Do not be content with the outward knowledge that you have. Seek inward knowledge as you seek outward knowledge. Use means to acquire both of them. May Allah give you success! Be among the people of hearts and limbs. Do not be among the people of limbs alone. "Allah does not look at your forms or your bodies. He looks at your hearts" as has come in tradition. It says in the Book of Allah, *"The eyes are not blind, but the hearts which are in the breasts are blind."* It also says, *"Hearts which do not understand,"* and other things. Beware of putting most of your energy in action as the speaker said: "Today there are only the people of the outward. As for the people of the inward, that is a community which has passed away." Many of the people of knowledge, may Allah be pleased with them, were quite explicit about this. By Allah, the matter is not what they have. It is the opposite of what they have.

> They eye may reject the light of the sun because of
> ophthalmia,
>> And the mouth may reject the taste of water be-
>> cause of illness.

By Allah, my friend, according to the statements of Shaykh Abu'l-'Abbas, Sayyidi Ahmad Zarruq and others, Allah has bestowed inward knowledge and great opening on a large number of the people of knowledge and others. Whoever wants to realise what is true and what is false should expel the love of this world from his heart and should not be pleased with himself because luminosity is strengthened by leaving this world. Certainty is strengthened by strengthening luminosity. When certainty is strengthened, himma rises above created beings. When himma rises above created beings, the Maker of being is reached. Reaching him is reaching knowledge of Him. This is our belief and we will believe it until we meet our Lord. We do not believe other than it because whoever belongs to Allah, Allah is his. Whoever has Allah, how can he be lacking in good and baraka? This is impossible. By Allah, we tell you: set aside a time for Allah without any portion for anything else because the one who gives his entire attention to Allah always has lights and secrets. Whoever has lights and secrets, has election. Whoever has election, recognises the true from the false. Recognition of the true from the false is a sublime rank. This is different from the one who has no election, and has commonality. He only sees what the common see.

I think that Shaykh Ahmad Zarruq said, "When a man blocks off the people of instruction before he recognises them and before Allah has given him an opening as He has given them, he will only have an opening at the end of his lifetime and he will only live a short time after the opening. The one who lives for many years after the opening is not like the one who dies shortly after it." We could say that the one who enters the land and lives in it until he knows its common, and its elite, and what it contains is not like the one who enters it in the morning and leaves it in the evening.

Peace

97

The greatest wonder is the one who only sees distance when, in reality, there is no distance. There is nearness since Allah-ta'ala said, *"We are nearer to him than you,"* and *"We are nearer to him than the jugular vein."* It is as one of the realised said, may Allah be pleased with them, "Had I been obliged to see other-than-Him, I would not have been able to do it since there is nothing else with Him, so how can I see it with Him?" One of them said:

Since I have recognised the divinity, I do not see other-than-Him,

Similarly, other is forbidden with us.

Since I have gathered together what I feared would separate, today I have arrived gathered.

One of them said, "Those who are realised refuse to see other-than-Allah." One of them said:

Say' 'Allah!' and leave existence and what it contains if you have any doubts about reaching perfection.

If you are exact, all except Allah is non-existence in detail and in sum.

Know that had it not been for Him, all the worlds
would have been obliteration and extinction.

Had it not been for Him, the existence of the one
whose existence is not by his own essence would
have been the impossible itself.

The gnostics are annihilated and do not see anything
except the Great, the Exalted.

They see that other-than-Him in reality is perishing in
the present, past and future.

The lofty Shaykh, the wali of Allah-ta'ala, Abu Zayd Sayyidi
'Abdu'r-Rahman al-Majdhoub, may Allah be pleased with
him, said:

My sight has disappeared into His sight, and it is
annihilated to every vanishing thing.

I realised that other-than-Him does not exist, and
departed in delight immediately.

How remarkable and yet more remarkable are those people
among the people of nearness who see only distance! There is
no distance, as we said. There is nearness.

Peace

98

As for the dream which you saw, we ask Allah-ta'ala to
make it a cause for great guidance for you. There are many
to whom Allah has given opening through a dream. The first
command of the Prophet, may Allah bless him and grant him
peace, was a vision. However, faqir, always draw near to the
people of good and go far from the people of evil. Leave
what does not concern you and take on the character of your
Prophet, may Allah bless him and grant him peace, and you
will see wonders.

Peace

99

Know, faqir, that I would like you to take on the opposite of the character which most of the fuqaha' of our time have, may Allah be kind to them! They have abandoned noble character and taken on blameworthy character. They know and do not act. They are proud and not humble. They are greedy and not content. They desire and do not do without. They are miserly and not openhanded. Allah is greater! How far they are from knowledge and how near they are to ignorance! My brother, flee! flee! Do not turn aside! If you want to inherit from the prophets, peace be upon them, then take on their character and travel their way. The secret, overflowing favour, baraka, and good deeds lie in leaving this world – that is the business of the prophets, blessings and peace be upon them, and the awliya, may Allah be pleased with them! Divesting oneself of it, outwardly and inwardly is the path of the Prophet, peace be upon him. You must have the one who clings to his sunna and is on a clear sign from his Lord. May Allah give you success!

Peace

100

Going straight is desired from us, outwardly and inwardly. None of us acquires it, no matter what he does, unless he expels love of this world from his heart. By Allah, no knower goes straight unless he leaves it. No one who fasts all day and prays all night goes straight unless he expels love of it from his heart as we said. The sign of the departure of its love from his heart is that it is constricted when it exists and expanded when it does not exist.

Peace

101

May Allah have mercy on you! Know, that the shaykhs of the Path, may Allah be pleased with them! who join attraction and wayfaring — or if you like, you can say intoxication and sobriety — are the means between us and our Lord. It is not the one who is wayfaring without attraction, or the one who is majdhoub (mad-in-Allah) without wayfaring. We could say, that it is not the one who is intoxicated without sobriety, nor the one who is sober without intoxication. Whoever attaches himself to them is saved. Whoever stays away from them is drowned. The People, may Allah be pleased with them, said, "Whoever has no shaykh, his shaykh is shaytan."

We urge you by every possible means to have respect and esteem for your shaykhs, your brothers, and all of the slaves of your Lord. When you have esteem for those whom we mentioned, they have esteem for you. If you disregard them, they disregard you:

I looked at them, they looked at me. My eyes shone.

As was said by the wali of Allah-ta'ala, Sayyidi Muhammad ash-Sharqawi, may Allah profit us by him! Be on your guard against exerting all of your energy in recalcitrance towards them. The people, may Allah be pleased with them, said, "There is no tawba for recalcitrance to the masters."

Peace

102

May Allah have mercy on you! Know that I have written you many letters and I do not know whether they have reached you or not. Now you have written a letter to me, and its carrier will not turn to anything until he brings it to us and its answer is returned to you. That is the outward aspect. If it is from you to us and from us to you without any barrier, it is water which flows from me to you and from you to us. If it is not without a barrier, then it is not like that. For us and all of the people of the station of annihilation, may Allah be pleased with them, the sensory is the source of the meaning. If it is released, then it is the meaning. If it is not released, then it is not. We are content with the letter from you, provided that it is from you to us and from us to you without any barrier as we said. The people, may Allah be pleased with them, said, ''The one who profits only profits by the company of one who has profited. The one who loses only loses by the company of one who has lost.'' Our company will be firm by writing, Allah willing, provided that it is from us to you and from you to us without any barrier as we stated.

Peace

103

As you love us, we love you. Allah is the authority for what we say. May Allah bless you! We would like for you to draw near to mercy always. We could say, always to be immersed in mercy. The Messenger of Allah, may Allah bless him and grant him peace, was the source of mercy. Draw near him with a lot of prayer upon him, peace be upon him, as we told you some days ago. Go far from all that distracts you from your Lord and do not go near it. Disregard your inward and your outward as much as you can. Among the benefits of disregarding them is the breaking of norms. It is clear to me that whoever is content with little of this world, weans his self constantly from it, and disregards his outward and inward, performs the obligatory prayer and confirmed sunna, and leaves what does not concern him, by Allah, he is embraced by the sunna of Muhammad, blessings and peace of Allah be upon him. Whoever is not like that — and they are many — does not follow the sunna, and Allah knows best.

Immense mercy will spread over existence, Allah willing, as it spread over existence in the time of al-Junayd, al-Ghazali, ash-Shadhili, al-Hatimi, and their likes, may Allah be pleased with them. All of them in existence were in the position of the pure jewel-like heart in the body. Because of that, their good qualities were manifested in existence so there existed what good deeds there were. If the heart is full of good qualities, then certainly its good qualities will be manifested in the limbs. If it is full of ugly qualities, then certainly its ugly qualities will be manifested in the limbs. This is a well-known tradition.

Peace

104

The sickness which has befallen you is that which befalls the one who is beloved with Allah. "The people with the most affliction are the prophets, then the awliya , then those like them." Those like them should not be grieved because of it because in general, it is inflicted on the people of true sincerity and love. By it, they obtain increase towards their Lord, and by it, their hearts are purified and made into jewel-essence. Had it not been for encounter-perceptions, gnosis would not be given to anyone. Far from it! Far from it indeed! "Had it not been for the arenas of the self, the way of the runners would not be realised" as Ibn 'Ata'Illah said in the Hikam. He also said in it, "By the variety of traces and transformations of states, I knew that what you desired from me was to give me perception in everything so that I would not be ignorant of You in anything." The people, may Allah be pleased with them, said, "It is in the transformations of states that men are recognised from men." It says in the Immense Qur'an. *"Do people reckon that they will be left alone if they say, 'We believe,' and they will not be tested?"* Also in it is *"Dutiful obedience is not...."* to the end of the ayat.

Listen to what the people of gnosis of Allah have. It was said to Sayyiduna 'Umar b. 'Abdil-'Aziz, may Allah be pleased with him! "What do you desire?" He said, "Whatever Allah decrees." Shaykh Mawlana 'Abdu'l-Qadir al-Jilani, said, may Allah be pleased with him!:

If affliction arrives, it is not up to me to turn away
    from it.
If bliss arrives, it is not up to me to revel in it.
I am not one to be consoled by part of my desire.
    For another part. I am content only with the whole.

Shaykh Ibn 'Ata'Illah said in his Hikam, "The pain of affliction should be lightened for you by your knowledge that He – glory be to Him! is the Afflictor." There is no doubt that with the people, may Allah be pleased with them, the best moment is the moment of their poverty, i.e. their need. By that, they obtain increase. Shaykh Ibn 'Ata'Illah, may Allah be pleased with him! said in his Hikam, "The best of your moments is the moment in which you see the existence of your poverty, and in it, you return to the existence of your abasement." He said, "You may find increase in poverty while you do not find it in prayer or fasting." Poverty (faqa) designates intensity of need. The shaykh of our shaykh, Sayyidi al-'Arabi b. 'Abdillah called it "urging-on" or sometimes "woman's prodding" because it urges on the one who has it to his Lord. Our Master, may Allah be pleased with him, said, "Had people known what secrets and blessing were in need, they would not have needed anything except need." He said that it stood in the place of the Greatest Name. He, may Allah be pleased with him, interpreted power as weakness.

We see that gnosis repels affliction as it repelled it from others, such as the prophets, blessings and peace be upon them, and the awliya', may Allah be pleased with them. Allah ta'ala said, *"We said: 'Fire! Be coolness and peace for Ibrahim.' They wanted to snare him, so We made them the losers and rescued him."* Allah-ta'ala said, *"It is said to those who have taqwa of Allah, 'What did your Lord bring down? They say, 'Good.' This is even though there is great affliction. Allah only brings it down on them out of love for them and concern for them.* It says in the Immense Qur'an: *"How many a prophet there has been with whom vast numbers fought...."* to the end of the ayat. Also *"If a wound touches you, a wound like it has touched people "* and so on. Their gnosis of their Lord and their absorbtion in the contemplation of the immensity of His essence has made them withdraw from good and evil since they, may Allah be pleased with them, see neither good nor evil. They see their Lord. As they, may Allah be pleased with him, see Him in blessing, they see Him in adversities since He is the Blesser, and He is the Avenger. They also see Him in giving as they see Him in witholding, and so on. Shaykh Ibn 'Ata'Illah said in his Hikam, may Allah be pleased with him. "When He gives to you, He shows you His kindness. When He witholds from you, He shows you His force. In all of that, He makes Himself known to you, and advances to you by His lutf."

The upshot is that He is the Majestic with them and He is the Beautiful. They do not recognise affliction and it does not recognise them, may Allah be pleased with them, since that only belongs to the people of the veil. It is not for the people from whom the veil has been lifted. The cause of punishment is the existence of the veil. The completion of bliss is by looking at the noble face of Allah. The sorrows and worries which the hearts experience are because they are barred from eye-witnessing as Ibn 'Ata'Illah says in the Hikam.

Peace

105

Illusion is baseless, but Allah gave it form by a great wisdom. Every matter has a great secret and a clear aspect as

Allah–ta'ala said, *"Our Lord! You did not create this in vain. Glory be to You!"* *"Do you suppose that We created you as a sport?"* Far be it from our Lord to create that. Our Lord is high above that! If you do not get control of illusion, i.e. put your own view on it, it will certainly get control of you and put its view on you. If you do not reject its view, it will reject your view. It is nothing. If you listen to its conversation it will weaken your certainty and pull you from it to the side. If you do not listen to its conversation, your luminosity will grow stronger. When it grows stronger, your certainty will grow stronger. When it grows stonger, your himma will rise. When it rises, you reach your Lord. Your reaching Him is reaching knowledge of Him, glory be to Him!

For those who travel to Allah and do not listen to its conversation or follow its opinion, it is like a strong wind released for sailors. In one hour, it makes them arrive whereas others arrive there after a month or a year. Allah knows best. When someone halts with its conversation and opinion, by Allah, he remains becalmed, at a standstill, as occurs to sailors. Such is its nature. We think that the one who leaves what does not concern him will find that the least of means is enough for him. If he does not leave it, nothing will be enough for him, no matter what he does.

Peace

106

All good is in the dhikr of Allah. Allah–ta'ala said, *"Those who remember Allah often, men and women, Allah has prepared forgiveness for them and an immense wage."* Allah ta'ala said, *"Remember me, I will remember you. Thank Me and do not be ungrateful to Me."* Allah–ta'ala said, *"Woe to those who are hardhearted against the dhikr of Allah. Those are in clear misguidance."* The Prophet, peace be upon him, said in what He related from his Lord; glory be to Him! *"I sit with the one who remembers Me, and I am with Him when he remembers Me....''* to the end of his words. This is enough about the virtue of dhikr and censure of heedlessness. If what we mentioned of ayat and hadith is not enough for us about its virtue, then nothing is enough for us and there is no good in us. Allah exalts our wages and we do not need anything else. What we need to do is oppose our passions. That will open up knowledge by divine gift. Knowledge by divine gift will result in great certainty. Great certainty purifies us of doubts and illusions and brings us to the presence of the King, the Knowing. Glory be to Him! There is no god but Him!

Peace

107

Injustice inevitably kills the one who perpetrates it when the end of its term comes because it appears to people that he does it deliberately. So they kill him because of the error which they see from him. By Allah, I used to think that it was people who despised me, thought me a fool, belittled me, demeaned me, abased me, considered me ignorant and did not recognise my worth. When Allah opened my inner eye and illuminated my secret by His generosity and openhandness, then I found that my self was the one doing that to me, and no one else. I found a large number of ayat which indicated this. Allah—ta'ala said, *'Allah does not change a people until they change themselves.''* *''Allah does not wrong people at all. People wrong themselves.''* *''Whatever evil hits you comes from your self ,''* etc. When I recognised this, I saw that the one doing the injustice was myself. I did not see it as coming from my fellow men. This was so much the case that when someone came to complain to me about anyone, we saw that the injustice was only from himself. We did not see it from any other direction.

May Allah bless you! Know that when you recognise your

worth and the height of your position in reality, all of existence recognises your worth and the height of your position. If you are ignorant of it, existence is ignorant of it and does not recognise your value at all. This is because your self, faqir, believer, in as much as it is knowing or ignorant, right-doing or vicious, is, in reality, the whole cosmos with the one who recognises, not with the one who is destroyed. You see only the cosmos which everyone sees. You also see that the cosmos injures you while only your self injures you. By Allah, if you were to overcome it — or we might say, kill it, you would overcome all created beings, great and small. Allah is the authority for what we say.

Peace

108

The root of the self is very good indeed. However, it has become foul after its goodness, low after its height, abased after its might, poor after its wealth, ignorant after its knowledge, weak after its strength, turbid after its purity, powerless after its power, lonely after its intimacy, constricted after its wideness, defeated after its victory, routed after its attack, belittled after its greatness, enslaved after its freedom, exiled from its homeland and people after it was in its homeland and people, dead after its life, and so on. The reason for what has befallen it is that it relies on a world other than its own. That is the world of turbidity in which we remain without any movement on our part to something else, or any repose. There is no power nor strength except by Allah, the High, the Great. "We belong to Allah and to Him we return." My brothers, this is the reason and the cause. If we want to return to our homeland from which we came — and it is the world of purity, or we could say the resplendent world, the celestial world, or the spiritual world, then all we need to do is to wipe out all the turbidities with which our hearts are bedaubed, or we could say, the others which are engraved on it. All we need to do is to strip off the world of turbidity as the sheep is stripped of its skin. We would forget and never remember it. This is the path of return. Oh for the one who does not fear hunger, nakedness, thirst, lions, eagles, snakes, and other things! My brothers, look at how we have exchanged the higher for the lower and yet we are not ashamed before our Lord and we do not reprimand ourselves for what we have done.

We have opened the door for you and removed the veil for you. We have let you sit down in the presence of the lovers. May Allah have mercy on you! Return to us and remember us with good, Allah will remember you with good. Come to us and do not cut yourselves from us. Allah-ta'ala will bring you to Him by pure generosity. He is Openhanded, Generous, Compassionate, Merciful, with immense overflowing favour. Glory be to Him! There is no god but Him!

Peace

109

People only look at the majdhoub with the eye of esteem. They do not look at him at all with the eye of contempt, even though he does not pray, fast, or do anything that Allah has commanded. He has lost his intellect because of his contemplation of the immensity of his Lord. His reality is a luminous reality. By Allah, it is not dark. By Allah, whoever is like this, is the wali of Allah.

My brother, the state of divestment which you have is the state of those who are majdhoub, may Allah be pleased with them. If you do not remain in it, people will call you a fool, despise and abuse you. They will not wrong you because you have not remained in the state of attraction after you have had it. You have not moved from the state of wayfaring after you had the state of attraction. While you are in the state of wayfaring, you fall upon the state of attraction as

when you are in the state of attraction, you fall upon the
state of wayfaring. Certainly you will be abused from the
direction of the people of wayfaring, and certainly you will
be abused from the direction of the people of attraction.
Both of them will abuse you, and they will not wrong you.
You have wronged yourself because of your vacillation. You
belong neither to these nor those. Had you remained in the
state of attraction, abuse would have restrained you from the
people of wayfaring. Had you joined attraction and wayfaring – or we might say, the outward and the inward, there
would have been no abuse towards you from either direction. You would have been like al-Junayd, al-Ghazali, ash-
Shadhili, al-Hatimi, Ibn Mashish, the Ghawth, or their likes
who joined intoxication and sobriety like our master, may
Allah be pleased with him, and his shaykhs, the masters, the
sons of Fez, and the masters, the sons of Ibn 'Abdillah at the
city of Fez. May Allah-ta'ala be pleased with all of our
masters! By Allah, I was accepted with all of the people of
wayfaring and all of the people of attraction, may Allah be
pleased with them.

Peace

110

Faqir, if your sensory is weak, your meanings will certainly be strong. If your outward is constricted, your inward will certainly be expanded. If your outward is in ruins,
your inward will certainly be built up. Look at the state of
the common people. When they adorn their outward, Allah
makes their outward and their inward ugly. After you have
smelled them for seven days or years, you do not smell the
scent of meanings in them. You only smell the odor of sweat
on them. That is the repayment for leaving the root, and the
root is the action of the heart, and taking the branch which is
the action of the limbs. They are denied arrival since they
have neglected the roots. Sensory things are the opposite of

meanings. Two meanings are not joined together. Whoever
wants the meanings, must leave sensory things. Whoever
wants sensory things, pleasures, and appetites, does not desire
the meanings since the only way to them is by the door of
leaving the sensory.

Peace

111

May Allah have mercy on you! Know that I want you to
remind each other about what will kill your self and give life
to your hearts as the people of the Path did before you. Be
on your guard against the machinations of the self so that
help will not be cut off from you. Whoever wants constantly
to have help, should not exalt his self. He should abuse
it, fling it aside, knock it down, and make it travel by the
things it dislikes, in spite of itself. This is always the method
of the people of true sincerity with it. They make it travel
only with what it dislikes, finds heavy, and abhors so that
loved and disliked things become the same for it. They are
not veiled to its ugly qualities, or we might say its faults, or
machinations, by being always pleased with it.

The state of divestment which you have is only related
to the great inward, i.e. the great heart. If the matter is not
like that, that which it has of form in its means is a better
state for it and more praiseworthy end. Allah knows best.
The shari‘at of the people confirms to us that our poverty is
greater than our reputation. Today our repute is greater than
us. May Allah heal us! Whoever wants help to remain with
him, should not speak about it with every one. He should
speak about it with his people.

Peace

112

One day, one of the rejectors said to me in the presence of a group of the brothers, may Allah be pleased with them, "You are our masters and lords." I told him, "I will not hear that from you or anyone else! I do not accept it from anyone! For Allah is my Lord and Master! As for my self being my lord and master, I will not hear it or accept it." Then I also said to him, "The moment in which Allah — glory be to Him! is my Lord and Master, in it I am the lord and master of existence in spite of it, whether it likes it or not. The moment in which my self is my lord and master, in it existence is my lord and master in spite of myself, whether I like it or not. All of it belittles me, demeans me, abases me, overpowers me, neglects, is unconcerned about me, and does what it likes with me. How then can we turn to this by your praise and blame, and the praise and blame of anyone else. This is to no purpose.

Peace

113

One day we were involved in teaching the brothers, may Allah be pleased with them! There was a man near us and it was as if he did not see us and had not heard us. I spoke to him in a strong state which had come to me, "Leave us or sit with us! May Allah have mercy on you! Our gathering is one which has been shown mercy, and mercy will not leave us as long as we are in our gathering. At this moment it is seen more and more. My brother, come near us, your Lord will show mercy to you with us as He shows mercy to all who are created for the sake of our gathering. Whoever doubts what we say, should neither sit with us nor come near us."

Peace

114

One day I was at the zawiyya of the shaykh, may Allah be pleased with him, speaking with the brothers, may Allah be pleased with them, about silence. We were urging them to have it. Part of what I said to them is: "Make silence one of the confirmed parts of your wird, its favoured part, and main part. It truly results in reflection. An hour of reflection is better than seventy years of 'ibada as you know from hadith.

At that time I was in great intoxication and great sobriety. I joined them and was strong in both of them with great strength. Then one of the people of knowledge, may Allah be pleased with them, from our brothers, the people of Fez, began to laugh and mock me. Look at what Allah did to him at the end. The precious things which Allah has honoured us with will be mentioned, and, Allah willing, you will see what will delight you and strengthen your certainty and love for the people of the Path, may Allah be pleased with them.

Peace

115

I would like you to abandon your dispersed love since it will keep you away from the secret, good, overflowing favour, and baraka. We see some people who are attached to this thing at one time, and attached to something else at another time. This is like the one who is digging for water, and digs a little here and a little there. He dies of thirst and does not find water. He is not like the one who digs in one place, trusting and relying on Allah. He finds water and drinks and lets other people drink. Allah knows best. The people, may Allah be pleased with them, said, "Persist at one door, and many doors will be opened for you. Surrender yourself humbly to one master, all necks will bow to you."

Part of this business also is that sometimes he loves the

East and travels there. Another time, he loves the West, and travels there. Sometimes he does without and sometimes he desires, and is distant. Had he obtained nearness, he would be still and at peace. The lofty Shaykh Sayyidi al-Majdhoub said, may Allah be pleased with him:

> The day rose on the moon and only my Lord re-mained.
> People visit Muhammad while he dwells in my heart.

Peace

116

I urge you to be on your guard as much as you can against meeting with the people of claims among the people of our time and speaking with them. If they speak with you and de-sire to converse with you, then the answer to them is like silence towards them. Our master said, may Allah be pleased with him, "Real opposition to the enemy is truly your oc-cupation with the love of the Beloved, for when you are oc-cupied with opposition to the enemy, he has obtained what he desires from you and love of the Beloved has missed you."

Peace

117

The one who remains with opinion will certainly never ac-quire realisation. Then stop remaining with it and do not judge anything by your supposition or your own opinion. Judge it after you have realised the matter since true sin-cerity in words and deeds banishes doubts and illusions, and establishes tawhid in the heart permanently. It even banishes the opposition of the self. When the opposition of the self is banished, the opposition of fellow-men is also banished. When the opposition of fellow-men is banished, it is your

turn and Allah–ta'ala will help you. If you refrain from injuring the slaves of your Lord and endure their harm, then
your realisation will be greater and your character will be
greater. That is the state of the perfected among the awliya
of Allah, may Allah be pleased with them.

Peace

118

The patched jelaba, begging, uncovering the head, walking
barefooted, sitting on rubbish heaps while being careful
about impurity, eating in markets, sleeping in the road and
others states which some of the sufis have like the people of
our tariqa, may Allah be pleased with them! – none knows
whether they are real or baseless except for the sincere. We
think that pure sincerity is what throws the people there,
since they, may Allah be pleased with them, are not concerned with themselves and they do not choose any state in
preference over another. They are also drowned in the seas of
exaltation as Shaykh Abu Sa'id Ibn al-'Arabi, may Allah be
pleased with him said when he was asked about annihilation.
He said, "Annihilation is that immensity and majesty appear
on the slave making him forget this world and the next...." to
the end of the quote which is previously cited.

Allah knows best, but they were like that before they
were drowned in the seas of exaltation because their true sincerity would not let them look at anything except what was
between them and their Lord. They did not look at all at
what was between them and His creation. This is their state,
may Allah be pleased with them. We see that the people of
pure sincerity have many great and varied strange states.
They are only perceived in reality by the person who is like
al-Khidr. Look at the states of al-Khidr, peace be upon him,
in the Book of Allah and you will see wonders. He made a
hole in the ship while it was being of good use to its owners

172

and their baggage. He killed the boy but did not kill him on behalf of his own people or for anyone else and there was nothing against the boy in the shari'at of Muhammad. He set up the wall after his owners had not offered them hospitality when they had requested it. He did all this in the presence of the Messenger of Allah to whom he spoke, Sayyiduna Musa, peace be upon him, since he would only accept the truth and only perform what was true, so understand! May Allah give us and you understanding!

Peace

119

The actions which people display today are very numerous. However, they have no fruit because of the love of this world which dwells in their hearts and remains with them and does not leave them. Had they been content with a little of it as others have been content, a tenth of a tenth of their actions would have been enough for them and the fruits of their actions would have been present as they were present for others. An atom's worth of actions by the heart is better than mountains of actions by the limbs. There is no doubt of that. The actions of hearts are many, even if they are few. The actions of other than the hearts are few, even if they are many as Ibn 'Ata'Illah says in the Hikam: "An action which comes from a heart which does without is not little. An action which comes from a greedy heart is not much."

Peace

120

With the perfect awliya, may Allah be pleased with them, majesty is the source of beauty since for them, majesty is the essence and beauty is the attributes. How can you distinguish between majesty or beauty, or we could say the essence and the attributes when you see might in abasement, strength in weakness, giving in witholding, blessing in adversity, life in death, well-being in affliction, the lover in the enemy, and the great in the small? A man said to Shaykh Dhu'n-Nun al-Misri, may Allah be pleased with him, "Show me the Greatest Name!" He rebuked him and said, "Show me the least name and I will show you the Greatest Name!" since he, may Allah be pleased with him! only saw immensity and greatness. They appear in tajalli-manifestation in what is hidden and are hidden in what is manifest. They are manifestation and they are hiddenness. They are near in what is far, and far in what is near. They are nearness and and they are distance. They are high in what is low and low in what is high. They are height and they are lowness. They are great in what is small and small in what is great. They are greatness and they are smallness. They are strong in what is weak and weak in what is strong. They are weakness and they are strength. They are aboveness and they are belowness. They are the separated and they are the gathered. They are separation and they are gatheredness. They are the part and they are the whole. They vary with every variety of created being, whether that variety — or we could say, that thing, were above or below, or high or low, speaking or not speaking, still or not still, known, or unknown, and so on:

> My beloved encompasses existence. He has appeared
> in the white and the black.
> In the Christians and the Jews, in the pigs and the
> monkeys,
> And in the letters with the dots. Do you understand
> me at all? Do you understand me at all?

This is what the famous wali, the great gnostic, Abu'l-Hasan Sayyidi 'Ali ash-Shushtari said, may Allah be pleased with him and give us the benefit of his baraka and the baraka of his companions!

Peace

121

The self and the spirit are two names for the same thing from the source of light, and Allah knows best. It became double by being described by two attributes: they are purity and turbidity. As long as the self is turbid, only the name "self" is true for it. When its turbidity goes, and it becomes pure and jewel-essence, the name "spirit" is true for it. We see that they always love each other because they are near to each other, and both of them possess excellence, beauty, stature, and harmony. When Allah wants to make one of His slaves a wali, he joins the two of them together for him, i.e. places one in the other's hands. That occurs when the self returns from its passions which have seized it and made it far from its family and homeland, and stripped it of its excellence, beauty, radiance, nobility, height, elevation, and whatever its Master had extended to it. Its passions made it reject its source and not search for it. It does not remain in this state. It leaves it and completely returns from it. Then the spirit comes to it and helps it. It has its meanings and secrets with which Allah helps it and they are endless. According to the amount of its passions which are abandoned, the help of the spirit becomes stronger from its Lord. The marriage and offspring become more and more. These are the knowledges by divine gift and the actions resulting from them. The pleasure of that is such that it can only lead one to oppose the self and make it go by what it dislikes, finds heavy, and abhors. That is easy for him because of what he sees of its lights, secrets, and benefits.

Peace

122

I said to one of the people of knowledge of the people of Fez, when he denied our divestment, and thought it unlikely and difficult, and disapproved of it and did not find it good: Among its people, divestment is like the red elixir with its people. None rejects it except the one who is ignorant of it and does not recognise its value. Shaykh Ibn 'Ata'Illah, may Allah be pleased with him, called it high himma. He said in his Hikam, "When Allah establishes you in divestment, your desire for means is falling from high himma." Sayyidi Abu Yazid al-Bistami, Sayyidi al-Junayd, Sayyidi Abu Ya'za al-Maghribi, Mawlana 'Abdu's-Salam b. Mashish, and their likes had it, may Allah be pleased with them. They are numerous. It has only appeared to you that it is error because you are ignorant of it and because of the scarcity of its people in this age which has few good points and numerous ugly points. Its people are few only because it is difficult for the self since none can divest himself of means, clothes, and habits unless Allah takes him by the hand and gives him trust of Him, or we could say, reliance on Him.

If you said, "The people of divestment flee from people to mountains that are far from habitation and to caves," we said: They are like that, but not all of them, some of them only. Most of them are like us. One of them who is with people in the markets and other places while he has broken the habits of his self, is stronger than others, and stronger still. There is a great difference between him and the one who has cut himself off from creation. He is weak. The strong one is the one who does not leave them while he is safe from them. The one who is in the wind — and the wind is people — while the lamp of his heart is alight and not extinguished by the wind of people is not like the one who is in a house with the doors closed. When the wind blows on him, he may remain occupied and maybe not. This is different from the one who is in the wind and it blows on him and does not extinguish him, so understand!

If you said, "The affair is confused for us. We do not know the one who is true from the baseless one," we said: Whoever wants to recognise that should have good opinion of his Lord and His slaves since the Prophet, may Allah bless him and grant him peace, said, "There is nothing better than two qualities: good opinion of Allah and good opinion of the slaves of Allah. There is nothing worse than two qualities: bad opinion of Allah and bad opinion of the slaves of Allah." By Allah, no one profits who has profited from the beginning of the world to its end except the one who has intention, love, true sincerity, good opinion, and submission. No one loses who has lost from the beginning of this world to its end except the one Allah leaves empty of what we have mentioned. The one who has intention and its sisters profits in the place of loss – and Allah knows best – let alone the place of profit. The one who has no intention or love loses in the place of profit – and Allah knows best – let alone the place of loss.

If you said, "Isn't there any other way for us to reach our Lord except by the door of divestment which you have? Isn't it enough for us to divest our inward rather than our outward?" We said: There is no way for any of us to reach our Lord except by the door of divestment of the outward and divestment of the inward because divestment of both directions was the path of the Messenger of Allah, may Allah bless him and grant him peace, the path of his companions, and whoever has followed them up to this very day. None divests his inward in reality unless his divestment appears on the limbs. If it does not appear on the limbs, then it is of no consequence. The wali of Allah, our master, Sayyidi 'Ali al–Jamal, may Allah be pleased with him! said: "Divestment is divestment of this world in the sensory, and not in the meaning alone since divestment of meaning has no benefit until sensory divestment is obtained. If one obtains divestment of meaning, he should pay no attention to it nor turn to it nor judge by it. It has no benefit unless the sensory appears. 'I am commanded to judge by the outward and Allah takes charge of the secrets ' because the outward is firm and it is that which is rejected. If nothing is firm for him outwardly, then he has nothing. The inward is the basis of the outward, and it is built on it." Shaykh Abu Madyan may Allah be pleased with him, said, "When you see someone who claims to have a state with Allah while he has nothing that testifies to it on his outward, then watch out for him." We said, "Had the meanings been connected to other than the sensory, the people of iman would have been content in as much as they believe that they have iman in their hearts and they would not have articulated the shahada on their tongues. Since meanings are only connected to the senses, we are commanded to articulate the shahada on our tongues, and it is not hidden.

We think that whoever purifies his heart of love of this world in reality and of all that does not concern him, by Allah, his limbs will be purified. Sayyidi, look at the states of the Companions, may Allah be pleased with them, and others among the people of pure sincerity. By Allah, you see that what they have inwardly appears on their limbs since they, may Allah be pleased with them, only have the provision of a rider from this world. Some of them have nothing of it. When he finds something, he is content with it and does not choose or store up. He follows the Messenger of Allah, may Allah bless him and grant him peace, and takes on his character. Had one of them chosen, he would have been constrained. Had he been constrained, he would have resisted, since the Prophet, may Allah bless him and grant him peace, said: "I and those of my community who have taqwa are free of constraint."

Some of the Companions and other people had this world, but their hearts were free of love of it and filled with love of Allah and love of the Messenger of Allah, may Allah bless him and grant him peace. Whoever is like that, is not harmed by it. It benefits him since he feeds the hungry and clothes the naked with it. It also says in hadith, "This world is the mount of the believer," but not for everyone. It is only for some.

178

Our master, Shaykh Sayyidi 'Ali, may Allah be pleased with him! said: "None of us can avoid that which must support his structure as none of us can avoid urine and faeces. When we have finished fulfilling what we need, we should leave it immediately and go about means. No one should be delighted by the proximity of that for an hour. It is like that with this world. When the believer fulfills his need of it, he leaves it and turns to his Lord. No one can turn to his Lord unless he turns his back on whatever distracts him from Him." Shaykh Ibn 'Ata'Illah, may Allah be pleased with him said: "Your turning to Allah is your turning away from creation. Your turning to creation is your turning away from Allah."

Our master, may Allah be pleased with him, said, "The truly sincere faqir is the one who is such that his enemy cannot find a way to injure him. This is his sign since his only constant occupation is his Beloved. His occupation with his Beloved veils him from his enemy. The Lover and the enemy are never joined." There is no doubt that if the faqir obtains divestment in reality, he will obtain pure sincerity. If he does not, then he will not obtain it. Divestment is ruins. If the ruins of this world and its means and appetites do not appear on the limbs of the faqir, he is a small child and not a great man. If the ruins appear on his limbs and he is established in the state of ruins, he is among the great men. This is the sign of his maturity, or we could say, his reaching his Lord. When light is strong in the inward of the believer, it drives out everything from it. When it drives out everything from it, his Master – glory be to Him and may He be exalted! remains in his inward part. Whoever is like that, is one of the awliya of Allah.

The one who says he is divested inwardly and not outwardly has no proof since the word of Allah, the Mighty, the Majestic is true for the one who is divested inwardly and not outwardly: *It is very hateful with Allah that you say what you do not do"* and other statements. The word of Allah, the

179

Mighty, the Majestic is true for the one who is divested outwardly and not divested inwardly: *"They say with their mouths what is not in their hearts."*

It is best that the faqir purify himself of the illusion of the existence of other until he begins to take and is not taken, to overcome and is not overcome, to pull and is not pulled, to own and is not owned, and so forth. Then there is no objection whether he is divested outwardly or not. How remarkable! Our Prophet, may Allah bless him and grant him peace, died and he had not placed one brick on top of another. The 'ulama of our time, may Allah be kind to them, although it is ours and theirs, do not accept the state of ruins at all. They accept the state of building. Very few among them will accept the state of divestment although the great Imam Sayyidi al-Junayd, may Allah be pleased with him! was truly among the people of divestment. The qutb Mawlana 'Abdu's-Salam b. Mashish was among the people of divestment. The great shaykh, the wali of Allah-ta'ala, Abu Yazid al-Bistami, may Allah be pleased with him, was among the people of divestment, and he had about 4,000 of the people of divestment with him. They had left means and clothes, and put on the patched robe.

Those, may Allah be pleased with them, all of them have lofty value and immense importance with Allah and all the slaves of Allah. May Allah be pleased with them, they are practically prophets, blessings and peace be upon them and our Prophet. In spite of that, they do not accept what they have and they do not listen to it, let alone know it. How remarkable! If we do not follow those people, then who could we follow among people? We would demonstrate a vicious, proud, arrogant self. By Allah! By Allah! By Allah! The only one who can oppose his passion is the one whom his Master strengthens. The only one who is generous with his own portion is the one who is purely and sincerely for his Lord. The prophets, blessing and peace be upon them, and the awliya, may Allah be pleased with them, have been purified for their Lord. They do not have divestment of means or anything, great or small, not even the bliss of the Garden. The contemplation and eyewitnessing of the King, the Judge, has made them withdraw from it. So how can they remain with means or divestment or anything? They are always drowned in the contemplation of their Lord. They do not see hardship or ease, poverty or wealth, health or sickness. May Allah honour us with their remembrance and make us die with love of them.

Peace

123

May Allah have mercy on you! Know that I heard a statement from the people of knowledge, may Allah be pleased with them! from Fez. He said, may Allah be pleased with him! "Knowledge only extends as long as this world." That which appeared to him appeared to me as well. After that, I scrutinised what he had said and I found the opposite of it. My brother, knowledge only extends because of the lack of someone to hear it. Had someone to hear it been present, the expression "knowledge" would have been insufficient.

A certain individual pressed me to give him the wird, so I gave it to him. Then after that, I observed him as Allah willed to see if he had done it or not. He was the same as before we gave him the wird. I said to him, "Do you do dhikr or not?" He said, "Yes." I said, "The one who does dhikr is not hidden from us since the Noble Name has great force and well-known virtue. It is the Sultan of the names. It does not leave the one who does it in the same state. It moves him from it immediately if he is of the nature of Adam. If he is animal, he may remain in that state. If you do the dhikr, it is better to do it when you are pure in body, clothes, and place, and pure inwardly from the forbidden, and your tongue is free of lies.

Then I said to him, "I was inspired to remember my Lord without intermediary. It was by His pure generosity, glory be to Him! There is no god but Him! I would do this dhikr night and day. I was never silent at all. I recited Qur'an and I fled from the people of heedlessness as a man flees from his enemy. I did not like anyone to distract me from the remembrance of my Lord, even if it was my father, my mother, my uncle, a loved one, or anyone else. The teacher Sayyidi Muhammad b. 'Ali al-Lajadi wanted me to go along with him in taking one of the people of the time as a shaykh since he had no shaykh just as I had none. He, may Allah have mercy on him, loved me dearly and was one of the shaykhs who taught me Qur'an. When he encouraged me to go with him to the shaykh he wanted, I said to him, "Should I go with you to him and take him as a shaykh as you have taken him? What benefit would we have from him? The prayer, recitation of Qur'an, dhikr, retreat, and the actions which the people of the outward have, I always do them. Praise be to Allah! What then? If he is of the outward, its people are numerous. If he is of the inward, I have not heard about him from any of the people of this time. If I do not know them, I know most of their companions and we know what they have. By Allah, we only see them like the common people. As far as gnosis is concerned, they do not have it. Had their shaykhs had it, they would have had it. What we need is gnosis of our Lord!"

"I remained in that state until Allah opened me to recognition of my master and he took my hand, Allah-ta'ala was enough for him. My brother, how is it that you only do dhikr when we tell you, 'Do dhikr!' By Allah, you are like the beast which only moves by the prod. One who is always with those who do dhikr does not need someone to tell him, 'Do dhikr!' when he has eyes and ears. The ignorant man follows people and the sheep follows people. People say: He needs someone to watch him in the stations of dhikr since it is dhikr by the tongue and dhikr by seeing.

Peace

Faqir, listen to this story and remember it and do not forget it! Recall it frequently to the people of your path, may
Allah take you by the hand!: I was with a group of visitors
among the brothers who had taken me before that visit as
one of the shaykhs of the tariqa, may Allah be pleased with
them. They were from within the city of Taza. Then two of
the men said to me, "We would like to go by way of the city
of Fez." I told them, "Return with your brothers. It would be
better and safer for you since the gathering has baraka."
They told me, "We want to buy a small bucket there." I
told them, "This is the time the Haji comes. He has resolved to travel and will pass by you. He has small buckets,
long-necked bottles, small pots and other things. You can
get your small bucket and other things from him." They told
me, "We intended to return through it and no other way,"
I told them, "Do you say that I am your shaykh?" They told
me, "Is there any doubt of Allah?" I told them, "Then you
must strip off your will about yourselves and surrender it to
me. Stripping off the will and surrendering it to the shaykh
is, in reality surrendering the will to Allah. Surrendering the
will to Allah is the great election. Shaykh al-Haddad, the
shaykh of al-Junayd, may Allah be pleased with both of
them! said, "For forty years I have desired to desire to
leave what I desire. I have not found what I desire."
Another of the shaykhs of the tariqa said, may Allah be
pleased with them, "For the past forty years my Lord
established me in a state. I disliked it and he did not move
me from it, so I resented it." Shaykh ash-Shurayshi, may
Allah be pleased with him, said in his poem in Ra':

> Whoever does not have the attribute of stripping
> away his will does not desire to smell the scent
> of poverty.

After this, I told them, "Learn! Listen to me!"

A certain individual pressed me very strongly to give him

the wird, so I gave it to him. Then he said to me, "I want to travel to my land or to such-and-such a land." I told him, "The form of entry is the form of departure. It was like that before you took me as your shaykh. Now I choose for you. You do not choose for yourself." Another one came to me and the same thing happened as had happened with the other one before him, no more, no less. We tell this to everyone who resolves to travel on the Path at the hand of its shaykhs, may Allah be pleased with them and give us the benefit of their baraka. Amin.

Peace

125

If the faqir desires to take the Path in its reality, he should be a slave owned by its people. He does not keep their company at all unless he fulfills all of their inconvenient demands as much as he is able. The Prophet, may Allah bless him and grant him peace, said, "I and those of my community who have taqwa are free of constraint." If he keeps their company, or we could say, is near to them, and does not pray the obligatory prayer with them in their mosque and attend their circles of dhikr, he certainly falls from their sight. There is no doubt that this is only done by those who are hated. He should also call to mind the benefits he has from them and what he does not have so that his actions will not be useless without being aware of their uselessness. Then his reality will be luminous, not dark. He will also have taken the Path in its reality since he knows its shari'at and fulfills it. The reality without the shari'at of Muhammad is paralysis as the shari'at of Muhammad without the reality is paralysis. Joining both of them is realisation.

It is good to obtain the intoxication which withdraws you from the sensory and which is not hidden from people. Then your reality is a reality of light, even if it is without shari'at.

Perfection is joining intoxication and sobriety. If someone withdraws from what we mentioned, and the cause of his withdrawal is ignorance and heedlessness, it will not profit him at all unless he knows it, calls it to mind and acts by it. If the reason is incapacity, laziness, arrogance, and lack of interest, what door is better and more fitting if he fulfills it since he knows it and does not act by it? Consult your hearts. Whoever leaves his family, work, tribe and land, and keeps the company of the people of the Path, may Allah be pleased with them, and then does not leave off socialising with people and conversing with them about this world and its affairs is of no consequence. He will never have success. The one with this state exists and has many followers because they are turned upside down every moment. Sometimes they talk to them about their selves and its necessity, and sometimes about leaving it and being attached to other than it. It is like that until they die while they have acquired nothing except doubt. We seek refuge with Allah! Had they done what we said and done it in earnest, and not in jest, Allah would have taken them by the hand since Allah-ta'ala says, *Had they been true to Allah, it would have been better for them.*"

Whoever has a shaykh and his shaykh says something to him while he says something contrary to his shaykh and thinks that his opinion is greater than his shaykh's opinion, should refute what his shaykh says and say that directly to him as one of the brothers, may Allah be pleased with him, said so directly to us when I told them, "The path of dawn is the path of the sun." He said, may Allah turn to him! "There is nothing to prove these words." He must do that since the only cure he has is the moving storehouse which teaches him. Then one hopes for good for him. May Allah give us and our brothers success. Amin.

Peace

126

There must be a realised shaykh in every discipline. If not it is generally useless. Listen to what will confirm what we say, may Allah give you and us success! May Allah have mercy on you! Know that one of the people of knowledge, may Allah be pleased with him, recognised many of the shaykhs of his time and learned from them. In spite of that, whenever he met me, he would complain to me about his debts and his state was very constricted because of it.

One day I said to him, "Listen to what I tell you and always base yourself on it, you will see wonders. In the moment of adversity, both good and evil are present and not absent. near and not far. If you remember your Lord in it and forget yourself, you will profit. If the reverse happens, you will lose. Whenever poverty gets the better of you and comes to you, occupy yourself with the means your Lord has commanded you to, and do not turn to anything else at all. Always be like that at the moment of adversities. Then evil will leave you and good will come to you. If you strip away your will and surrender yourself to your Lord at the moment of your loss, or we could say, your adversity or affliction, and do not help yourself by any means, that is the highest station and the clearest secret. There is nothing above it except the station of prophecy. Allah is the authority for what we say."

May Allah be kind to him! He said to me after this, "I have such-and-such dhikr of 1000. Some of it I took from shaykh so-and-so and some of it I took from shaykh so-and-so," until he had mentioned a large number of shaykhs of the people of his time. I told him, "Listen to what I tell you and base yourself on it, and you will see wonders. I tell you that in reality the shaykh is the one who teaches you what I have taught you.

Peace

I strongly urge you to be occupied with your Lord. Do not concern yourselves about what distracts you because if you do not come to your own assistance, Allah-ta'ala will help you and take charge of your affair. May Allah curse whoever lies to you. If you come to your own assistance and take charge of your affair He will let you take care of it. You have no power to do anything. He — glory be to Him! "has power over everything." Know that if you master yourselves, you master whoever abuses you and all of the cosmos. Allah knows best. Only the one who masters his self masters people. Only the one who has been freed from the opposition of the self drives away the opposition of his fellowmen. None is freed of the opposition of his self unless he opposes his passion and obeys his Master. If you control your self as we have stated, you control people and all created being. All is under your force and power, and you can dispose of it as you like.

Beware of being ignorant or being ignorant of your ignorance. That is compounded ignorance. You suppose that you master something while you do not master your self. By Allah, that will never be yours. If you control your self, Allah will give you control over all created being as we have told you. He — glory be to Him! is Generous and His generosity is great. None of us can bestow himself on Him, i.e. be generous with it for Him, without Him, glory be to Him! bestowing His sublime self on him to repay him. When we give our vicious imperfect selves to Him, He - glory be to Him! gives us His precious self to repay us for them. He covers our abasement with His might, our poverty with His wealth, our weakness with His strength, our ignorance with His knowledge, our anger with His forbearance, our incapacity with His power, and so on. If you like, you could say that He covers our attribute with His attribute and our quality with His quality. How remarkable! The Kingdom belongs to Him, but He buys it from us by Himself and yet we do not sell it.

By Allah, by Allah! Whoever is shy cannot listen to this, let alone do it. Listen to what our Master, the Majestic, the Mighty, said to the one who was generous among us with himself for Him, glory be to Him!: *"Slave, are you generous to Me? Generosity is mine and I have it. Here is Myself in yourself!"*

Peace

128

I advise you to draw near your Prophet with the prayer and peace upon him as we told you many days ago. We think that the reality of the prayer of blessings and peace upon him is only obtained by the one who follows his sunna and takes on his character. Many people bless him constantly while they swim in darkness. That is because they are ignorant of his sunna. They take on the character of innovation. May Allah have mercy on you! take note of this deep hole and avoid it. May Allah save us and you from falling into it!

Peace

129

If you wish to join your meanings to our meanings, then join your sensory to our sensory, or we could say, bring your sensory near to our sensory if you can do that. If not, then the least amount of increase you can direct to us, even if it is only once a month in order to connect your meanings to our meanings as we have said.

Peace

130

About the states which you have — and they are the breaking of normal patterns — if you do not have the inner eye in them, they will certainly put you far from the sunna and bring you near to innovation. Then affliction will be generated. We seek refuge with Allah! You only break the normal patterns of your self by what is heavy for you, as long as it is neither forbidden nor disliked by the shari'at of Muhammad. The statement of the right-acting wali, Sayyidi Ahmad Zarruq, is: "As long as dislike is not very strong, it is not fitting for us to use it at the moment in which loved things are few and disliked things are many, and following is little and opposition is great since Allah-ta'ala said, *'If you love Allah, then follow me. Allah will love you.'* "

I advise you to perform the obligatory prayer and the confirmed sunna. You should not travel any road without knowledge since the Prophet, peace be upon him, said, "It is not permitted for a believer to set his foot on a matter until he knows what Allah's judgement in it is." Sayyidi Abu Sulayman ad-Darani, may Allah be pleased with him, said, "The one who is inspired to do something good should not do it until he hears about it in tradition." We say that the one who knows is not like the one who is ignorant since Allah-ta'ala said, *"Are they equal — those who know and those who do not know? Are darkness and light the same?"* We have said before this: Whoever knows what he does is not like the one who does not know it. We see many fuqara and others who do good actions while they do not know that they have done them. They do bad actions while they do not know that they have done them. The reality of these is dark, not luminous. Whoever knows what he does and is on his guard against opposing the command of his Lord, by Allah, his reality is luminous, not dark. There is no doubt that knowledge is light and ignorance is darkness, and knowledge is day and ignorance is night, and so on. As far as the nobility of knowledge, its height and elevation is concerned, it is enough for us that it is the attribute of Allah-ta'ala as the Prophet said, peace be upon him, in what he related from his Lord — glory be to

Him! *"I am Knowing. I love every knower."* There is no good in the one who does not learn and the one who does not recognise the value of knowledge since he does not recognise his Lord. He is only worshipped by knowledge. The Prophet, peace be upon him, said, "Every action which is not based on Our command is rejection." My brothers, the Muhammadan sunna is the sunna. Shaykh al-Busayri, may Allah be pleased with him, said in his Burda:

> He called to Allah. Those who cling to him, cling
>   to an unbroken rope.
> You will not see any wali who is not helped by
>   him, nor any enemy who is not broken.

Peace

131

Contemplation is meaning. The meanings are only bound by the sensory. They only last by teaching through mutual reminding, visiting (awliya) and breaking habit. When one feels at home in his state, then there is slackness and a pause inevitably. Do not be incapable of movement, or we might say, means, since contemplation is strengthened by them. Our master, may Allah be pleased with him, used always to say to me, "The meaning is very subtle indeed. If man is not intelligent with inner core, then it slips from his hands while he is unaware of it.

Peace

132

There is nothing in existence except Allah. Allah-ta'ala said, *"Everything perishes except His face." "All that is on it vanishes, and the face of your Lord remains, the One who possesses Majesty and Nobility." "That is Allah, your Lord, the Truth. What is there after the Truth except misguidance?"*

190

"That is because Allah is the Truth and what they call on apart from Him is false." "Say; the Truth has come and falsehood has disappeared. Falsehood always disappears." "Say Allah, and then leave them plunging in their playing." "He is the First and the Last, the Outward and the Inward." Our Prophet, peace be upon him, said, "The truest verse uttered by the poets is:

'Everything except Allah is false.' "

The Prophet, may Allah bless him and grant him peace, said, "I have not seen anything except that I saw Allah in it." We say, may Allah pardon us! that it is impossible for our Lord to be seen while something other-than-Him is seen as all the people of realisation know. The one who has not set foot on the Path does not perceive it. One of them said:

Since I have recognised the Divinity, I do not see other than-Him. Similarly, other is forbidden with us.
Since I have gathered together what I feared would separate, today I have arrived gathered.

Allah knows best, but it means that since I have recognised my Lord with the recognition of the people of contemplation and witnessing, not the recognition of the people of proof and exposition, I have not seen anything except Him in every thing as the Prophet, may Allah bless him and grant him peace, saw Him. He also said, "Since I have gathered together what I feared would separate, today I have arrived gathered." It means, and Allah knows best, that since I have seen unity in multiplicity, I do not fear that I will see multiplicity in unity as I did before I saw my Lord in everything. There is no doubt that there is nothing in existence except Allah. It is illusion which veils us from seeing Him. Illusion is baseless. Shaykh Ibn 'Ata'Allah, said in his Hikam, "Had the veil of illusion been rent, eyewitnessing would have occured in the absence of sources and the light of iman would rise and shine and cover the existence of created beings. Sayyidi al-Majdhub, may Allah be pleased with him! said:

My sight has disappeared into His sight, and it is an-
    nihilated to every vanishing thing.
I realised that other-than-Him does not exist, and de-
    parted in delight immediately.

Your intellects should not conceive of the existence of something with Allah since there is nothing except Allah with
Allah as all the people of realisation know. The one who has
not set his foot on the Path is not aware of it.

Do not dislike the thoughts of the self when they try to
get the better of you, and pile up with their armies on your
hearts. Strip off your own will and surrender it to your Lord
when they try to overwhelm you. Be still. Do not move.
Relax about them and do not be constricted by them. Sleep
if you can until you have had your fill since among the
benefits of sleep at the time of adversities is the breaking of
habits. It is surrendering the will to Allah. Whoever surrenders his will to his Lord, He takes him by the hand. So do
not dislike the thoughts of the self when they increase against
you. Be as we have told you. Then they will profit you and
give you a lot. Because of that, tawhid will be firm in your
hearts and doubts and illusions will leave you. By it, travel
occurs and good is obtained. By it, the disappearance and
purification from every misguidance is obtained. Be on your
guard against being worried about many impediments, or we
could say barriers, for the good – may Allah strengthen it! –
will make you pass quickly through them if you do what we
have told you.

One of the fuqaha' said to me, "Appetite has struck me."
I told him, "This is what benefits me. I only have the favour
of Allah and its favour. By Allah, we do not forget its
beauty." The people of knowledge of Allah do not flee from
things like others do since they see their Lord in everything.
Others flee from them because the contemplation of created
beings veils them from the contemplation of the Maker of
being. Similarly, the people of knowledge of Allah are veiled

by contemplation of the Maker of being from the contemplation of created beings. For that reason, Shaykh Ibn 'Ata'Allah, said in his Hikam, "The worshippers and those who do without alienate themselves from everything since they are withdrawn from Allah in everything. Had they seen Him in everything, they would not alienate themselves from anything."

Listen to what happened to one of our brothers, may Allah be pleased with him! while he was travelling on the road. The contemplation of the Maker of being had veiled him to created beings. He was with some people at a certain road and whenever he saw or heard something he said to the one who was with him, "This, what is it?" whether he had heard people speaking, birds, beasts, the wind, or anything. Whenever he heard or saw any of that, he would say to the person with him, "This, what is it?" The one who was with him was amazed at what he said. A similar thing happened to one of them at Alexandria. A crow cawed above him and he said, "At Your service, Allah, at Your service," and he did the tawaf — the ritual seven-fold circling of the house of Allah, Ka'ba, in Makkah — of the shari'at of Muhammad! This is because he spoke of the outside-endless time of the in-time and its going-on after endless-time. Far be it that other-than-our Lord should have that.

May Allah have mercy on you! Know that nothing prevents us from seeing our Lord except remaining with the appetites of our self. Be on your guard against saying that it is created being which veils us from the Maker of being. By Allah, nothing veils us from Him except the illusion whose result is ignorance. Did we know, our knowledge would result in certainty for us. Indeed it would keep our hearts and all of us from seeing others as we normally do. "Had the veil of illusion been rent, eyewitnessing would have occured in the absence of the sources, and the light of iman would rise and shine and cover the existence of created beings."

Listen to what happened to one of the murids in 1183. When his witnessing was strong, he set out for the people of heedlessness intending to hear what they did of plunging into discussion about created beings. Perhaps by this he would be tempted, or we might say, his contemplation might be weakened. Then because of that, his contemplation of his Lord would become stronger so that he would almost leave his sensory experience and flee and seek refuge with his Lord. His contemplation was very strong when he returned to what he had in the days of his heedlessness of diversions and passions. Allah desired to make him one of the people of sobriety, so he became sober. He is still alive now, may Allah be kind to him and his loved ones. Amin.

Contemplation is by the inner eye, not by the eye itself. Whoever claims that things prevent it, has no knowledge of it since nothing stops it except for illusion. Illusion is baseless. If illusion departed, he would find that everything is a means to Allah and there is no means to Him except Him. I recognised my Lord by my Lord. Had it not been for my Lord, I would not have recognised my Lord. Shaykh Ibn 'Ata'Illah said in his Hikam, "When were You absent so that there is any need of a proof to guide one to You? When were You far so that there should be traces which lead one to You? Created beings are not set up so that you see them. You should see their Master in them."

Peace

133

As for the people of love and gnosis, whenever someone injures them and gets the better of them, they have *"the sunna of Allah which has passed before. You will not find any change to the sunna of Allah."* Injury to the awliya, may Allah be pleased with them, is an immense business. Some of them were imprisoned. Some of them were whipped. Some

194

of them were forced to keep moving from place to place. Some of them were killed. We and others have enough of this meaning in the death of the qutb, Mawlana 'Abdu's-Salam b. Mashish and the death of Sayyidi al-Hallaj and others, may Allah be pleased with them. It is like that with the death of the Companions, may Allah be pleased with them, and with the death of the prophets, peace be upon them. Allah-ta'ala said, *"There has been many a prophet, with whom thousands fought, and they did not faint at what befell them in the way of Allah and they did not weaken or humble themselves. Allah loves the steadfast."*

We think that the injury which the prophets, peace be upon them, experienced is greater than the injury which the Companions, may Allah be pleased with them! experienced. The injury which they experienced is greater than the injury which other awliya have, peace be upon them. It is according to stations as has come in tradition from the best of mankind, may Allah bless him and grant him peace, "The people with the most severe affliction are the prophets, then the awliya then those like them." By Allah, it is a sign of honour from Allah to them. It is a favour and a blessing from Allah. It is great guidance from Allah for them.

Know that if you control yourselves, Allah-ta'ala will give you control over whoever injures you from your fellowmen and others, and all created beings as we have told you time and time again. The only one who masters people and all created being is the one who masters himself. We could say, the only one who is freed of the opposition of his fellowmen is the one who is freed of the opposition of his self. The only one who is freed of the opposition of his self is the one who opposes his passion and obeys his Master with sincere obedience. If you want Allah to take you by the hand, then surrender your will to Him. He will take charge of your business as He has taken charge of the affairs of others. May the curse of Allah be upon whoever lies to you. Allah willing,

He will make an opening for you so that you have no doubt at all about anything we have told you.

Peace

134

If the believer is constant in his dhikr and says "Allah, Allah, Allah," he will obtain nearness to Allah, and he will obtain might from Allah, and he will obtain victory from Allah. May the curse of Allah be upon whoever lies. The root of all good qualities such as they are, is freeing the heart from this world.

Peace

135

Only the one without intellect resists power. The man of intellect does not resist it. Do not be sad about a state which you do not have and do not be joyful about a state you have. Choose what your Lord choses for you, whether it is finding or loss, giving or withholding, might or abasement, health or sickness, wideness or narrowness, expansion or contraction, wealth or poverty, height or depth, life or death, and so on. It is the state of the people who surrender their will to their Lord, and the state of the one who wants to be connected to them and wants to be among them. As for the one who chooses above Allah and wants what he wants, he remains the prisoner of his passions.

Surrender to Salma, and go where she goes.
Follow the winds of the Decree, and move where she
  moves.

This is what we would like to hold on to and to rival each other in. It is the goal of the Path and the end of realisation. None is purified of passion except for the one who is calm at the time of affliction.

Peace

136

There is a great difference between the one whose heart is with the Maker of being and the one whose heart is with created beings. As far as the one whose heart is with the Maker of being, created beings are in his possession and subject to his force and strength. As for the one whose heart is with created beings, he and his heart are in their possession, and subject to their force and strength. They always have mastery over him, i.e. they always make him move and afflict him unless Allah frees him of them by His pure generosity. If not, he dies a captive in their hands.

The people of means who distract one from Allah and make one go far from Him criticise divestment which is distance from preoccupations. They praise preoccupations. There is no power nor strength except with Allah.

Peace

137

One day I prayed the prescribed prayer at the Qarawiyyin mosque. After it, everyone was occupied with their 'ibada. Some of them were praying. Some of them were reciting Qur'an. Some of them were doing hadith. Some of them were studying. Some of them were reciting Dala'il al-Khayrat, and so on. There was a man near me who laid claim to election. We knew him since he had been attached to our shaykh as we were. This world had stripped him of the robe of poverty and it only left him the claim by his clothes. It had cut him off from the shaykh and us. It left him the least of people.

I said to him after the prayer, "Are these people doing dhikr or are they heedless?" He was confused about what to tell me for a bit since he understood that the meaning was directed at him. He said, "They only seem to be people doing dhikr to purify the self." I said, "Those doing dhikr are with the heedless, and the heedless are with those doing dhikr because they have what you see of the means of this world while they are poor in two directions — poor in this world and poor in the next world. They have neither of them since they are not at peace with their Lord. Had they remembered Him, or we could say, worshipped Him truly, they would have been at peace with Him and every harm would have left them. Harm and dhikr of Allah are not joined together. Whenever dhikr of Allah is present, harm departs. Whenever harm is present, dhikr of Allah departs. Whoever claims that they can be joined together is ignorant of the virtue of dhikr of Allah, the secret of dhikr of Allah, or the rank of dhikr of Allah. Dhikr of Allah has great value and a great secret. How can it not have? The one who is at peace with dhikr of Allah will not be grieved by the greatest terror on the Day of Rising, let alone the afflictions and trials which befall him in the abode of this world. What dhikr or 'ibada is there for the one who is immersed in the sea of doubts and illusions; by Allah, we do not think that he has any good.''

Peace

138

Wilaya is a noble state of the presence of lordship and a sublime state of delegation. People's intellects are bewildered about it. Only the strong astute ones among them perceive it. Allah has not left this world in them. How could it be when the wali is the one whom Allah has taken charge of, so He has covered his attribute with His attribute, and his quality with His quality i.e. his incapacity with His power, his weakness with His strength, his poverty with His richness, his abasement with His might, his ignorance with His knowledge, and so on. No one should be ignorant of its rank or overlook its people. It is imperative that he recognise it and not be ignorant of it so that his himma will be high and his heart will rise.

We see that most people do not believe in wilaya from one aspect as they do believe in it from two other aspects. One of them is that of the people of attraction (jadhb) without wayfaring. The other is that of the people of great striving. The matter is not as they believe because jadhb is wilaya, but it is not joined with striving. It is strength and striving is strength, and strength cannot be in two directions as we have said many times. Perhaps whoever hears us and follows us, will profit and give profit.

Jadhb is reality-intoxication. Wayfaring is shari'a-sobriety. The reality veils one to the shari'at of Muhammad as the shari'at of Muhammad veils one to the reality as in the Hikam of Ibn 'Ata'Illah. The one with reality withdraws from creation by the contemplation of the King, the Real. He is annihilated to causes by witnessing the Maker of causes. This is a slave who is brought face to face with the reality and its radiance appears on him. He travels on the Path and he has mastered its distance although he is drowned in lights and his traces are completely obliterated. His intoxication has overcome his sobriety, his gatheredness has overcome his separation, his annihilation has overcome his going-on, and his withdrawal has overcome his presence. Our lady 'A'isha, may Allah be pleased with her, was so intoxicated that she withdrew when she said, "By Allah! I will thank only Allah!" However, she became sober immediately and returned to the state of perfection which she had. It is joining intoxication and sobriety, the shari'at of Muhammad and the reality, jadhb and wayfaring, the outward and the inward, and presence and withdrawal. This is the state of the perfect, may Allah be pleased with all of them. Shaykh Ibn 'Ata'Illah, may Allah be pleased with him! said in his Hikam: "More perfect than him is a slave who drinks and is increased in sobriety, and withdraws and is increased in presence. His gatheredness does not veil him from his separation nor does his separation veil him from his gatheredness. His annihilation does not veil him from his going-on nor his going-on from his annihilation. He gives everything with a due its due and he gives everyone with a portion his full portion."

One becomes so intoxicated here that many of the awliya of Allah, may Allah be pleased with them, have withdrawn. The right-acting wali, Abu Yazid Sayyidi 'Abdu'r-Rahman al-Fasi known as the gnostic of Allah, may Allah be pleased with him! said, "I used to retain 14 knowledges. When I obtained the knowledge of the reality, all those knowledges departed and all that remained of them was Qur'an and hadith." When I myself acquired what Sayyidi 'Abdu'r-Rahman had obtained, I was stripped of every bliss that I had enjoyed. I left all my habits and all my passions. Nothing at all remained in my heart except Allah. Had I relied on Him by my limbs alone, that would have been my contentment with my Lord. Praise and thanks be to Allah! When Shaykh al-Junayd, may Allah be pleased with him! obtained it, he said:

> Purify yourself with the water of the unseen if you
> have a secret.
> If not, then do tayammum with sand or stones.
> Step forward if you are the imam, and pray the dhuhr
> prayer at the beginning of 'asr.
> That is the prayer of the gnostics of their Lord. If you
> are among them, then moisten the dry earth with
> the sea.

When Sayyidi al-Wasiti, may Allah be pleased with him, acquired it, he said, "Those who do dhikr are more heedless in their dhikr than those who forget His dhikr because His dhikr is other-than-Him." There are more statements to that effect among the people of annihilation, may Allah be pleased with them in this meaning. It is as they said:

> I only have to remember You and my spirit, my heart,
> and my secret begin to curse me in Your remem-
> brance!

It is almost as if there was a watcher from You calling
to me, "Look out! Woe to you! look out! look out
for remembrance!

Now you see that the witnesses of the Real shine, and
all has reached your meaning from His meaning.

As for the people of attraction without wayfaring, they are
as they believe them to be since the luminosity of their
Lord directs them. It brings out their inward to their outward and whatever happens to them happens as Ibn 'Ata'Illah
says in the Hikam, "When the divine waridat come to you,
they destroy your habits. *'Kings, when they enter a city,
destroy it and make the mighty among its people abased.
Such will they do.'* "

In addition, another obscure matter for people is that of
election among the people of means, let alone the people of
begging among them. They do not know that the famous
wali, Sayyidi Abu Silham, may Allah be pleased with him,
had the weakest means. It was fishing by the hook. In spite
of that, the sea was pulled by his himma and he disposed of
it by his force and power. Our master, may Allah be pleased
with him, used to beg for money in Fez al-Bali from shop to
shop like someone in great need although he had lived as a
ghawth for most of his life, and he was over 80 years old.
Allah knows best. It is as if people think that trust and
reliance on Allah are only obtained by the one who leaves
his worldly means. They do not know that the Prophet, may
Allah bless him and grant him peace, had such trust in his
Lord that no one in his community or any of the previous
communities had the like of it. In spite of that, he would
use worldly means and divest himself of them. He would not
fast and he would fast. He would sleep and he would stay up
in prayer. It was all to give a shari'at to his community.
Among his community are those who follow in his footsteps
in trust in his Lord until they meet their Lord. We have
mentioned some of them and their likes, may Allah be

pleased with them. Another obscure matter is the one who has few practices, and is content by them with his Lord. They do not know that constriction is absolutely not necessary among the noble, so what about constriction among the noble one of the nobles? The reality indicates the Real. The Real is Allah, the Mighty, the Majestic. The shari'at indicates the giver of the shari'at – that is our Prophet, may Allah bless him and grant him peace.

Peace

139

Allah can only be reached by the door of the death of the self, no matter what you do. Its death is by opposing it and completely leaving its opinion and following the opinion of the people of the sunna, may Allah be pleased with them. As for the one who remains with his opinion and thinks that he will only reach his Lord after the annihilation of his bad qualities and the obliteration of his claims, he will never reach Him. Reaching Him is only by His generosity alone. Allah-ta'ala said, *"Had it not been for the favour of Allah to you and His mercy, you would have. . ."* to the end of the ayat. *"Had it not been for the overflowing favour of Allah to you and His mercy, none of you would have been pure. . ."* to the end of the ayat. The Prophet, may Allah bless him and grant him peace, said, "None of you will enter the Garden by his actions." It was said to him, "Not even you, Messenger of Allah?" He said, "Not even I unless Allah covers me with His mercy." There is more to that effect.

I urge you to lower the position of your self and to be careful in your striving not to fall into the forbidden and disliked things which your Lord has forbidden you. This is is so that your luminous reality will not be transformed into a dark reality. You should not take on what is not on your backs by being occupied with your management and choice, and being very worried about what Allah has guaranteed you — that is provision. You should take on what will direct you away from people and from disliked things. You should restrain your harm from people since it is well-known that the pole of sufism is withholding injury and enduring injury. You should leave whatever attributes of the commonality are left in you. You should vie with each other in their opposite. Your himma should always be high, not low. There are very few people in this time who have high himma. You do not see any faqir, scholar, or sharif, but that you see that his himma is low, not high since all people are only fixing their himma on the low. It is this world, and love of rank. There is no power nor strength except by Allah. For that reason, they fall lower and do not rise above.

My brothers, therefore travel with your hearts from the world of perishing appetites to the world of lasting appetites. Advance to it and do not delay. Only the people of heedlessness delay. As for the people of wakefulness, they have advanced, or we could say, travelled there and alighted there.

Peace

140

The self of the one of Adam is like the earth. If you do not cultivate goodness in it, then certainly wrongness will grow in it and it will be left for the plants. How wrong! How far off! If the good does not come, then the ugly comes. You must have what will benefit you and what will give you a return of good in the two worlds. Go always from the rights of your Lord to the rights of yourselves, and from the rights of yourselves to the rights of your Lord if you desire your heads to be safe and your outward and inward to be straight.

If no good is bestowed on you and no harm comes to you, then you should leave means, clothes, lack of practices, and remaining in those things without being immersed in the contemplation of the immensity of the essence of your Lord, and the contemplation of the immensity of your Prophet, and not withdrawing from the sensory, while you are still aware. This is useless. It is not hidden because the one who relinquishes is adorned. The one who does not relinquish is not adorned.

It is good to acquire the matter as we said. No one has what he says since it is arrival, and one who has arrived has a strong proof. It is his contentment with Allah. Allah-ta'ala said, *"Isn't Allah enough for his slave?"* or isn't it enough that your Lord sees everything? *"Doesn't he know that Allah sees?"* The one who is content with Allah has many proofs. When he is parted from what he loves, he is not lonely. He is calm at the time of affliction. If something is lost, he finds in his loss. If he is abased, he is exalted in his abasement. If he is impoverished, he is rich in his poverty. If he is weak, he is strong in his weakness. If he is powerless, he is powerful in his incapacity. If he is constricted, he is wide in his constriction. If he is broken, he is mended in his brokenness. If he loses, he profits in his loss, and so on.

Also, we see someone who has left his worldly means. When he wakes up from his sleep, then what direction does he turn to with his heart? We only see him turning his heart to plunging. This is different from the one who has worldly means. Whenever he wakes up from sleep, he immediately gets up and goes to his means without plunging into anything, managing, or choosing. Therefore, be occupied with what will benefit you and what will bring you good in the two worlds. "Move, and you will have provision" as your Prophet, may Allah bless him and grant him peace, told you. Do not be lazy.

Listen to how I strengthened one of the brothers. He was afraid of marriage and thought that it would tempt him as many of the people of the Path, may Allah be pleased with them, have feared temptation. I strengthened him when I said: "We see some people who have many occupations, and in spite of that, it is as if they had no occupation. They are not among the elite of the people. They are among the common. We see that some people have nothing except their own heads, but they sink into the mire with them and are always in extreme difficulty because of it. That is due to their management and choice and the intensity of their anxiety about the business. Allah knows best, but it is clear to me that nothing tempts real men (rijal) away from their Lord. The family is the last thing to tempt them. What does the one among you who desires arrival rely on? He has given up the means of this world and the next. How remarkable! Someone blames his worldly means for the fact that he has not put himself right! He says, 'Had I abandoned my worldly means and been occupied with my Lord, it would have been better for me than what I have.' In spite of that, he has wasted many moments in not being occupied with his Lord. He does not see them and he does not blame them. This is disappointment. This is loss. It is not proper for a man to blame his worldly means about putting himself right and taking care of his family until he does not waste any of his moments in respect to the due of his Lord.

Peace

141

Whoever wants to be adorned must relinquish passion. Allah-ta'ala said, *"Man only has what he strives for."* Allah-ta'ala also said, *"Shake the trunk of the date-palm. . ."* to the end of the ayat. The Prophet, may Allah bless him and grant him peace, said, "Move, and you will have provision." Ibn 'Ata'Illah says in the Hikam, "How can normal patterns be broken for you when you have not broken the normal patterns yourself?" How can the heart shine when the forms of created beings are stamped on its mirror? How can it travel to Allah when it is shackled by its appetites? How can it desire to enter the presence of Allah when it is not purified of the janaba (major impurity) of its heedlessness? How can it hope to understand the fine points of the secrets when it is not safe from its own lapses? Help comes to them according to predisposition, lights shine according to the purity of the secrets. You must have high himma and free your goals. The Prophet, may Allah bless him and grant him peace, said, "Actions are by intentions, and a man has what he intends. Whoever emigrates for Allah and His Messenger, his emigration is for Allah and His Messenger. Whoever emigrates to obtain something of this world or for a woman he wants to marry, his emigration is for that to which he emigrates." He said, "Do not travel from created being to created being. You will be like the donkey at the millstone. That from which he travels is that to which he travels. Travel from created beings to the Maker of being. The end is to your Lord."

Therefore be among the people of high himma. Do not be among the people of low himma. There is no doubt that the people of high himma are few and their openhandedness is the goal. You do not see any scholar, any faqir, or any sharif but that you see his himma alighting on this low world and love of rank. These two things are forbidden for the people of Allah. For that reason, I cast my net, this teaching of mine and others, over the fuqara. We did not cast it over the 'ulama and other people because we see that all of the fuqara claim to be on the path of poverty. By Allah, they will not have it until their self and this world are nothing. This is the reality of poverty and its path.

The fuqara are also our companions. From us and to us, they have what we have. They own what we own as opposed to our master, the 'ulama. They are not among our companions, not in the outward path nor the inward path. That is from them, not from us. Allah watches us closely. It is because they make us far from them in both directions. We are not among the people of distance. We are among the people of nearness since we and the favour belong to Allah. We have the fullest portion in the path of the outward and the greatest share in the path of the inward. Had they opposed their passions and been purified of their portions, they would have found that most of us are people of knowledge and most of them are ignorant in spite of the existence of our ignorance and their knowledge. Shaykh Ibn 'Ata'Illah said in his Hikam, "What knowledge does a knower have when he is pleased with himself?"

As for the common they are as our noble master said to one of the salihun of the city of Fez. This man laid claim to the greatest election when he said to him, "In your opinion, what group am I in? The group of the common or the group of the elite?" Our master told him, "The common people are our masters and your masters since they do not lay claim to anything." He replied, "In your opinion, I am not among the common or the elite, so then who am I among in your opinion?" The shaykh told him, "In my opinion, you are among the long-eared donkeys of Egypt." For that reason, I did not remind them and I did not cast my net over them. There is no doubt that whoever is ignorant of something opposes it. Had he tasted something of what the men have tasted, he would have said the like of what one of them said:

> My heart had various passions. My passions are gathered together since I saw that You are the source.
> The one I used to envy began to envy me. When You became my Master, I became the master of mankind.
> I have left people their deen and this world. I am occupied with You! You are my deen and this world!

Peace

I do not know whether or not you recognise that shaytan has influence over the people of the path. The Path has a living shaytan who has sway over its people always. He injures them. He had influence over the awliya, may Allah be pleased with them, as well as the prophets, blessings and peace be upon them. His harm becomes greater according to the greatness of the stations. "The people with the most severe affliction are the prophets, then the awliya, and then those like them." The wisdom in his injury is that by it they become pure for their Master, glory be to Him! That happened before them, and happiness also came to the prophets, peace be upon them, and the awliya, may Allah be pleased with them, before them. Ibn 'Ata'Illah says in the Hikam, "Whoever finds the fruit of his action soon, that is a proof of the existence of acceptance." Allah-ta'ala says in His book, *"There is no fear on the awliya of Allah, neither do they sorrow." Those who believe and have taqwa, they have good news in the life of this world and the next. There is no change to the words of Allah. That is the great victory.*

There is no doubt that shaytan has no power over them or anyone else, since he has no power to benefit or harm himself. Had he been able to harm or benefit himself, he would have been able to harm everyone. He is far from being able to do that, nor can anyone else do that. That belongs to Allah alone. However, it is a wisdom of the divine presence of lordship and one of the secrets of lordship for whoever has recognition. Opposition to him is truly turning to Allah and turning your back on him as our master said, may Allah be pleased with him!: "The real attack against the enemy is your occupation with the love of the Beloved. When you are occupied with attacking the enemy, he gets what he wants from you and the love of the Beloved passes you by. It is as Shaykh Qasim al-Khassasi said, "Do not be occupied at all with the one who abuses you. Be occupied with Allah and He will drive him away from you. He is the One who makes him move against you in order to test your claim to true sincerity. Many people have erred in this matter. They were occupied with the abuse of the one who abused them , and the abuse continued along with wrong action. Had they returned to Allah, He would have driven them away from them, and their proper business would have been enough for them."

That is the opinion of the great sufis, the people of teaching. We think that the shaytan who has sway over the people of the Path is from among human beings, not the jinn. We also think that the one who is like him is stronger than the shaytan of the jinn. Outwardly, both of them influence the sons of Adam. It says in the Book of Allah-ta'ala, *"The device of shaytan is weak."* We have told you that opposition to the enemy truly is turning to Allah and turning away from him.

Peace

143

Whoever performs the obligatory prayers and confirmed sunna and frees himself of traces of urine, and persists in the state of cleanliness, bereftness, and contentment has the best state and will obtain what the men of Allah have obtained, may Allah be pleased with them. The tongue said to the head, "How are you this morning?" The head said to it, "Well, if I am safe from you!" Whoever wants his deen to be safe and his shaykh to be safe, should occupy himself with dhikr of Allah or be silent or sleep since the moment and the people of the moment are in very great difficulty.

We urge our brother to remind the slaves of Allah as much as he can. Allah ta'ala said, *"Remind. The Reminder benefits the believers."* However, he should make them go on to their means from it, and not neglect to push them until there are many people gathered together with him. If one of them spends the night with him, he should urge him to come again, and so on until the feet of the brothers are firm in the path of Allah. Then that which we warned him about will not harm him. It will benefit him and help him with increase to his Lord. Similarly, we would like him not to be dominated by nature so that he leaves his opinion for the opinion of others. It is better for you and for other people when it pleases Allah, not when it pleases the slave. Pleasing people is a goal which can never be obtained.

You must absolutely, catergorically be on your guard against the opinion of the fuqara, the opinion of others, and your own opinion. That goes straight to the point since Allah ta'ala said, *"Man has an inner eye on himself." "If you follow many of those who are in the earth, they will misguide you from the way of Allah."* If you are confused in any matter and do not know whether good lies in doing it or leaving it, then you should do the Istikhara of the Prophet without delay, or pray two rakats and recite two short suras in them like Expansion or Power, do the prayer on the Messenger of Allah, may Allah bless him and grant him peace, at least three times morning and evening, and say "Allah is enough for us, and He is the best Protector" and "There is no power nor strength except by Allah, the High and the Great" the same number of times. Then Allah will prove the truth for you and nullify the false. Allah is the authority for what we say.

We think that when the wayfarer (salik) uses this and consults his heart as the Prophet, peace be upon him, said to one of his Companions, may Allah be pleased with him, "Consult your heart," then only the truth will be established in his heart. It is best that you verify it by the inner eye of one of the fuqara or someone else more than your own inner eye. The correct way is to follow the one with inner eye, be he a faqir or not. Allah will strengthen your help and help you Himself.

Peace

144

I advise you to be on your guard against letting time slip away while you have not obtained what the people of attraction in every time and age have obtained. You absolutely must always expose yourselves to the fragrant breezes of your Lord. Do not be incapable or lazy! What has slipped away from most people from their Lord might slip away from you! There is no power nor strength except by Allah! Whoever wants to expose himself to the fragrant breezes of his Lord, should not give his self what it desires and what is light for it. He should give it what it does not desire and what is heavy for it. Then the distance of the Path will be covered quickly and he will pluck the fruit of his action. If he is preoccupied with actions and his attention is not returned to Him, then he will not join the men of Allah and he will not be free of misguidance, no matter what he does. One of them, may Allah be pleased with them, said, "Leaving one appetite of the self is more beneficial to the heart than fasting and praying for an entire year." One of them said, "I prefer to leave a mouthful of my supper than to eat it and stay up to pray for the entire night." I said: This is how you expose yourselves to the fragrant breezes of your Lord if you want to cover the distance of the Path quickly, your moments to be pleasant, and to have nearness to your Lord which others do not have.

You must visit the living shaykhs of the tariqa, may Allah be pleased with them! if you find them. This world is not lacking them. Whoever lacks them is empty of baraka and every good, whatever it is. Only the one who is in very great need of them, may Allah be pleased with them, finds them. The need of the one in great need of them will join him to them wherever they are, in the land of Islam or the land of the Christians. He comes to them or they come to him. Power moves him to them and it moves them to him. The one in great need of them may find them in his own house or near to it as happened to us. We were in great need of someone to take us by the hand. We found him near to us. He was nearly in the same house as us. Allah would take account of us if we were to tell you something other than what happened to us. That is the secret of great need. How many do not perceive what secrets there are in Allah's kingdom!

May Allah have mercy on you! Know that a certain person had strong need of one of the awliya, may Allah be pleased with him, to show him the Messenger of Allah, may Allah bless him and grant him peace. He was extremely insistent about it with him. Finally, he ordered him to eat some fish until he had his fill. Then he was to keep himself from drinking water that night until morning. He did what he told him to do and went to sleep. For the entire night, all he saw was water and plunging into water. Ibn 'Ata'Illah says in the Hikam: "Glory be to the One who directs people to His awliya in order to direct them to Himself, and who only leads a person to them when He wants to bring him to Himself."

You must also visit the dead awliya like the shaykh, our master, may Allah be pleased with him, Shaykh Mawlana 'Abdu's-Salam b. Mashish, may Allah be pleased with him, and Shaykh Sayyidi al-Ghazali, and their likes, may Allah be pleased with them. You should also visit places that are respected by people like the Mountain of Tazyan at the tribe of Ghamara, Banu Yafrah at the tribe of al-Akhmis, the Hadrat la ilaha illa'llah of Targha at the Ziyatiyya tribe, al-Mansura at the Ahmadiyya tribe, and different ribats and other respected places. By Allah, whoever lifts his himma above this world, will be joined to the awliya. Among the benefits of high himma is breaking habits. Among that is that one who has high himma says to a thing, "Be!" and it is. Allah is the authority for what we say.

My advice to you is that whenever someone confronts you with one of the attributes of freedom, confront him with one of the opposite attributes of slaveness. If he confronts you

212

with speech, confront him with silence. If it is with might, then confront him with abasement. If it is with strength, then confront him with weakness, and so on. You will conquer him, abase him, and inevitably overcome him. Allah is the authority for what we say.

Peace

145

That which happened to you happened to two of the men of the people of the Garden. When they entered it, they found a valley of milk or wine in it. They began to drink like someone terribly thirsty. It was said to them, "If you go on a bit, you will find something sweeter than that." They said, "Your father! Certainly not! This is what we need!" You are like that, may Allah be kind to us and you! When you turn to your Lord, this world presents itself to you and it takes you with your patched jelabas, your prayer beads, you staffs, and all you have while you are not aware of what has happened to you of enemy capture. If you were aware, then transient appetite has control over you in spite of yourself.

My brothers, none of the people of the Path have said that there should be constant begging. You have become very excessive in that since you have found that it is a door to this world. Among the appetites you have obtained by it is breaking normal patterns. The fine man among you desired one appetite and did not obtain it. There is no doubt that there is no good for you in obtaining appetites. Good for you lies in distance from appetites. The people, may Allah be pleased with them, said, "Whoever consents to his appetite lacks his best part." They said, "Leaving one appetite of the self is more beneficial to the heart than fasting and praying for an entire year." One of them said, "I prefer to leave one mouthful of my supper than to eat it and stay up to pray for the entire night." I said that there is no doubt that whoever recognises what the goal is, whatever he leaves is easy for him. Whoever recognises Allah-ta'ala, does not turn to the bliss of the Garden, so what do you think about the bliss of this world? Whoever is ignorant of Him, he is the one who is owned by the appetite of this world and the appetite of the next. So refrain from begging and travel the roads of the men of Allah if you desire arrival and safety from misguidance. Loss is also extension of gifts. You have locked its door and denied its baraka. It refers to intense need. The shaykh, our master, may Allah be pleased with him, said, "Had people known the secrets and blessings that there are in need, they would not need anything except need." It is said that it is in the position of the Greatest Name.

My brothers, come near to the one your Prophet, may Allah bless him and grant him peace, has come near. Flee from others since he will rescue you and is safer. Shaykh al-Busayri, may Allah be pleased with him, said in his Burda:

> The proud mountains tried to tempt him with gold. He showed them a widower of pride.

If you are content with what you have, Allah ta'ala will delight you with it. I am free of the one who asks any being unless he abandons importunate behaviour and does not desire anything at all as is the case with the People, may Allah be pleased with them. Since all of the greatest portion of the fuqara have begging, then begging is a dark reality. It is not luminous. Whoever is made turbid by injury to creation and lack of something will never profit.

Peace

146

If you have resolved to visit us as one of the brothers has informed us, may Allah give you strength and support you with His overflowing favour. The secret lies in having less to do with people. Only whatever Allah wills should come with you. Many people results in fame. There is nothing more harmful to the murids than fame. There is also discomfort with a lot of people. Our Prophet, may Allah bless him and grant him peace, said, "I and those among my community who have taqwa are free of constraint." Obscurity is also a blessing. As far as its virtue is concerned, the word of Allah, the Mighty, the Majestic, is enough for us, *"We desired to show favour to those who were oppressed in the earth and to make them imams and to make them the heirs."* Whoever wants to visit us other than those who come with you, after you return, Allah willing, they can come to us little by little.

My brother, for a long time — 43 or 44 years, and Allah knows best — I have been speaking to the fuqara and making them remember Allah ta'ala. I looked at their states and found that they had many desires. I wanted to please them, and it was clear to me that pleasing people is a goal which is never obtained. The stupidest of people is the one who seeks what cannot be obtained. Part of their desires is love of position, or we could say, elevation. Lowering position is a necessary condition of the Path as Ibn 'Ata'Illah says in the Hikam, "Bury your existence in the earth of obscurity. That which grows from what is not buried does not have complete fruit." It is as one of the shaykhs of the tariqa said, may Allah give us the honour of their dhikr, "This Path of ours is only useful for people who sweep the rubbish heaps with their spirits." There are more statements like that of Shaykh 'Umar Ibn al-Farid, in his poem in Ta':

> Had abasement been exalted in it, how sweet
>   passion would be for me!
> Had it not been for abasement in love, I
>   would have had no might at all.

Another said.

> If you are not steadfast in abasement in passion,
>   You will be parted from the One you love
>   in spite of yourself.

Another said:

> Abase yourself to the One you love – you will
> obtain might. How many men have obtained
> might by abasement!
> If the One you love is Mighty and you are not
> abased to Him, then say goodbye to arrival.

Another said:

> Abase yourself to the One you love. Love is not
> easy. If the Beloved is pleased, then arrival is
> permitted to you.

There is more like this. There is no doubt that abasement is
slaveness. Slaveness is the door of freedom. Allah ta'ala says,
"Come to houses by their doors." The upshot is that I urge
you not to let them go unrestrained in their desires as many
of the muqaddams have done with the fuqara. Their business
should be confined to you unless you are pleased with it and
choose it. This is correct action. It is clear to us that the
noble faqih, Sayyidi so-and-so of such-and-such is among
those pleased with that. We would like you to advance only
his like.

Peace

147

I am one of those who love you for Allah, Sayyidi
Muhammad b. 'Abdillah al-Buhlani. I do not know whether
you know that or not. The reason for my love of you is that
I was in the Misbahiyya madrasa in Fez al-Bali, when you
were there in 1217. I used to hear the students speaking well
of you while there were strong doubts about you. What had
seized them seized me and I have been the same from that
very moment up to now, and will be until the time when
Allah inherits the earth and what is on it, Allah willing. We
have only heard good about you. Allah is the authority for
what we say.

The outcome is as you have counseled us — may Allah repay you with good from us — and you, sincere believer, know that error dominates people at the beginning, especially if they are not constantly in the presence of one who teaches them. The only one who profits is the one who keeps the company of one who has profited. The only one who loses is the one who keeps the company of the one who has lost. My master, may Allah be pleased with him! used to tell me, "Seize your hand and clench your teeth. If you see something which you do not like, then close your eyes so that we will not fly away and leave you."

Rescue certainly lies in following the Messenger of Allah, may Allah bless him and grant him peace. Passion overcomes everyone except the one for whom Allah has had previous concern. Whoever you see among us who opposes accidentally or deliberately, be quick in reminding him as Allah ta'ala has commanded you. Allah ta'ala said, *"Remind! The Reminder benefits the believers."* He — glory be to Him! said, *"Call to the way of your Lord by wisdom and excellent warning and argue with them by that which is better."* That is not like what was done by the qadi, Sayyidi al-Mustafa b. Jallul who was there. By Allah, now I ask you — is it firmly established in your opinion that the great Imam Malik, may Allah be pleased with him, pulled out the beard of any of the muslims? Or was it done by the Shafi'i, the Hanafi, the Hanbali, or any of our Imams, may Allah be pleased with them? Or in their time, was there not anyone who rebelled against Allah? We seek refuge with Allah from that happening! By Allah in every age there is obedience and rebellion, tawba and forgiveness. Allah is greater! Where is knowledge? Where is forbearance? Where is patience? Where is unhurried action? Where is doing-without? Where is trust? Where is scrupulousness? Where is leniency? Where is moder-ation? Where is bereftness? Where is self-restraint? Where is compassion? Where is mercy? Where is fear? Where is humility? Where is modesty? Where is generosity? Where is noble character? Where are the immense good qualities? Ibn 'Ata'Illah says in his Hikam: "Whoever becomes acquainted with the secrets of the slaves and does not have the quality of divine mercy, his knowledge is then a temptation and trial for him. It is also a cause for unwholesomeness which comes to him." He also said, "The best knowledge is that which has fear with it. If fear is parted from knowledge, it is up to you. If not, you must have knowledge with fear. What knowledge does a knower have who is pleased with himself? What ignorance does the ignorant man have who is not pleased with himself?" It was said to ash-Sha'bi, may Allah be pleased with him! at the beginning of his business, "Oh knower!" He said, "Do not say 'knower.' Say 'faqih.' The knower is the one who fears Allah."

There is no doubt that the only thing which impelled the faqih Sayyidi al-Mustafa to disgrace the people who are affiliated to Allah is lack of fear and modesty before Allah. Had it not been for the lack of fear and modesty, he would have been concerned about himself and distracted from the slaves of his Lord. Would that he had been concerned with his own writing-board and left the boards of people like our great Imams and best masters, may Allah be pleased with them. We do not dislike it being said to him, "Why don't you take care of your own behaviour so that you go straight? Then you could govern other people. Have you left your self in the difficulties of appetites and oppositions, while you lord it over the weak bereft exiles who are affiliated with their Lord and who have turned from their appetites?" We also would not dislike it if it was said to him, "The one who has no helper to help him, Allah, the Blessed, the Exalted! will help him."

Peace

148

We would not dislike it if you order all the brothers, may Allah be pleased with them, who are in those areas to do the dhikr of the Greatest Name silently constantly until they are purified of their passions. Then they can do it silently or out loud and not be concerned. We also do not dislike it if you always order them to silence unless speech is confirmed for putting this world or the deen right. Among the benefits of silence is the breaking of habits. The least amount of actions will be enough for them if they abandon what does not concern them and take on the character of their Prophet, may Allah bless him and grant him peace. By Allah, when we took on the character of our Prophet, he was not absent from us wherever we were. How can we desire to see our Prophet when we have bad character. By Allah, we will not have that and we think that we will only be increased in distance from him. There is no meaning in our striving when we have bad character. It was said to the Messenger of Allah, may Allah bless him and grant him peace, that such-and-such a woman fasted all day and prayed all night while she had a very bad character. She injured her neighbours by her tongue. He said, "There is no good in her. She is among the people of the Fire." Whoever is made turbid or we could say, overcome by injury to creation and lack of something will never profit as we have stated before.

Peace

149

People disagree about the master al-Khidr, peace be upon him. Some say that he is a wali. Some say that he is a prophet, and some say that he is a messenger. That which I say about him is that which has already reached you except for countering the one who thinks that it is unlikely that he, peace be upon him, had taught the Messenger of Allah,

Sayyiduna Musa, peace be upon him. He did teach him as Allah reported when Allah ta'ala said, *"How can you be patient with that which your knowledge has not embraced."* He said, the Great! *"As for the ship, it belonged to some poor men who worked the sea.........As for the boy, his parents were believers.........As for the wall, it belonged to two boys...."* to the end of the ayat. Is this not teaching? We seek refuge from Allah that this should not be teaching! By Allah, it is the great teaching since the like of it is not heard in the Book of Allah or the hadith of the Messenger of Allah, may Allah bless him and grant him peace! The great trusty ones among his community said in the hadith of the Messenger of Allah, may Allah bless him and grant him peace, "Allah was merciful to my brother Musa. Had he been patient, we would not have benefited...." to the end. The like of what he taught him paved the way for a hundred questions. Allah knows best. This is enough.

It is not inconceivable that a wali or a prophet might know what a messenger does not know, even if the messenger is better and has more knowledge. This is because if the knower is not incapable, he is not supported. He would be claiming the attribute of lordship. There is no way for him or anyone else to have that as Ibn 'Ata'Illah said in the Hikam: "He forbids you to claim anything that is not yours from that which creatures possess. Then how can it be permitted for you to claim His attributes when He is the Lord of the worlds?" It says in the Book of Allah ta'ala, *"You have only been given a little knowledge."* It is also said that part of protection is what you do not find. Allah ta'ala supported His messengers, blessing and peace be upon them, with incapacity and force. He also helped them with His attribute, i.e. He supported them with His help. He — glory be to Him! is the Wise, the Knowing. He has power over everything. He helped all the prophets, awliya, and slaves as He helped His messengers, peace be upon them. Had it not been for His constant support, all of us would be swimming in darkness.

Know that when the Jews, may Allah curse them! resolved to question our Prophet, may Allah bless him and grant him peace, about the reality of the spirit, they said — may Allah curse them! "If he cannot answer us, then he is a Prophet. If he does, then he is not a Prophet." Then he did not answer them until Allah had taught him what to say as it says in the Book of Allah-ta'ala, *"They will ask you about the spirit. Say: the spirit is from the command of my Lord."* There is no doubt that incapacity is the attribute of the slave. Slaveness is the very limit of nobility. For that reason, Allah praises His Prophet, may Allah bless him and grant him peace, with it when He says in His Book, *"Glory be to the One who travelled with His slave by night."* He did not say, "His Prophet" or "His Messenger."

Peace

150

By Allah, truly nobility lies only in slaveness. For that reason, Allah praised His Prophet, may Allah bless him and grant him peace, with it when He said in His Book, *"Glory to the One who travelled with His slave by night."* He did not say "His Prophet" or "His Messenger," and anything else. He chose the name "slave" for him since he, may Allah bless him and grant him peace, was truly His slave in reality. He praised other prophets, peace be upon them, with slaveness. Allah ta'ala says in His Book, *"He was an excellent slave, frequently returning."* *"Remember Our slaves Ibrahim, Is-haq, and Ya'qub."* One reading has *"Our slave Ibrahim."* It is absolutely clear and evident to the one who has had his inner eye opened by Allah and his secret illuminated, that slaveness is the nobility of every being, no matter who he may be. So grab hold of it! Take on what is heavy for your self, not what is light for it. Allah-ta'ala says, *"Whoever is in the heavens and the earth comes to the Merciful as a slave.* There is a great difference between the one who devotes himself to

221

his Lord by choice and not compulsion, and the one who devotes himself to Him by compulsion and not choice. There is no doubt that the only way to freedom is by the door of slaveness.

Peace

151

Allah ta'ala has removed the prayer from the menstruating woman and the woman with lochia after childbirth. It is one of the obligations which He demands of His slaves, so how can it be abandoned? Women should leave what does not concern them and perform what Allah has made obligatory for them. They only perform what superogatory things they are able to do. Then they will be happy, Allah willing, and not wretched or burdened because they grind flour, sieve, plait, knead, season, bandage, untie, sweep, give water, gather firewood, spin, milk, go into labour, bear their children, and raise them. These are all great deeds and well-known striving. With these deeds, they only need the prayer, fasting, and what Allah has made obligatory like zakat for the one who has the minimum of property subject to zakat, or the hajj for the one who is able to make it.

It is like that with men when they have what concerns them and are occupied with what concerns them in the obedience of their Lord. We do not like for any of them to be constrained since the Prophet, peace be upon him, said, "I and those of my community who have taqwa are free of constraint." He said, peace be upon him, "Compassion does not enter a heart but that it adorns it." Compassion persists for the one who has it, as you know.

Know that man only benefits by the action which he does by knowledge. As for the action which he does without knowledge, it does not benefit him. The shaykh of our shaykh, Sayyidi al-'Arabi b. 'Abdillah said to our Shaykh

Sayyidi 'Ali, may Allah be pleased with both of them. "This state of yours (and it was the state of divestment) joins the outward and the hidden for you. I only mention this to you so that you might benefit by it." My brother, in the same way I am only reminding you about what I have mentioned concerning women so that you can inform them. Most of them do not consider this to be action. By Allah, it is among the greatest of actions. Allah wipes out evil deeds by it and elevates degrees. Tell them about it so that they can leap up to it, and so they will not resent it. It is very great with Allah. That is absolutely definite.

As for whoever yearns for our wird among the people of that area, I gave you permission to give it to them when you were with us some time ago. Perfection belongs to Allah and one should rely on Him. You can give the Unique Name which is what most of the people of the tariqa, may Allah be pleased with them, have, provided there is purity of body, clothes, and place, and the belly is free of forbidden things, the tongue is free of lies, slander, and calumny. He should also leave forbidden and disliked things, and what does not concern him, whatever it may be.

Peace

152
The faqir without a heart is certainly not free of turbidity since he is always complaining, always weeping, and always trembling. He will not be free of his turbidity or his sickness or his whisperings until he finds his heart. We do not see any cause for the immediate appearance of the heart like the breaking the habits of the self, i.e. leaving its habits of constant speech, constant satiety, and constant socializing with people. As for sleep, it does not harm him. It benefits him if it is at its proper time. By Allah, the fuqara are not hindered from being immersed in the meaning of the past and future

by anything except constant speech, constant satiety, and constant socializing with people. If the faqir were to have the nature of the opposite of speech – and it is silence, the opposite of satiety, and it is hunger, and the opposite of socializing with people – and it is alienation from them, and then delayed, i.e. returned from following the sensory which is the opposite of meanings, he would have become so immersed in the meaning that he could not leave its sea. This is what happened to the Imam al-Ghazali, the Imam Ibn al-'Arabi al-Hatimi, Imam ash-Shadhili, and others like them, for instance our master and others, may Allah be pleased with them. We have told you before that the sensory has overwhelmed people and seized their hearts and limbs so that they are only occupied with the sensory. They discuss it alone and they recognise only it. It is as if Allah-ta'ala had not given them the meaning although He – glory be to Him! has made each of them a part of it as He has given the sea waves. Had they known the meanings, the sensory would not have distracted them from them. Had they known them, they would have found that there are seas without any shore in themselves. Allah is the authority for what we say.

Whoever is destroyed among people, is destroyed in respect to what he is ignorant of, because all people recognise that constant speech, constant satiety, and constant socialising with people truly corrupts the heart and does not put it right. It harms it and does not benefit it. What then do the people of knowledge think? However, passion has overwhelmed them, disgraced them, deprived them, rent their honour. It has blinded them and completely finished them. It has left them deaf, dumb, and blind. They have no intellect at all except for the rare exception among them. *"We belong to Allah and to Him we return."*

Peace

For a long time I have been meaning to write a short letter which will contain the discipline of the Path for us so that all of us can have its reality. I have not seen anything which is succinct except something which has not been written down. Now Allah has given me a reason, so the distance has become near for me without any hardship or trouble. That is because I heard one of you speaking without any benefit at all for the length of time in which he could have prayed eighteen rakats, recited five hizb of Qur'an, or harvested three measures of wheat. The result is that he, may Allah be kind to him! spent the entire time between the sunset-prayer and the night-prayer talking about something which had no benefit in it at all. The faqir who is like that is not truly sincere, and he never will be

Listen to how people behave! Sayyidi Abu'l-Qasim ash-Shatibi, may Allah be pleased with him, would only speak when necessity forced him to do so. Sayyidi 'Umar az-Ziyati, may Allah be pleased with him! did not speak. When he spoke, he would say, "Allah, Allah. *'Say: Allah! and leave them playing in their plunging.'* " Sayyidi 'Ali al-Hajj al-Baqqal, may Allah be pleased with him, whenever he finished one 'ibada, would start another. These and their likes, may Allah be pleased with them, are the people. They are the masters. They are *"those who say 'Our Lord is Allah' and then go straight." "They are those upon whom there is no fear nor do they sorrow." "Those who say: 'Our Lord is Allah' and then go straight. The angels descend on them. They do not fear nor do they sorrow."* "He said, glory be to Him! *"Those who believe and have taqwa, they have good news."*

As for those who say "Our Lord is Allah" and then do not go straight, they have wasted their lives in other than what their Lord commanded them. By Allah, they are not people, nor masters. Fear is on them and they sorrow. So leave whatever has no benefit. Always be on your guard against it. Do not waste your lives in other than what your Lord has commanded you to do. May Allah take you by the hand! Shaykh al-Hasan al-Basri, may Allah be pleased with him, said, "I have known people who were more concerned about their hours than you are about your dirhams and dinars." He said that as none of you spends a dirham or dinar except on that which will bring benefit to him, so they only like to spend an hour of their lives in what will bring them benefit. It says in tradition, "No hour comes to the slave in which he does not remember Allah but that it is a regret and distress for him on the Day of Rising." May Allah have mercy on you! Take note of your states and do not be deceived by the states of the people of uselessness among the people of your time!

What I have mentioned to you will keep the tariqa in order for you so that all of you have its reality, especially if you attend to cleanliness of body, clothes, and place, and free yourself of urine as is obligatory. You should also keep on visiting your shaykh and the people of the Path, be kind to your parents, and abase the self when its worries recur in every moment. The people, may Allah be pleased with them, say, "This Path of ours is only useful for people who sweep the rubbish heaps with their spirits."

If it has no benefit in it for his deen or this world, he is not occupied with it and does not turn to it. He should perform what are established of the commands of his Lord, provided, of course, that he does not burden himself beyond his limit. This follows the Book of his Lord and the sunna of his Prophet, may Allah bless him and grant him peace since Allah-ta'ala said, "He has not placed any constriction for you in the deen." The noble hadith says, "I and those of my community who have taqwa are free of constraints." There is more to that effect. There is no doubt that if the faqir only moves for benefit and is only still for benefit, and he is not occupied with what has no benefit in it, his meanings will become strong. Whoever finds that his meanings have become

strong, has been enriched by them and is free of burdens —
except what is absolutely necessary. He is drowned in the
seas of reflection. "An hour of reflection is better than
seventy years of 'ibada" as has come in tradition.

Peace

154

If you are scrupulous in your words and actions, and consider as the same the one who exalts you and the one who
abases you, the one who gives to you and the one who with-
holds from you, the one who makes you arrive and the one
who cuts you off, the one who loves you and the one who
hates you, the one who affirms you and the one who rejects
you, the one who recognises your value and the one who is
ignorant of your value, the one who scratches you like a
hedgehog and the one who treats you like a newborn, then
we have no doubt about your perfection. This is because we
know that there is no one who moves in the knowledge of
the people like you move, and there is no one who has a
heart like you. May Allah bring the tariqa to life by you!
May He protect you from the evil of the one who envies you
by His overflowing favour!

I only mention this to you so that you will recognise the
favour of Allah to you above the fuqaha of your time. We
see that their water is stopped. It is stopped by bad opinion,
malignant secret, arrogance, pride, stubbornness, self-con-
tentment, ignorance, and ignorance of their ignorance. Had
they made their opinion good and bowed their heads to the
people of their time, Allah would have released their water.
It is also stopped because of their low himma and their claim
that they are like the people. They are not, by Allah, like the
people. If they had been like the people, they would have
had what the people have. Whoever claims that he is like the
people and has what the people have, his measure is the

measure of the people. That is, that he is not concerned with himself. He abases his self and does not exalt it. He lowers it and does not elevate it. He belittles it and does not make it great. He disgraces it and does not cover it up. That is also because he trades in the markets like people. He takes care of their needs with his own hand, whatever the need may be — meat, intestines, the head, tripe, chicken, eggs, saddle, handful of garlic, bundle of onions or the like of this. He carries it in his hand, on his neck or on his donkey or cow. By Allah, I do not think that any of them will do this. If he had done it, he would have been like the people. If he had been like the people, he would have been stripped of what he believed about himself because he is on the same level as the people and he and they are the same. The matter is not like that with him: The matter is that people are common and he is elite, as far as he is concerned. He does not see that he is better than them by his 'ibada or his character or his humility. He sees that he is better than them since he is disconnected from the states which they have, due to their direct contact with their means in their hands and protecting their manliness. He does not want anyone to see him except with what he likes and is pleasing among the high states. They are not hidden. He, may Allah be kind to him, does not know that one of the masters, may Allah be pleased with them, used to give water at the markets. One of them used to auction donkeys. One of them was a blacksmith. One of them traded while riding on his donkey with his wife following behind him. There is more of that. The people, may Allah be pleased with them, say, "This path of ours is only useful for people who sweep the rubbish heaps with their spirits."

May Allah have mercy on you! Know that Shaykh al-Majdhoub, may Allah be pleased with him! was among our shaykhs and the paragons of the men of Allah in North Africa. He said, may Allah be pleased with him, "All of the water of Morocco is cut off except for our water. It will not be cut off until the last day." Sayyidi Yusuf al-Fasi drank it from the shaykh. His brother, Shaykh Sayyidi 'Abdu'r-Rahman al-Fasi, the gnostic of Allah, had it from him. Shaykh Sayyidi Muhammad b. 'Abdillah had it from him. Shaykh Sayyidi Qasim al-Khassasi had it from him. Shaykh Ahmad b. 'Abdillah had it from him, His son, Shaykh Sayyidi al-'Arabi b. 'Abdillah had it from him at Hawmatu'l-Makhfiyya, may Allah be pleased with them and give us the benefit of their baraka. From him, it was drunk by the great shaykh, our master, Abu'l-Hasa Sayyidi 'Ali b. Sayyidi 'Abdur'r-Rahman, the Hasani 'Imrani sharif known as al-Jamal, may Allah be pleased with him. Al-'Arabi b. Ahmad, the Darqawi sharif, had it from him. There is no doubt that many people other than those we mentioned took from each of the shaykhs, may Allah be pleased with them!

Peace

155

If you want the favour of Allah to appear on you, then persevere in your wayfaring, being always attentive to what will benefit you and what will bring good back to you in the two worlds. Recognise the shari'at of your path and act by it. Do not dive into what does not concern you. Do not follow what is light for you. What is heavy for you is better for you since that is what has no portion for your self. That in which there is no portion for your self is pure for your Lord. Do not turn to the one who blames you or praises you. Say with the tongue of the state: "That which you dislike from me is that which my heart desires."

Would that You were sweet while this life is bitter.
Would that You were pleased while people are angry.
Would that what is between You and me were filled
and flourishing, and that what is between me and
the worlds were a ruin.

If Your love proves true, then all is easy, and all which
is on the earth is earth,

There is no doubt that the people of true sincerity only look
at what is between them and their Creator. They do not look
at what is between them and creation: If you desire to free
yourself of the appetites of your self, then you must have
what pleases your Lord. You do not need people, whether
they blame or praise you, or see you doing what they dislike or they like.

Peace

156

Whoever is destroyed among people, is destroyed only in
respect to what he knows, not that of which he is ignorant.
Each of them truly recognises that action-by-knowledge is
what is needed. It is not knowledge. Some of them do not
recognise this, and think that knowledge is what is needed.
The matter is not as he thinks. It is the opposite of what
he thinks. The lofty Shaykh Sayiddi Ibn 'Ata'Illah, may
Allah be pleased with him! said in his Hikam, "It is not
feared that the paths will become confused for you. What is
feared, is that passion will overwhelm you." Therefore take
note and always expose yourselves to the fragrant breeze of
your Lord. Do not slacken in travelling your path as we see
many of you doing. Help is according to predisposition as in
the Hikam of Ibn 'Ata'Illah, "Help arrives according to predisposition, and lights shine according to the purity of the
secrets. The only one who belittles the wird is the one who
is ignorant of the warid which exists in the next world. The
wird will last as long as this world. It is more proper to be
concerned with that, the existence of which is not disputed.
There is no replacement for whatever of your life you have
missed, and that which you have obtained of it is worthless."

I tell you that the wird is what the slave has of means of

his Lord. The warid is what comes to His slave from Allah of gifts. You absolutely must expose yourselves to the fragrant breezes of your Lord. But you should always be on your guard against what will harden your hearts like constant speech, constant satiety, and constant socialising with people. Your outward should always have the state of humility. You should leave every state which leads to arrogance and pride. You should not desire any of the states of the proud at all. You should have the state of humility, cleanliness, bereftness, contentment, and so forth.

Peace

157

Each faqir with intellect must have adab. If he loses his intellect, adab falls away from him. The people, may Allah be pleased with them, say:

> The adab of the slave is abasement. The slave must not abandon adab
> If his abasement is perfected, he obtains love and draws near.

May Allah be pleased with them! They also say, "Make your action salt and your adab flour." I say that whoever dissipates his adab while he still has his intellect has been misguided from the path, even if he is annihilated in the contemplation of the immensity of the essence of the Lord from seeing himself while his intellect is still present. Absence and presence are two states of the perfect among the people of the Path, may Allah be pleased with them. The only one who knows them is the one who has obtained them. All that is recognised is that when he obtains absence, he does not obtain presence and when he obtains presence, he does not obtain absence. They are two opposites, and two opposites can only be joined for the man whose foot is on that of the Messenger of Allah, may Allah bless him and grant him peace.

Faqir, perfect adab is that you have the reality inwardly and the shari'at of Muhammad outwardly without having one exceed the other. This is like the prophets, blessing and peace be upon them and the perfect awliya, may Allah be pleased with them. Do not be deceived by the one who has his reality overcome his shari'at — and they are very many, and the one who has his shari'at overcome his reality, and they are very many. If you said, there is no one is this world whose reality does not dominate his shari'at or his shari'at his reality, I say that baraka will exist in this world as long as this world endures. The only one who lacks it is the one who has a bad opinion and does not lower his head to the men of Allah.

You must have adab with Allah, with the Messenger of Allah, may Allah bless him and grant him peace, and with all the muslims, may Allah be pleased with them! May Allah give life to the one who gives life to the tariqa and let us die in the goal of realisation! In our area, we have seen the tariqa brought to life with a clear sunna from the sunna of the Messenger of Allah, may Allah bless him and grant him peace. Shaykh 'Abdullah, the sharif, and the ancestor of the sharifs, the people of Wazzan, brought it to life, may Allah be pleased with them and give us the benefit of their baraka. That sunna is feeding the visitors with couscous, or wheat or barley or pearl barley mixed with water, salt, and a bit of ghee or some other condiment. There is no good for the faqir in appetites. He has good in leaving appetites. There is no good for him in satiety, even with grass. Had there been any good in it, our Prophet, may Allah bless him and grant him peace, would have had his fill of food. He did not have his fill of food for any two consecutive days. His affair is well-known among the elite and the common people. Whoever says other than this is lacking in the Messenger's sunna. The one who has the sunna is not disappointed or deficient. Good is not far from him. This is our belief and we will have it until the meeting with our Lord. The rare exception is not needed. What is needed is other than the rare exception.

We saw a clear sunna of the Messenger of Allah, may Allah bless him and grant him peace, which was given life by the shaykh, our master, may Allah be pleased with him. It is the state of divestment which was the state of our masters, the Ahl as-Suffa who were the Companions of the Messenger of Allah, may Allah bless him and grant him peace, and the dearest of people to him. May Allah be pleased with them! Sayyiduna 'Umar b. al-Khattab, may Allah be pleased with him! and others shared their states with them during the life of the Prophet, may Allah bless him and grant him peace. He was divested in his worldly means, earning in his divestment. He was purely sincere in his means and his divestment without turning to what his Lord had forbidden. This is enough of a proof for the one with worldly means and for the divested one. Whoever rejects divestment, has rejected reliance and trust. Whoever rejects means, has rejected the sunna. Whoever finds divestment heavy, finds it heavy to follow the Companions, may Allah be pleased with them.

Before these two immense famous parts of the sunna, he also saw a clear sunna which was given life by the ancestor of the sharifs, Mawlana Idris b. Idris b. 'Abdillah al-Kamil, may Allah be pleased with them and give us the benefit of their baraka. That was: working from the time of duha until noon only outside of the city of Fez, not inside of it. This is what we have seen.

Peace

158

May Allah have mercy on you! Know that I tried very hard to find recognition of the bereft among people. By Allah, I only found it truly in what the Messenger of Allah, may Allah bless him and grant him peace, said, "Injustice is under everyone's wing. Perfection belongs to Allah-ta'ala." I used to believe that the 'ulama did not wrong people or commit unjust aggression against them. When they saw someone who acted unjustly to them, no matter who that was, I thought they would hurry to help and protect him because of their forbearance. I thought that they only watched for Allah and only feared Him.

However you, faqih, are among the worst people in injustice towards them and the worst in pride and arrogance towards them! Do you not know that every warning mentioned in the Immense Qur'an is for the unjust? Every curse in it is for them? Do you not know that forbearance is the business of the people of knowledge and the deen? Its opposite is the business of the people of ignorance and lack of deen? Do you not know that baraka lies in compassion and seeking shelter in Allah, not in severity and forgetting the Master, the Blessed, the Exalted? Do you not know that the believer looks for excuses and invents seventy excuses for the mistake of his brother? Do you not know that the people of knowledge have the fullest portion and greatest share of the attributes of the prophets, peace be upon them? They are their heirs. Their attributes are the attributes of the prophets and their quality is from their quality. Or is the expression in the head while loss is in the seats?

I ask you by Allah, is it established in your opinion that the great imam, our Imam Malik, or the Shafi'i, Hanbali, or Hanafi imams in spite of their lofty value and high position, may Allah be pleased with them! ever pulled out the beard of any of the muslims? Or were there not any who deserved that in their time while they do exist in your time? I ask you by Allah, did you do that by the command of Allah or did you do that from your own opinion? No, by Allah! Allah did not command that! He commanded the opposite of that. Allah-ta'ala said, *"Call to the way of Allah by wisdom and excellent warning. Argue with them by that which is better."* Allah-ta'ala said, *"Go to Pharoah. He has become excessive. Say gentle words to him. Perhaps he will remember or fear."*

Allah is greater! This is with Pharoah! In spite of his claim to lordship, Allah commanded His prophets, peace be upon them, to say gentle words to him. What about the weak bereft believer, the sharif, the knower affiliated with his Lord? You have reached the very limit in harming him and terrifying him. You had no shyness before Allah nor before His creation.

Allah is greater! "Where are you in relation to knowledge? Where is knowledge in relation to you? By Allah, there is as much distance between you and it as there is between the East and West. May Allah have mercy on the one who says to the like of you: "I have not reached the station of Pharoah! no matter what act of rebellion I have done. You have not reached the station of the Messenger of Allah, may Allah bless him and grant him peace, Sayyiduna Musa, no matter what your obedience." Do you have knowledge in this case which we do not have? Then please bestow it on us, may Allah repay you with good from us! If you have nothing, then turn in tawba to your Lord and occupy yourself with your own faults. If you have freed your self of its appetites and all its portions and desires, there is no harm if you are then occupied with purifying people. If you are occupied with people before you purify your self, then that will not be of any profit for you and will not be accepted from you. You will be rebuffed and it will be thrown in your face. It says in the Book of Allah-ta'ala, *"Do you command people to dutiful obedience while you forget yourselves? You recite the Book and do you not understand?"* The speaker did well when he said:

> You who seek to teach someone else! Do you yourself
>   have that teaching?
> Do not forbid a quality and then do the same. Shame
>   on you! If you do that, it is terrible.
> Begin with your self. It is full of error. If you give it
>   up, then you are wise.

Then the person will hear when you warn. He will be
guided by your action, and teaching will profit.

Another said:

How can you desire to be called wise while you pursue everything you desire

You are always playing around upside down. You per-
petrate wrong actions and do not turn in tawba

If Allah guides you and you are occupied with purifying
people, then begin with your family, then your neighbours,
then the people of your city, then whoever is human like
you. First get rid of the great wrong actions and then the
small ones. It is only valid to get rid of small wrong actions
after the great ones. There is no great wrong action in what
'Abdu'l-Qadir did. No, by Allah! There were only marvels
and odd things among ugly things and scandals. All you saw
there were the faults of the people of affiliation with Allah.
You attach little importance to injuring the people of Allah.
Do you not know that the Messenger of Allah, may Allah
bless him and grant him peace, said, "The muslim is the one
from whose hand and tongue the muslims are safe." They
said, "Who is the believer?" He said, "The one the believers
trust with themselves and their property." They said, "Who
is the emigrant?" The Prophet, may Allah bless him and
grant him peace, said, "The one who separates from evil and
avoids it." The Prophet said, "It is not permitted for a
muslim to indicate to his brother with a glance to harm him."
He said, may Allah bless him and grant him peace, "Whoever
forgets the fault of a believer, Allah will forget his fault on
the day of rising." He said, may Allah bless him and grant
him peace, "Do you not know the one for whom the Fire is
forbidden?" They said, "Allah and His Messenger know best."
He said, "It is forbidden for the plain, simple, humble near
one."

Listen to the advice of one of the 'ulama of action, may Allah be pleased with all of them, to one of the kings, may Allah be pleased with them: "Have the best intention toward the one who is affiliated with Allah. Do not expose him to any evil. If he is true, then you will benefit by him. If he is a liar, Allah will give you benefit because of your intention." "Listen to our advice to your like: The people of the presence of Allah such as they are – if you have a good share, then honour them with it for Allah-ta'ala. If not, then leave them and beware of them very much. Counsel is for Allah. If you accept it, Blessed is Allah! If not, the matter belongs to Allah, the Lord of the worlds, not to you or us or any creature.

Peace

159

We urge you to teach every one who takes you as a shaykh. We have given you permission in that as our master, may Allah be pleased with him, gave us permission and as my Master – glory be to Him! and my lord the Messenger of Allah, may Allah bless him and grant him peace, gave us permission. My brother, recognise the virtue of the permission, and its secret and worth. Do not be ignorant of it. The one with permission is trustworthy since he has the surety of Allah, the surety of the Messenger of Allah, may Allah bless him and grant him peace, and the surety of the shaykhs of the tariqa, may Allah be pleased with them! Recognise this and believe it! Do not be ignorant of it. Be firm in teaching the slaves of Allah. Do not be shy towards anyone in dealing with the right of Allah as we are shy. There is no power nor strength except by Allah.

I also strongly urge you to get the fuqara to refrain from the circle of dhikr which they perform in the markets. Is dhikr outside of the markets not enough for them? Who do they think did that or have they heard it from the beginning of time to the end? No, by Allah, the circle of dhikr is not in the markets! The markets are the place for buying and selling. That is for markets which are empty of buying and selling and all occupations. You absolutely must tell them to stop that. They must make themselves inaccessible to the shayatin of jinn and men by the Messenger's sunna. Heaps of money will not work to bring them to it. Do they not know that this world is filled with enviers. Have they not heard the word of Allah-ta'ala. *"Do not be thrown by your own hands to destruction...."* You absolutely must warn them about what will harm them. Allah has more knowledge of them.

May Allah have mercy on you! and be pleased with you! Know that I have not seen anything disliked or harmful for the past forty-four years — and Allah knows best— but that I was grieved for their sake since they were exposing themselves to afflictions. I used to warn them, but they were not put on their guard until one of them was imprisoned, and one of them was flogged, and one of them became ill and one of them died because of their bad adab. Allah is the authority for what we say.

Peace

160
Allah-ta'ala does not leave the one with certainty for anyone except Him. None harms or benefits him except Him. Nothing distracts him from Him and he does not turn to obedience if he performs it or rebellion if he falls into it. May Allah have mercy on you! Have high himma which is above this world and its appetites, and the Garden and its bliss. Allah, Allah. He is the goal of obtainment. No one has what he says.

Peace

161

We have love of Allah, and may Allah-ta'ala put us among those whom Allah shades on the day when there is no shade except His shade. May Allah bless you, we want you always to expose yourself to the fragrant breezes of your Lord. That is so that your movements and stillnesses may be joined to the dhikr of your Lord as He has commanded you and to love of the people of Allah and constant kindness to them. Our prophet, may Allah bless him and grant him peace, would not go to anyone the way he went to the Ahl as-Suffa who were the Companions of the Prophet, may Allah bless him and grant him peace, and the dearest of people to him, may Allah be pleased with them. They did not have any business, and no occupation distracted them from their Lord. Every divested faqir follows them. They, may Allah be pleased with them, wore the patched robe. However, their patched robe covered them in such a way that their imam could not go in front of them out of fear that they would expose their private parts. He went to them and he was equal with them in the row. Their affair was outwardly manifest. It was not hidden. Sayyidi, then draw near to the One to whom your Prophet and beloved drew near, may Allah bless him and grant him peace. Flee from the one he fled from, may Allah take you by the hand!

We urge you not to listen to the words of one who does not fear Allah among those of means to Allah. We only see them objecting to the sunna by innovation, not objecting to innovation by the sunna. Allah is the authority for what we say. Part of the sunna, Sayyidi, is trust in the weak, the bereft, the orphans, the exiles, and the people of Allah, such as they are. Part of the sunna is also love for them, kindness to them, helping them, and the like of that.

Peace

162

There is no disagreement among the people of knowledge, may Allah be pleased with them, about people seeing their Lord in the Garden as it is in the sound hadith. As for this world, it is permitted and not deemed impossible among the people of the sunna, may Allah be pleased with them. The people of the sunna have enough of a proof when they say that had the vision been completely impossible and forbidden, Sayyiduna Musa, peace be upon him, would not have asked for it since he was the Messenger of Allah and the one to whom Allah spoke. The Messenger does not ask for the impossible. He asks for what is permitted since he is protected. Protection keeps him from doing what is not correct. The vision is not obtained by anyone until after the annihilation of his self, its obliteration, disappearance, departure and extinction as has been the case with all of the shaykhs of the tariqa, East and West, modern and ancient, may Allah be pleased with all of them.

When anyone acquires it, by Allah, that person departs and everything departs. Nothing remains except Allah since it is impossible for anyone to see Him while he sees other-than-Him with Him. The lofty shaykh, the wali of Allah-ta'ala, Abu'l-Qasim al-Qushayri, may Allah be pleased with him, said in at-Tajir, "It is related that a man knocked on the door of Abu Yazid. He said, "Abu Yazid is not in the house," It is related that a man said to ash-Shibli, "Where is ash-Shibli?" He said, "Dead, may Allah not have mercy on him." It was said that Dhu'n-Nun al-Misri sent a man to learn about the states of Abu Yazid al-Bistami and to describe them to him when the news reached him. The man came to Bistam and asked to be shown to Abu Yazid. He was shown to him while he was in his mosque. The man came in and greeted him. He said, "What do you want?" He said, "I want Abu Yazid." Abu Yazid said, "Where is Abu Yazid? I am looking for Abu Yazid." The man said to himself, "This man is mad. My journey has been a complete waste of time." He returned to

Dhu'n-Nun and described to him what he had seen and heard. Dhu'n-Nun wept and said, "My brother Abu Yazid has departed with those who depart in Allah." It is related from Sahl b. 'Abdillah at-Tustari, may Allah be pleased with him, that he said, "Since such a year I have been speaking to Allah – glory be to Him! while people imagined that I was speaking to them." They composed on this meaning:

> They supposed that I praised them before. You were my goal when I praised them.

The difference between contemplation and vision is that knowledge precedes contemplation and vision is not preceded by knowledge. It is as the greatest Shaykh Sayyidi Muhyi'd-din b. al'Arabi al-Hatimi, may Allah be pleased with him, said in al-Yawaqit wa'l-Jawahir fi Bayan 'Aqa'id al-Akabir (The Rubies and Jewels in the Clarification of the Beliefs of the Great). We see that the people of the station of going-on, may Allah be pleased with them, after they obtain annihilation and after they obtain going-on by their Lord, have fear and hope. Fear and hope are two of the attributes of the self, and it is dead. I say: They have fear and hope like that. The difference is that when fear comes to them, hope comes to them. When hope comes to them, fear comes to them. They are always between fear and hope. Hope does not dominate fear and fear does not dominate hope. They are a protection that keeps them from feeling safe from the device of Allah or despairing of the spirit of Allah. This is the state of the prophets, blessings and peace be upon them, and the state of the perfect awliya, may Allah be pleased with all of them.

We do not think that the one who sees his Lord in this world will see Him any differently in the Garden from how he sees him in this world. After the vision, we do not see him turning aside to anything else at all. The one who is immersed in the contemplation of the immensity of the essence of Allah, by Allah, he withdraws from his passion, from this world, and from the next world.

Peace

163

Every faqir who is not concerned with what he says or does and is completely taken up in what Allah has forbidden and is not concerned about the acts of rebellion which issue from him is not a faqir. He is a donkey. May Allah have mercy on you! Take note and be on your guard against what Allah has forbidden you. Beware of forbidden things and disliked things. I do not fear anything the way I fear the effects of lying, slander, and calumny on you. We have seen many we have had good thoughts about and believed to have baraka and secret who were not concerned with what they said or did. They were completely caught up in what Allah had forbidden and were not at all concerned about the acts of rebellion against Allah which issued from them. The faqir who is like that is not truly sincere and never will be. You must absolutely be on your guard against lying, slander and calumny, and all forbidden and disliked things. Do not listen to anyone slandering another. If that happens and you hear it, hurry to answer him back and reprimand him as much as you can. If he stops it, Blessed is Allah! If not, then part company with him as long as he persists in it.

Also speak well of the dead as the Prophet, may Allah bless him and grant him peace, said, ''Speak well of your dead.'' Have modesty towards each other and towards all people. Have good character, good opinion, and abandon greed. Do not be the opposite and have lack of modesty, bad opinion, bad character, and greed. Always pay attention to keeping yourself free of urine as much as you possibly can. Have modesty before Allah, before the Messenger of Allah, may Allah bless him and grant him peace, and every believer,

male, or female, among men and jinn. May Allah take you by
the hand.

Peace

164

Shaykh, do not hope for any good for a faqir as long as
you see that he is not concerned about the shari'at of the
tariqa or the shari'at itself, whether that is intentional or
unintentional on his part. The Messenger's shari'at is the door
for the one who desires to come to Allah. There is no other
door. Whoever neglects it and wants to enter by another
door, cannot expect to enter, ever. There must be recognition of the shari'at of Muhammad, keeping in mind and
acting on it if you want to enter, or we could say, arrive
or be accepted.

Shaykh, know that I saw a faqir who took one of the
shaykhs of the Path, may Allah be pleased with them. He
used to talk about the knowledge of the people, may Allah
be pleased with them, and mention the station of annihilation and the station of going-on. These are two great
stations. In spite of that, a certain person wanted him to
travel with him to a nearby place for Allah-ta'ala. He intended to take care of something which he needed there. He
went with him. When they returned, he took his fee from
this man against his wishes, whether he liked it or not. He
had entrusted him with what Allah willed of dirhams, so he
took them for himself as a fee after he had gone with him for
Allah. What deen is this? What school? By Allah, we do not
think that he has anything!

Peace

165

Faqir, stupidity will belittle you in the eyes of people

even if you are great. It will abase you even if you are mighty. It will make you ugly even if you are beautiful. It will make you hated even if you are loved by them. It will put you far from them even if you are near to them, and so on. Turn in tawba to Allah immediately without any hesitation. Allah turns to all of us. Beware! Beware of confronting anyone on the Path among the slaves of your Lord, or betraying him, being dishonest to him, demeaning him, hating him, slandering him, or breaking a contract with him if you have made one, and so on. Similarly, right guidance will make you great in their eyes even if you are small in them. It will exalt you even if you are abased. It will adorn you even if you are ugly. It will make you beloved even if you are hated. It will bring you near, even if you are far. Allah is the authority for what we say.

Peace

166

One of the sharifs of Fez, and one of its masters and great men denounced me very strongly in the presence of a gathering of the brothers, may Allah be pleased with them. I was silent before him and did not speak until his rancour had reached the brim, ebbed and abated. I was silent. I did not speak or answer him at all. After this had gone on for some time and I still had not answered him at all, he said to me, "Speak with me so I can speak with you." I said, "I recognise the generous. They brought me up, may Allah repay them with good from me." He told me. "How is that?" I said, "If I speak with you and plunge into discussion, I fear then that I may become involved like you. If both of us become involved, then what good will there be between us? By Allah, we do not think that there will be any good between us if I join my plunging into discussion with your plunging." He said to me with great strength, "That is what people have told me about you! They said that you are a great faqih!"

Then he regretted the ugliness which had come from him and apologised to me profusely and began to have great love for me. Good character — or we might say, noble character, my brothers, is sufism with the sufis and the deen with the people of the deen.

Peace

167

By Allah, the people of Allah, are only in the presence of Allah. They are not in this world or the next. I heard Shaykh Sayyidi 'Ali, may Allah be pleased with him, say, "When the intercession for the wrong-doers among the community of the Messenger of Allah, may Allah bless him and grant him peace, occurs, they will leave the Fire and enter the Garden. They will recognise each other. There are certain people whom they will find neither in the Garden nor the Fire. They will have the confusion of the people of the Garden in the Garden until their Master gives them a tajalli-manifestation. All of them will see Him as it says in the two books of the Sahih. Allah knows best. They will say to Him "Our Lord, there are some great people whom we used to know in the world. They are not here in the Garden and they are not in the Fire. Lord, where are they then? You have more knowledge of them." Allah — may His majesty be exalted and His attributes and names be pure! will say to them, "They are My guests. They used to worship Me with pure sincerity for My face. Now they are with Me as they were in the world." The proof of this is in the Book of Allah. It is clear and manifest. Allah-ta'ala said, *"Those who are certain are in a garden and a river in a seat of true sincerity with a Powerful King."* There is also a proof in the sunna when the Prophet, may Allah bless him and grant him peace, said, "This world is forbidden for the people of the next world, and the next world is forbidden for the people of this world. This world and the next are forbidden for the people of Allah." May Allah not forbid us and whoever follows us and is from us to us! Amin.

Peace

168

I wrote to some of the students who were studying in Fez al-Bali. After I greeted them, I said: "We do not see anyone who plunges into the mercy of Allah as the one with knowledge plunges into it. We do not see anyone who is in the good pleasure of Allah-ta'ala like the one who is occupied with learning his deen and leaving what does not concern him. Do not be lazy or incapable or slacken or leave your knowledge for any of the professions which we see that many of the heedless students do, let alone the common people. There is no profession greater than learning knowledge for Allah."

I said to them after this: "We would not dislike it if you were to give a copy of this warning to the people you love."

Peace

169

Whoever surrenders his face to Allah and turns from his passion, he is the wali of Allah. We could say, whoever is truly sincere in his turning to Allah, all created beings or existent things of Allah call him by the tongue of their state — each and every thing calls him always by the tongue of its state: Give me your hand! You who have turned from your passion and turned to your Master! There is no beloved like Him and there is no sincere friend like Him. People are heedless about this and think that it is created beings or existent things which distract them from their Lord and that they are what cut them off from Him and stop them from travelling to Him. We seek refuge with Allah from the matter being as they believe! By Allah, it is as we have stated. By Allah, by Allah, by Allah! People, whoever reflects on this question until they recognise it as we have recognised it, will weep for themselves for the rest of their lives.

Peace

170

Faqir, I strongly urge you not to divulge my knowledge to other than its people. It is the knowledge of the people, may Allah be pleased with them. Its people are like that. They do not squander. As for the one who contradicts me, and does not obey my order and thinks it to be of no consequence, ignores and pays no attention to it, i.e. the knowledge of the people, I am free of him in this world and the next. He is not from me and I am not from him. There is no doubt that whoever thinks it to be of little consequence, and ignores it and pays no attention to it, nothing comes from him and nothing exists from him. Allah knows best. The one who sees me will not be mistaken about me. I will think him of little consequence, ignore him and not be concerned with him since I was disappointed and despised in that. May Allah disprove me! This is what I say to every follower. This is my reason for counseling him.

Peace

171

I was teaching the children there at the 'Uyun quarter. I would recite the Immense Qur'an while the children in front of me would read from their writing-boards. Suddenly I found myself on a boat in the sea near the city of Tunis, may Allah defend it. I was reciting Qur'an as I had been reciting Qur'an in front of the children. All those who were in the boat were delighted by my recitation. Then there were many Christian ships. They rushed at us to capture us. Then everyone on the boat clung to me since for them, I was truly one of the awliya of Allah-ta'ala. Allah covered my attribute with His attribute and my quality with His quality. I compelled the boat towards their boats by himma. I surrounded them by my force and attention. Some of them sank, some of them were broken up, and some were captured. Allah has command of His affair. Then I found myself at the school. I was like someone ill or who had been struck by the evil eye. My bones felt as if they had been beaten and bruised by iron rods. I told the Shaykh what had happened to me. He put his hand over his mouth and smiled. He said, "Well, no one knows where the office of qutb is — whether it is in the mountains herding goats or in the school teaching children." Soon afterwards, news came about what had happened.

Peace

172

The beginning of my affair was at the time of the entry into al-Barija. The great sultan, Sayyidi Muhammad b. 'Abdillah b. Isma'il al-Hasani al-'Alawi, may Allah have mercy on him and be pleased with him, entered it in 1182. At that time we saw only the essence of the Messenger of Allah, may Allah bless him and grant him peace, in everything. I would see the essence of Allah in the essence of the Messenger and the essence of the Messenger of Allah in the essence of Allah. Created being was completely gone from me and we did not find it at all. Allah is the authority for what we say.

Peace

173

One night my self said to me, "The outward and the inward which are not like your outward and inward are not balanced." I told the fuqara about what my self had said to me after the dawn-prayer. One of them came near and he had on a hat exactly like my hat, no more and no less. My hat had a new bit of cloth around the bottom of it while the hat itself was old. The hat of the faqir had not been like that the previous evening. That morning he had found it looking exactly like my hat. Allah is the authority for what we say.

Peace

174

I used to stay up for the last third of the night and do the dhikr of the Majestic Name, Allah. I learned how to do this dhikr when I found it in one of the books of Shaykh Sayyidi ash-Shadhili, may Allah be pleased with him. My master also taught me how to do it in a different way which is more exact and more to the point. Allah knows best. It is that we were to visualise the five individual letters of the Name before our eyes when we mentioned them without writing them on a wall or stone. We would only visualise them before our eyes. Whenever I let their visualisation fade away, I visualised them once again. If I let them fade away a thousand times or more an hour, I would return to them. This state resulted in immense reflection for me, and it always brought me knowledges by divine gift. I paid no attention to them and did not occupy myself with them at all. Then my human-ness became weak and luminosity grew stronger every moment. One night the word of Allah-ta'ala came to me, *"He is the First and the Last the Outward and the Inward."* I turned away from this statement as I was accustomed to before this. It would not leave me alone. It said to me, *"He is the First and the Last, the Outward and the Inward."* I said to it, "As for His words that He is the

First and the Last and the Inward, I understand them. As for His word the Outward, I do not understand it since we only see created being outwardly manifest." It said, "Had He meant by His word, may He be exalted! 'the Outward', something other than the outward which we see, that would have been 'inward' and not 'outward'. I say to you, 'The Outward'.' " It overpowered me with its force and overwhelmed me with its attention so I was silent and did not answer it as I had no proof at all against it. Then I realised that there is nothing in existence except Allah, and there is nothing in created beings except Him. Praise and thanks be to Allah.

I told my master about that, and he was very happy and completely delighted with me. He began to talk to me about pure tawhid and was unrestrained. He, may Allah be pleased with him, used often to quote the words of the great realised wali of Allah-ta'ala, Sayyidi ash-Shustari, may Allah be pleased with him,"You! You! You! You! You! You! The lover is with the Beloved! The union is You!"

There was a period in my life
When I wanted to know what we could know of anyone
Then I saw that I was I
He is my Beloved and I do not know.

He also would quote the words of the shaykhs of the tariqa of the East, may Allah be pleased with them.

I am Your foundation and You are my foundation. The clarification
Is that I am You, if you understand the meanings.
Why do I withdraw from You when I know how You see me
Before today I was bound by the shackles of separation,
Veiled by illusion. We supposed the unique to be two.

When your beauty appeared, the rust left me,
And I saw my source by my source, and I be-
came the source of the source
All is beauty, the beauty of Allah. There is no
doubt about it.
Doubt overcomes the blotches of the intellect.
Oh you who come to the source, doubt vanishes
after realisation.
The essence is the source of the attributes. There
is no doubt about the meanings.

Peace

175

When my master saw my true sincerity in the Path, he
ordered me to break the habits of my self. He, may Allah be
pleased with him, told me, "As we gain knowledge of the
reality, so we gain acting on it."

I did not understand. So he grabbed my ha'ik with his
noble hand, may Allah be pleased with him, and pulled it off
my head and left it bare. Then he twisted it up a lot and
wrapped it around my neck. He told me, "Such is the test of
good!" My self was so terribly alarmed by that action that
death would have been easier for it than to be seen in that
state. He was looking at me without speaking until it was
nearly dead from the intensity of the weight of that state on
it. Then I got up before the shaykh had stood up. It was not
my habit with him. On the contrary, I would never stand up
until he had stood up. I walked away until I was hidden from
him by the wall of the zawiyya. My self said to me, "What is
the meaning of this?" I could not find any answer for it unless it was to put the ha'ik back on my head like everybody
else. I did not do so. I told it, "The shaykh recognises its
meaning, but why were you so alarmed and upset? You dis-

like being low? What are you? What station do you have that you are not content in being in this state? Do you want to remain only with your appetites and favourite things, being set loose in them without restraint? By Allah, no! You will not enjoy that nor will you have that as long as I have re-cognition of you and your destructive actions!" It despaired of the appetites it had when it realised that it would never have them after seeing my eyes red with anger against it. It obeyed me in what I desired of it. The greatest disappoint-ment of all is that the faqir should see the form of his self clearly and then not strangle it until it dies!

Peace

176

One day I was sitting in the Masjid al-Andalus in the third row. It was Friday. Then I took my hat off my head and left it bare. People were looking at me from every direction since I was not normally like that with them. My self was terribly alarmed like a blood-clot with salt on it. It said to me, "What have you obtained by this? Your self-respect is disgraced." I said to it, "By it, I have obtained recognition of you since I did not recognise you or your form. Now I recognise it, and I will only have this state which you dislike while I am with you." When it saw that my eyes were red with anger against it, it despaired of me ever having anything except that which was disliked, heavy, and abhored by it. Then it completely left me. When it left all the turbidity in my heart departed and only great purity remained.

Then many knowledges of divine gift came to me like the waves of the sea. It was such that had the 'ulama of the East and the 'ulama of the West gathered together and each of them asked me about something, I would have been able to answer all of their questions. We would have had no need of what we said to them since, by Allah, I had become like the

lamp. After each of them had lighted his lamp or candle from
me, it would not have diminished my light at all. It would
have remained as it was. That is how I was! Allah is the authority for what we say.

There is no doubt that each person is part of the meanings
as the sea has waves. However, the sensory has overpowered
them and snatched their hearts and limbs. It has left them
deaf, dumb, and blind. They have no intellect.

Peace

177

I found the excellent sharif, the arrived wali Mawlay
Ahmad at-Tahiri saying to the fuqara, "Mawlay al-'Arabi says:
Divestment! Divestment! By Allah, Ibn 'Ata'Illah in his
Tanwir preferred means to divestment." The good brother,
Mawlay at-Tuhami ar-Rukuni agreed with him and said to
him, "Allah loves the slave with gainful employ." I heard
what they said and analysed it and then said to them by the
generosity of Allah, "Yes, Allah loves the slave with gainful
employ, but the great profession is leaving professions. Allah-
ta'ala said, *"Whoever has taqwa of Allah, He will make a way
out for him and provide for Him from where he does not
reckon." "Whoever has taqwa of Allah, Allah will make his
affair easy." "Whoever relies on Allah, He is enough for him.
The command of Allah reaches the mark." "Had the people
of the villages believed and had taqwa, we would have
opened baraka on them from the heaven and the earth."*
Their argument was cut off. They were silent and did not
speak, may Allah be pleased with them.

Peace

178

My self said to me, "Sayyiduna Ahmad al-Khidr, peace be
upon him, will lean on that post." Then a man came and

leaned on it, as my self had told me. He looked at me with a beautiful look, and I experienced a great awe of him. I was sure that it was him, peace be upon him. He left me and I went after him but I could not find him.

Peace

179

A group of the fuqara were with me and then they were confronted by divestment. It was like what happens to people when they have something sour which they cannot stand. It is sour so they leave it. Similarly, when this group could not remain with divestment, they were constantly finding fault with it. They did not keep our company after that but they did not part with us completely. By Allah's command, we were all gathered together for a meal with some other people. A man there said, "Sayyidi, by Allah, had it not been that I was occupied, I would not have left you." I said, "What was that?" He repeated what he had said. By the generosity of Allah, I said to him, "This which you have told us, Sayyidi, is what our Lord tells all of us. He says to us: *By My Might and My Majesty, had it not been for your pre-occupation, I would not have left you.*" The words fitted the place, and by it, obedience appeared from error. The group had been praising wordly means which make people neglect dhikr of Allah. They were finding fault in divestment by which dhikr of Allah is obtained. There is no power nor strength except by Allah, the High, the Great.

Peace

180

After the drought, we also asked Allah to give us rain and He did not give us any. Then I said in my self, "Our supplication is urgent and this business is not hard for the people of Allah. It is easy for them." Then I looked closely at our brothers, the fuqara. I found that many of them inclined to ruin. Then I knew that the real token would inevitably appear in the sensory and it did appear. Then I wrote to the shaykh to bring them back from the state of ruin to the state of wayfaring. Then my self told me that rain was going to fall immediately, so I brought back the messenger from the road, and then it rained. Baraka was everywhere. Praise be to Allah, the Lord of the worlds, and thanks be to Allah, the Lord of the worlds.

Peace

181

One day I was doing a ghusl for janaba in an isolated ravine near to my home which was near the tomb of the good wali, Sayyidi Ahmad b. Yusuf, at Rub Bum'an at the Zarwali tribe. It was the beginning of the year 1209. Suddenly I found myself on an immense mountain surrounded by lowlands which was beyond anything I knew. It was green in colour. There was no habitation on it or near it. It was of great distance from any human habitation. I was doing the same thing there, washing as I was washing near to my house. It was exactly the same, no more, no less. I was very bewildered about this since I found myself in these two places at the same time. The distance between them was very great indeed. It was my habit to take a long time in my wudu and ghusl. Then as my confusion went on, I used my intellect carefully to examing my state. Was it as I experienced it, or was it a dream or fancy? I was convinced that I was at the Banu Zarwal and at the mountain Qaf at the same time. This went on for some time until I finished the ghusl and I left. Then the mountain was gone and I was at the Banu Zarwal. Allah is the authority for what we say.

Peace

182

I visited the tomb of the good wali, Sayyidi Abu 'Ali at
the tribe of Yusiyya. I wanted to see a secret from him. Then
there was a green dove — the colour of the tomb covering —
which came from the direction of his grave. It fluttered down
until its right wing touched my left cheek and its left wing
touched my right cheek. Then it kissed me in the face. Allah
is the authority for what we say.

Peace

183

One day I was walking in the Suq ar-Rasif in the city of
Fez. I was in a state of great intoxication and great sobriety.
I joined both of them and was strong in them. Then my self
said to me, "You are the qutb." None of its opponents contra-
dicted it at all. Then suddenly a man came swiftly toward me
until he was face to face with me. Then he said to me in excellent Arabic, "The qutb." Then he left. I left and did not
turn to him since I was rich with my Lord. His form
remained fixed in front of my eyes as if he were present before me and I was looking at him. He was of good stature,
beautiful form, black hair, and radiant face. It is as if I can
see him now. He did not say to me, "You are the qutb." He
said "The qutb." Allah is the authority for what we say.

Peace

184

I was in great intoxication and great sobriety, and joined
both of them and was strong in them. One night, I went into
the tomb of the good wali, the Husayni sharif, Mawlay
Ahmad as-Siqalli in Fez. It was the time of maghrib, and the
mu'adhdhan was in the minaret giving the call to prayer. I
had on an old patched robe and three old straw-hats on my
head since that was my state at that time. A voice said in my

secret that I should add a fourth hat. Just then, the mu'adhdhan came down with it from the minaret, laughing and running. A stork was taking it to her nest and it fell on him. He came with it laughing. I said to him, "By Allah, give it to me! It came only for me!" He gave it to me when he saw that I had three sisters just like it.

This is always the business of the people of true sincerity. Whatever emerges in their hearts, appears in the sensory world immediately.

Peace

185

As far as we are concerned, there is no one who hits upon correct action and is in harmony with the sunna and the Book like the one who flings away his self and does not elevate it. He abases it and does not exalt it since it is our worst enemy. One of the masters, may Allah be pleased with them, said, "The self is your worst enemy and the director of your destruction. Shaytan only reaches you through its appetites and you only leap into rebellion because of its ignorance. It is like the cave of darkness, the earth of appetite, the treasury of ignorance, and the spring of laziness. If it lays claim to true sincerity, it lies. If you examine it, it is exposed. If you make it go straight, it goes crooked. If you are indulgent with it, it seeks a safe refuge. If you lead it by the halter, it kneels. The only cure for it is to oppose it and give the whip of close examination power over it." Shaykh al-Majdhoub said about it:

> Self, if I am safe from you,
> I have no enemy to harm me.
> Oh my Lord, If I rebel against You,
> Where is the earth that will give me shelter?

Peace

186

Faqir, to speak when people are praying, studying knowledge, or reciting the Immense Qur'an, or doing the dhikr of Allah, the Majestic, the Mighty, is disguising behaviour and very ugly indeed. Going far away from them or sleeping is a thousand times better than being near them. If you cannot pray with those who pray, learn knowledge with those who are learning, or remember your Lord with those doing dhikr, then go far away from them and sleep with those who sleep or run away with those who run away. That is correct action.

Peace

187

Amir, Allah put a very precious robe on you. You do not recognise its value, and for that reason, you have torn it and cut it into pieces so that it does not all join together. If you understand my allusion and indication, then Blessed is Allah! If not, bring together the people you have separated who love and help you. Put right the affairs you have corrupted and you will see wonders.

Peace

188

Faqir, the real elixir is the one which inevitably actually transforms the sources. By it, man controls his self, men, jinn, and what his intellect cannot conceive of. By it, he wins the good of this world and the good of the next world. It is what the Messenger of Allah, may Allah bless him and grant him peace,brought us from Allah-ta'ala as in His Book: *"Take what the Messenger has brought you and leave what he has forbidden you."* If you like, you could say it is the fitra (naturally correct), intention, love, cleanliness, moderation, bereftness, true sincerity, passionate love, yearning, humility, good opinion, good character, generosity, modesty, fulfilling the contract, stopping at the limits, abasement to Allah, steadfastness in Allah, contentment with Allah, and exalting the shari'at of the deen of Allah. You could say, it is following the Messenger of Allah, may Allah bless him and grant him peace, following his noble Companions, may Allah be pleased with them, and following the trusty great ones of the community. They are many, alive and dead, may Allah be pleased with them and give us the benefit of their baraka. No one recognises them except the one who reaches their station or comes upon their tracks and it leads him to them. None recognises that except the intelligent man with an inner core among the people of knowledge and taqwa. None recognises it except him as we have said before.

Whoever is given this elixir which has no like, by Allah, he has been given great good and a clear secret. Whoever is denied it, has no good, no secret, no baraka, no excellence, and no deen since he, by Allah, is like the stones or the animals. Allah knows best, but we think that the green twig is better than him since it always glorifies Allah and is not obliged to do anything. The one we mentioned who is lacking the elixir is obligated and not excused! May Allah take the hand of every believer among the men and jinn.

My brother and my brothers, all of you! Drink this water which we have drunk and praise Allah as we have praised Him!

And after the end of it: Sumission! Submission! Submisson! Justice! Justice! Justice!

Peace

189

Faqir, know that one of the benefits of opposition to the

self is breaking normal patterns. Enough for anyone concerning that is the story of the Christian — may Allah destroy them! — who only did what was heavy for his self and never did what was light for it at all. Allah then gave him an immense power because of his opposition to it. It was that he would touch the disease of any of the Christians with his hand — and that person would be healed of it immediately. News of him spread through the lands until it reached one of the awliya of Allah-ta'ala. He, may Allah be pleased with him, said, "This is one of the miracles of the awliya of Allah-ta'ala which no one who is a kafir and rejects Allah-ta'ala can have. This is impossible. This is unheard-of. By Allah, we will go to him wherever he is and ask him about what he does." He said to him, "I only do what is heavy for my self and I never do what is light for it." He said to him, "If you are sincere in your claim, then show it Islam and see whether it is heavy or light for it." He showed it Islam and it was heavier for it than anything before it had been. He confirmed and admitted that to the wali, may Allah be pleased with him. He said to him, "Then become muslim if you are truly sincere in what you say." He could do nothing except become muslim immediately at his hand.

It happened to him, may Allah have mercy on him and be pleased with him, as it happened to the one who was at the bottom of the well and then suddenly he was on top of the minaret by a blessing and favour from Allah. By this, he recognised Allah-ta'ala and that He was greater than him, and still greater and more extraordinary. This story is well-known among the people of knowledge, may Allah be pleased with them, although it was not well-known to them before. It is not in Sayyidi al-Bukhari or Sayyidi Muslim, or any of the books of Sahih. Its excellence is like the sun on a guidepost since it has immense good and a clear secret.

Faqir, then test the knowledge of the realities of divestment. Whoever tests, hits the mark. Whoever lies is ruined.

The like of that happened to a man who had made a pledge with Allah only to have what opposed his self. He did that for a certain period of time, and then one day he was near a butcher's shop. He saw that he had excellent fat meat there and his self yearned for it and intensely desired it so that all he could do was to go and buy it. After he had brought the meat, he became aware of it and got control of it since he was involved in abandoning his appetite and fulfilling his pledge to Allah.

He quickly threw away the meat and went off. Then the butcher left his shop and caught up to him. He said to him, "Wali of Allah! I turn in tawba to Allah! I will not follow this profession as long as I am alive!" This was because he thought that the man was one of the awliya of Allah-ta'ala and that Allah had informed him that he was selling forbidden meat to the muslims. The butcher had had a fattened sheep which he found dead in the morning. He was selling the dead animal to the muslims since he coveted the dirhams which he had spent on it. When he saw what the man did, he thought that he was a wali of Allah-ta'ala and one of the people of unveiling. He admitted it and acknowledged his wrong action and turned in tawba to his Lord at his hands. Both of them were happy — the butcher and the man who had thrown away the meat after he had bought it and got control of himself. By Allah, opposition to the self was the reason for their mutual profit because the butcher turned in tawba to his Lord from his wrong action and the man was strengthened in opposition to his self when he saw some of the secret of opposition to the self. By Allah, the man was not a wali as the butcher thought. He was desiring and striving for wilaya by disciplining the self. It is an amazing and excellent story which strengthens one in opposition to the self which is the core of 'ibada. The only one who opposes his self is the one for whom Allah desires profit.

Oppose the self and shaytan and resist them. If
they offer you sincere advise, do not trust it.

This is what Sayyidi al-Busayri said in his highly-valued
Burda. Whoever allows the self what it desires, his passion is
his idol. It is what Sayyidi Ibn al-Banna said in his Mabahith,
may Allah be pleased with him!

Faqir, if you see that you desire an appetite, then look
carefully at it. You must do that. If it is from shaytan or the
self, then abandon it immediately if you are truly sincere.
If not, then you can choose. There is no doubt that the
people of true sincerity choose to leave it rather than take it
since pure sincerity lies in leaving it rather than taking it. The
portion of the self may lie in leaving it. In that case, it is
better to take it if it is permitted, and Allah knows best.

There is not doubt that the greater jihad is the jihad of the
self as the Prophet, may Allah bless him and grant him peace,
said, "We have come from the lesser jihad to the greater
jihad." He said this after returning from doing jihad against
the enemy.

To end with, "Leaving one appetite of the self is more
beneficial to the heart than fasting and praying for an entire
year."

To end with, "I prefer to leave one mouthful of my supper to eating it and praying for the entire night."

To end with, one of the masters, may Allah be pleased
with them, said that one of the prophets, peace and blessings
be upon them, was speaking with Allah-ta'ala. He said,
"Lord, where can we find You?" He said to him, "Leave
your self and come to Me."

Peace

262

If you desire to overcome illusion as it overcomes you, then hold on tightly to the sunna of your Prophet, may Allah bless him and grant him peace as long as you are alive and as much as you are able. If you desire to do anything important and fear its outcome, then hurry to do the Istikhara of the Prophet. It is to pray two rak'ats. In the first one, you recite the Fatiha and the sura of Kafirun. The second you recite the Fatiha and Ikhlas. You say the Basmala, both for the Fatiha and at the beginning of the other sura. You say "Amin" after "those astray (Dalleen)." You make supplication to Allah with the well-known supplication in every prostration. It is "Oh Allah! I ask You for good by Your knowledge and I ask You for strength by Your power. I ask You for some of Your immense overflowing favour. You have power and I have no power. You know and I do not know. You are the Knower of the unseen worlds. Oh Allah! If you know that this matter is good for me in my deen, this world, my livelihood, my daily affairs and the outcome of my affair, sooner or later, then decree it for me and make it easy for me and bless me in it. If you know that it is bad for me in my deen, this world, my livelihood, my daily affairs, and the outcome of my affair, sooner or later, then turn it away from me and turn me away from it. Decree good for me wherever it is and then make me pleased with it. You have power over everything." When you finish with the Taslim (greeting), then repeat your action from beginning to end seven times. Allah-ta'ala will confirm the truth and nullify the false. Know that from the time of my youth up until this very day —and it is a period of fifty years – I have not undertaken any important business without performing the Istikhara of the Prophet. In that entire period, I have experienced nothing but good. Allah is the authority for what we say.

Allah knows best, but we think that the repetition of the Istikhara befits the station of the people of heedlessness since every station has its vocal expression. There is no doubt that we consider this teaching to be for the common fuqara, not for the elite. The elite already do as we have mentioned and they are not ignorant of it. It is necessary. You must recognise the shari'at of the deen and not be ignorant of it. You must pay attention to it and not neglect it. You must always have esteem for it and esteem for the one who brought it to us. That is our Prophet, may Allah bless him and grant him peace. You must have esteem for those who took it from him and conveyed it to us exactly as it came without any alteration. Beware, and again beware of losing esteem for it and esteem for the one who brought it or you might fall from the eyes of the Merciful. We seek refuge with Allah from falling from the eyes of Allah!

Peace

191

At the time the muslims entered al-Barija — and the amir at that moment was the great sultan, Muhammad b. 'Abdillah al-'Alawi, I spent a night with a man from the Ashraga near to the famous wali, Sayyidi Abu'sh-Shita al-Khammar, may Allah give us the benefit of his baraka. With him, I found a good man of baraka who was more than 110 years old. He was called al-Hajj Mubarak Barghawth as-Silasi, may Allah strengthen his like in Islam by the rank of the Prophet, may Allah bless him and grant him peace. He, may Allah be pleased with him, was the first who recognised Mawlay at-Tuhami b. Muhammad al-'Alami at Wazzan, may Allah have mercy on him. We spent the night in the same room. However, the owner of the house had given the good man of baraka a raised and excellent bed, and a good lamp. I was under him on the ground without a bed. I did wudu, prayed the obligatory prayer, and occupied myself with dhikr of Allah on my prayer-beads for an hour.

Then the man of baraka thought of me and turned his whole attention towards me. I was occupied with what I was doing and did not turn to him. His feeling became very strong and he began to speak to me. I kept my words to a minimum with him. He asked me numerous questions and I answered each question with a short, excellent, useful answer. He spoke a lot with me until I directed an excellent shock to him. I said, "In my opinion, the shaykhs of this time should make a pronouncement that they are leaving the market places. They should say 'La ilaha illa'llah! Sayyiduna Muhammad is the Messenger of Allah, may Allah bless him and grant him peace. Slaves of Allah, listen! What you hear is nothing but good! Whoever of you takes a wird from us or takes us for shaykhs, no longer concerns us, because we cannot purify ourselves of passion, let alone purify others.' "

The man of baraka quickly got up from his place and swore to me by Allah that "You will sit in my place!" He sat down in my place on the ground. I obeyed his wishes until his alarm had subsided. Then I put him back in his place. However, it was after he had made a bed for me in my place. He apologised to me profusely. Then he called for the owner of the house where we were. We had affection for him and he had affection for us. We were linked to him and he was linked to us. He honoured us and we honoured him. He respected us and we respected him. He had a nephew who was like his own child. He had ample provision but had no children except for his nephew. He had taught our brother the Warsh recitation, the Qalun recitation, and the Ibn Kathir recitation as is proper and as he desired. This was also pleasing to his family and the people he loved. He also studied the al-Basri recitation with us as well. In spite of his love for us, it did not reach the degree of his love for the man of baraka. When he called him, he told him, "Ride and go to whatever druggist you find." It was the time of the evening prayer. "Bring me some paper from him. It is absolutely necessary." He went quickly and brought him the paper immediately, the man of baraka spent the night writing down all that he had heard from me because he recognised that what I had said was true and not false. This is because the shaykhs of the tariqa are nearly prophets or the children of prophets, blessing and peace be upon them. Ignorant men today and at other times judge by their own opinion. They make the common elite and the elite common. Would that Sayyidi Al-Hajj Maymun al-Mu'askari would hear this and look closely into himself to see where he is in it. Then he will give the Truth its due and the Truth deserves to be followed.

Peace

192

A countryman among the inhabitants of the city of Fez disputed with us about the possession of two oxen which we had bought with the intention of visiting Shaykh Abu'l-Hasan Sayyidi 'Ali, may Allah be pleased with him. We had purchased one of them from the Arab cart which was at Zaytun al-Matruh at the Waryagliyya tribe. The other was from some people from the Ashraga tribe, who were selling it at Fez al-Bali. It was not easy for them to sell it so they were going to take it back. We asked them about it when we met them at Lamta Gardens. They told us about it and we bought it from them. In spite of that, he did not accept our explanation. He disputed with us about them and continued to argue with us about them for almost three days until we were extremely troubled. There was a group of us and the Shaykh Sayyidi 'Ali was bewildered about this business of ours.

Then after three days, Allah, the Blessed, the Exalted! inspired me by a favour and blessing from Him, that I should say to the man who was arguing with me, "May Allah help me in what I say to you." He told me, "Say what you like." I said to him, "Go and do wudu and pray two rak'ats. Then do the prayer on the Messenger of Allah, may Allah bless him and grant him peace, ten times. Then come back to us. Then, Allah willing, there will be good between us." He went and did what we had told him to do. He came back to us and said to us, "I have returned from doubt to certainty: The oxen are not mine."

My brother, this is the secret of returning to Allah in all matters, great and small. This is the secret of gathering things to Him and from Him. I know what I am telling you and what I say to you. It is that each and every person needs many things, but in reality, they are all in need of just one thing. It is to turn to Allah and turn away from everything except Him. Shaykh Sayyidi at-Tustari recognised this when he answered his murid who had said to him, "Master, food." He said to him, "Allah." The murid was silent awhile and then said, "We must have food." Shaykh at-Tustari said, "We must have Allah." Whoever of you recognises this and is not at all ignorant of it, my brothers, should leave me. Whoever does not recognise it, should cling to us and not leave us until he dies or we die.

Peace

193

My brother, know that I heard the shaykh, our master, Sayyidi 'Ali al-Jamal, may Allah be pleased with him, say, "People say that there has never been such a disaster as the loss of the Prophet, may Allah bless him and grant him peace, from the earth, and like leaving Andulusia since it was a land of knowledge. Mawlay at-Tuhani b. Mawlay at-Tayyib living at Silimaniyya at the Sharra'a citadel: I say that the greatest of all disasters is that a man wastes his entire life in other than what his Lord has commanded him. Sayyidi, look closely at what you have from first to last! If it is what concerns you and what will bring you good in both worlds, then praise Allah and thank Him! If not, then have what Allah commanded you and always cling to the sunna of the Messenger of Allah, may Allah bless him and grant him peace. Whoever turns to Allah and turns away from his passion, is a wali of Allah.

Peace

194

When a certain person told me that it was difficult for him to cross a threshold in front of him, I said to him, "If you say the prayer on the Messenger of Allah, may Allah bless him and grant him peace, by Allah, you will cross seventy thresholds and you will cross the Sirat in the blink of an eye while you are not aware of crossing the threshold or the Sirat." He did not listen to me. He continued to talk about the threshold and was not silent. Then I said to him, "My brother, forget yourself by your Lord, and you will see wonders. Do not forget your Lord by yourself, and then die in sorrow, anxiety, and fear, i.e. forgetting your Lord. We seek refuge with Allah from forgetting the Lord, glory be to Him!

Peace

195

I said to one of the brothers, may Allah be pleased with them! "The root of happiness and good things is turning to Allah and always gathering oneself to Him. The root of anxieties, sorrows, turbidities, and loss is heedlessness to Allah and turning away from Him. We seek refuge with Allah! If a man looked carefully and turned to his Master and turned away from his passion, he would have the gifts of Allah which the awliya of Allah have. You absolutely and

categorically must direct your attention to what I have told
you and act on it. May Allah give us and you success.

Peace

196

I also said to one of the brothers, may Allah be pleased
with them, "If your wind has no direction and your state is
constricted and your situation is unbearable, then stop
plunging into yourself, do the prayer on your Prophet, may
Allah bless him and grant him peace as much as Allah wills,
recite what is easy of the Qur'an as much as Allah wills, say
"La ilaha illa'llah" as much as Allah wills, and pray two
raka'ts. Always be like that no matter what happens to you
and you will see wonders.

Peace

197

Sayyidi, know — may Allah teach you good! that the
water which always flows downward out of humility to Allah
was raised up by Allah. He made every living thing from it as
Allah-ta'ala said:

*"We made every living thing from water.", "He is the One
who created man from water and made him kindred by
blood and marriage.", "Have you not seen that Allah
sends down water from the heaven, and by it, brings out
fruits of different colours and in the mountains are streaks
of white and red, of different colours and pitch black, and
people, animals and beasts of different colours, and then
they wither...", "He sent down water out of the heaven
and so the valleys flowed with it, and the flood carried an
increasing froth.", "Allah created every animal of water."*

raise him. Bearing down on the self is the business of the people of knowledge and the deen. Always do that and you will see wonders.

Peace

198

I said to one of the brothers: In our opinion, and Allah knows best, sufism is observing the shari'at of the deen of Muhammad, surrendering will to the Lord of the worlds, and having good character towards the muslims. Discarding this world is a clear matter since love of it is the source of every error and affliction as the Messenger of Allah, may Allah bless him and grant him peace, said. My brothers, recognise the shari'at of the deen which the Messenger of the Lord of the worlds brought to us, may Allah bless him and grant him peace. Do not be ignorant of it. Pay attention to it and do not neglect it. It is the real elixir that inevitably actually transforms the sources. By it, man controls his self, jinn, men and all existence, the good of this world and the good of the next. Surrender your will to your Lord in whatever He decrees for you and only choose what He chooses for you. Surrendering the will to Allah is the great election, and there is nothing above the great election except for the rank of prophecy. There is no doubt that the end of the wali, may Allah be pleased with him, is the beginning of the Prophet, peace be upon him, and Allah knows best.

Listen to the words of one who surrendered his will to his Lord and only chose what He chose for him and only loved what He made him love. It was said to the Imam Sayyiduna 'Umar b. 'Abdu'l-Aziz, may Allah be pleased with him, "What do you want?" He said, "What Allah decrees." Sayyidi Abu Ja'far al-Haddad — and he was the shaykh of Imam al-Junayd, may Allah be pleased with both of them, said, "For forty years I have desired to desire to leave what I desire. I have not found what I desire." It was said to Sayyidi Abu Jida al-Fasi who was at the Bab Banu Musafir, when he came to the door of the garden of a certain person, "Ask Allah to send us rain." He knocked on the door of the garden quickly. The gardener said, "Who is it?" He said, "Water the garden." The gardener said, "What makes you bother with that, you meddler? The garden belongs to its master, not to you. Its master knows about it." Sayyidi Abu Jida said, "Listen to what he tells you!" It was said to one of the more recent awliya, from this town of ours, the town of the Banu Zarwal — and he was a majdhoub called Sayyidi Ibrahim al-Janati, "Ask for rain with us." He, may Allah be pleased with him, said, "We are slaves and will remain slaves. Allah does what He wants." One of them said, "Allah put me in a state which I disliked for forty years and did not move me to another, so I was annoyed about it." There is more like this which we do not know and we only know a little, no matter what we know. It says in the Immense Qur'an addressing the noble Prophet, may Allah bless him and grant him peace, *"You have only been given a little knowledge."* Oh Allah! Make us and whoever is pleased with us among the party of the people of Allah by the rank of our master, the Messenger of Allah, may Allah bless him and grant him peace.

We urge all of the people we love, those we write to and others as well, to learn it letter for letter until it is fixed in front of their eyes. We have no fear for the one on whom Allah has bestowed two qualities. The first is that he is always alert and discerning so that he will not miss the good and manliness which others have missed. The second quality is that whenever he is heedless about dhikr of Allah, he returns to dhikr of Allah. Whenever he rebels against Allah, he immediately turns in tawba to Allah. "The one who turns in tawba from wrong action is like the one who has no wrong action" as the Messenger of Allah, may Allah bless him and grant him peace, said.

We urge you to be careful about removing all traces of urine, about cleanliness, and persisting in wudu. I have pointed out what I say to you many times and we do not know whether you have taken any notice of it, or whether our words to you are like the wind which strikes and goes. I recommend noble character to you since it is the deen with the people of the deen.   I also advise you to be on your guard against causes which lead to falling from the eyes of Allah. We seek refuge with Allah! The sign of falling from the eye of Allah is that one's heart is empty of respect for the shari'at of the deen of Allah — we could say, the five things of Allah. May Allah take us, and you, and all of the muslims by the hand. Amin.

Peace

199

There was a woman who was one of the lovers of Allah — may Allah make many like her! Whisperings had got the better of her for many years and oppressed her greatly. It was so extreme that at certain moments she would almost stop speaking because of the intensity of her anxieties and sorrows. I used to remind her and warn her against listening to the chatter of the self throughout that entire period. Then her son wrote a letter to me about her. I answered him and said: "By Allah, there is only good in your mother. There is no evil in her except that she listens to all the illusions which come to her. Illusion is baseless. We have pointed it out to her, we have reminded her, and cautioned her about it as much as we can.   Part of what I told her is that whispering used to overwhelm me and make me conceive the impossible. It would say to me, 'Look at the sky. There are arrows of fire falling from it which will burn you up from head to foot.' I looked at the sky and, as the voice had said to me, it was falling on me. It was like that, I don't know how many times, until my breast was terribly constricted and I was distressed and grieved. Then I went to an isolated spot with the intention of killing myself. Allah is the authority for what we say. Then I said, 'The only thing I can do is to surrender my will about myself to Allah. He can do what He likes with me, be it happiness or wretchedness.' Then I completely avoided retreat and fled from it entirely. I used to talk with people and not leave them, and I would speak with them and not be silent for a certain period of time. Then I completely forgot those whisperings by the overflowing favour of Allah. Every harm left me, i.e. those impossible forms which illusion had been making me imagine withdrew from me and completely went away. Not a trace of it remained. I did not add anything to the obligatory and confirmed 'ibada which Allah has made obligatory. Then great favour and a clear secret appeared to me. The reason was that I had surrendered my will about myself to my Lord to do with as He liked. He could make me happy or wretched, show mercy to me or punish me, bring me near or put me far away, make me enter the Garden or make me enter the Fire. I had relief from what had afflicted me, and by Allah, I was completely delighted. Praise and thanks be to Allah!''

There is no doubt that whisperings are multiplied when one is in retreat or silent. If Mawlatna Amina is as we were, it will leave her. There is also no doubt that whisperings only impose themselves on the best of people. Listen to what happened to Shaykh ash-Shadhili, may Allah be pleased with him. He said, ''One night, I was reciting: *Say: I seek refuge with the Lord of men, the King of men, the God of men, from the evil of the slinking whisperer who whispers in the breasts of men, of jinn and men.* Then it was said to me, 'The evil of the whisperer is the whisperer who comes between you and your Beloved. He makes you forget His good kindness and reminds you of your evil actions. He makes little of that on the right and makes much of that on the left to make you turn from good opinion of Allah and His Messenger. Watch out for this door! Many people — worshippers, those who do without, the people of earnestness and striving — have been taken by it." It is also with Shaykh Ibn 'Abbad in the words of Ibn 'Ata'Illah, may Allah be pleased with him! "Whoever speaks from the carpet of his own goodness is silenced by evil. Whoever speaks from the carpet of the goodness of Allah to him, is not silenced when evil comes." Shaykh Ahmad b. Abu'l-Hawari said, 'I complained to Shaykh Abu Sulayman ad-Darani, may Allah be pleased with both of them! about the whisperer. He said, "If you want him to leave you alone, then whenever you sense him at any moment, rejoice. If you rejoice, he will leave you alone since shaytan hates nothing so much as the happiness of the believer. If you are distressed by it, it will increase." ' Part of what will confirm this is what one of the Imams said, " The one whose iman is perfect is afflicted by the whisperer. The thief does not bother to enter a ruined house." It is from al-Jawahir al-Hisan (the Beautiful Jewels).

Peace

200

Bring the Path of the people, may Allah be pleased with them! to life so that Allah will bring you to life. Travel it with knowledge so that Allah will make the distance short for you. I advise you that the day when its people come to you should be a day of feasting, a day of booty, a blessed day, and a happy day, since it says in the noble hadith, "Whoever looks upon his brother's face with love is better than the one who retreats in this mosque of mine for forty years." On that day, none of you should do anything except prayer, recitation, dhikr, and teaching, and what will bring you close to Allah-ta'ala after He has put you in a good position, whether it is a zawiyya or anywhere else. He has given you a place to sleep and food to eat without any trouble on your part to get them. This is as Allah commanded when He — glory be to Him and may He be blessed

274

and Exalted! said in His Mighty Book: *"Let the one with wealth spend from his wealth. The one whose provision is held back should spend out of what Allah has given him. Allah only burdens a self with what He has given it."* It is as the Messenger of Allah, may Allah bless him and grant him peace, said, "I and those of my community who have taqwa are free of contraint." "The only one who honours the guest of my Lord is the one whom Allah has honoured." We could say that the only one who honours him is the one who is gracious to Allah. As for the one who is not gracious to Allah, He does not care about him and does not want to see him. We seek refuge with Allah!

Whoever has not the capacity to do any of what we mentioned should give water, light lamps, clean the house, tie up the beasts when necessary, set them loose to graze, feed them, round them up and guard them at night, and cover the floor with sweet basil. This is an excellent thing to do. All of it is love for Allah and gathering and drawing near to Him. This counsel is what Allah has made easy about this matter. Allah – glory be to Him! gives success to correct action. Act on it and none other than it. Allah will help you and support you. Amin.

Peace

201

Give good news of great good and a clear secret to whoever takes notice and pays attention, and then turns away from his passion and turns to his Master. He is a wali of Allah. Or we could say, give good news to whoever takes notice and knows that the prayer is the buttress of the deen, the first thing that Allah made obligatory for His slaves, and the first thing He will question them about on the Day of Rising. It is not valid without wudu, purity of body, clothes, and place, covering the private parts, and facing qibla.

Similarly, wudu is not valid after going to the lavatory unless you have freed yourself of all traces of urine. We only see those people whom Allah wills doing this among the people of the cities and the people of the deserts. Whoever wants to see what we see should take careful notice of these people. Then he will see them as we see them.

My brothers, look after yourselves. The one who is misguided will not harm you if you are guided as Allah commanded when He said – glory be to Him and may He be Blessed and exalted! in His Mighty Book, *"Oh you who believe! Look after yourselves, you will not be harmed by..."* to the end of the ayat. Similarly, give the good news of evil to the one intoxicated by heedlessness. He continues in his intoxication while he is not aware of his heedlessness concerning his Lord. You could say that he is the one who squanders his deen until the Angel of Death comes to him and takes his spirit. He goes to Allah without tawba. We seek refuge with Allah! May Allah save us all from rebellion by the rank of the 'Adnani prophet, may Allah bless him and grant him peace, and his family and Companions.

Peace

202

I spoke to one of the brothers about the past. We prayed much, fasted much, recited much Qur'an, did much dhikr, and a lot of the prayer on the Prophet, may Allah bless him and grant him peace, and we did what we could. We did not obtain the fruit of our actions as others, past and present, had obtained it. This continued until we became aware of an inner sickness. This sickness is love of this world, the heart's attachment to it, and constantly plunging into its affairs. We left that and turned away from it and avoided it by success from Allah. Then we obtained the good that others have obtained. Praise and thanks be to Allah! Now we see people among those who love and follow us doing dhikr with this inner sickness. So give good news to whoever takes notice and pays attention. Persevere in getting up before dawn as slaveness to Allah since the one who is a slave to Allah is never disappointed. This is because praying at that time is extremely difficult for the self. What is difficult for the self is true and it is the best of actions. He should rely on his Lord, and not on his action. "Part of the sign of relying on action is decrease of hope when errors exist" as the great Shaykh, Sayyidi Ibn 'Ata'Illah, may Allah be pleased with him, said in the Hikam. I said that there is no doubt that there are many doors to happiness. They are the shara'i (pl. of shari'at) which the Messenger of the Lord of the worlds, may Allah bless him and grant him peace, brought us. What happiness! What good news for the one who knows it and is not ignorant of it, who performs it and does not neglect it. Countless people, ourselves included — the favour belongs to Allah! have profited from them. One of the doors from which profit comes is visiting the awliya of Allah-ta'ala, may Allah be pleased with them. I visited the 'alami sharif, the wali of Allah-ta'ala, Sayyidi Muhammad b. 'Ali b. Raysun at Tazrun at Jabal al-'Alam when I was young. I went seven times from the Banu Zarwal and once or twice from the city of Fez, and Allah knows best. He, may Allah be pleased with him, was always intoxicated. It was rare that his intoxication was accompanied by sobriety. On one visit, I visited him with a large group of the people of the Immense Qur'an. He gave me two loaves of bread filled with ghee. He gave them to me in particular and not to any of the rest of the group. I do not know whether he had them with him or he brought them from another place by high himma. That is not difficult for the awliya of Allah-ta'ala, may Allah be pleased with them. I was very happy about that and all who loved me were happy. Another time, I visited him with a group from Fez. He asked Allah to give me good. He had a great state of attraction. Sometimes he would recite the sura YaSin, sometimes the sura TaHa, invoking, and dancing, sometimes weeping, and sometimes laughing. We would help him in all that came from him. Then he came to me restlessly and hit me with his right hand on my left shoulder and said to me, "May Allah give you strength!" Then he repeated his action three times. Then he left me and pushed me away with his blessed hands and said, "Go! I have given you the great one." I was extremely happy with that and all who loved me were happy. He is our shaykh and our lord and master like the teaching Shaykh Abu'l-Hasan Sayyidi 'Ali al-Jamal, may Allah be pleased with him!

I also visited Shaykh Mawlay at-Tayyib b. Muhammad b. 'Abdillah b. Ibrahim al-Hasani al-'Alami the same number of times as I visited his cousin, Sayyidi Muhammad b. Raysun, may Allah-ta'ala have mercy on them both and be pleased with them. He asked Allah to give me good after he had placed his blessed hand on my forehead and recited what Allah wished of the Immense Qur'an silently. I had placed two small writing-boards in his room. Written on them was the first half of *"All that is in the heavens and the earth glorifies Allah, the King, the Absolutely Pure."* He gave them to me after he had done what he did of supplication for me and recitation on my forehead. I was very happy about that. Before that, I only had memorized a little. Then Allah opened my inner eye with a tremendous opening by his baraka. It was such that whoever knew me had their attention drawn to me instantly. Praise and thanks be to Allah.

I used to know the wali of Allah-ta'ala, Sayyidi Muhammad b. Harun al-Aghzawi. I loved him and respected him. I used to sit with him and did not want to leave him. At that time, he was staying in Fez. Sometimes he was in Taza and sometimes with his tribe. He went on hajj three times as he had been promised by his shaykh, the wali of Allah-ta'ala Sayyidi Muhammad Barhun az-Zajli. He, may Allah be pleased with him, was among the great majdhoubs. He was constantly intoxicated, and his intoxication was only rarely accompanied by sobriety like the wali of Allah-ta'ala, Sayyidi Muhammad b. Raysun. He died a martyr, may Allah have mercy on him, as his Shaykh Barhun had promised him. He had said to him: "You will go on hajj three times, and then you will die a martyr." When he came from his last hajj, he got as far as Wadi Wargha, and then, by Allah, he was drowned at Mashra' ar-Rukham at harvest time. I do not know what year that was. All I know is that it was a year or two after the entry into al-Barija. Allah knows best.

One day I met him at the door of the tomb of the great Imam, Mawlay Idris the younger, may Allah give us the benefit of his baraka. I asked him to make a supplication. He said to me, "May Allah-ta'ala let you enjoy looking at the face of the Messenger of Allah, may Allah bless him and grant him peace, in this world before the next. As far as I know, I have never seen a state more noble than his. He was a salik-majdhoub (wayfaring-attracted), or we could say, sober-intoxicated. He did not pretend passion and he was not dislodged from the state which he had. It made him firmer in his wayfaring without any excess in any of his actions. The upshot was that he was strong-weak, and he joined strength and weakness. There is no doubt and no dispute about the fact that it is a noble, precious, cherished, rare state. By Allah, in existence it is like the philosopher's stone. The only one who obtains it is the one for whom the face of election has been unveiled, and Allah knows best.

I used to know the master, the wali of Allah-ta'ala, Sayyidi Muhammad ibn Jami', may Allah be pleased with him. He was one of the wanderers as I had been informed by someone who had been his companion in the days of his travels. His place of origin was the tribe of Banu Azjal which is near Chauen. By Allah, he stopped because of a quarrel which occured between him and Shaykh Mawlay at-Tayyib b. Muhammad al-'Alami. They disagreed about the authority of the sultan, Sayyidi Muhammad b. 'Abdillah al-'Alawi. Mawlay at-Tayyib used to say, "The sultan is Sayyidi Muhammad b. 'Abdillah." Sayyidi Ibn Jami' would say to him, "That is absolutely impossible!" The quarrel between them grew intense until it reached the point where Mawlay at-Tayyib kicked Sayyidi b. Jami' out of Wazzan. He did wudu at the tomb of the famous wali, Abu'l-Hasan Sayyidi 'Ali Abu Ghalib at Qasr Kathama. He stopped there and remained there until he died. We heard that Shaykh Mawlay at-Tayyib died at the time of this quarrel. Ibn Jami' lived to be 125 or 126 years old, and Allah knows best. He died after the death of Mawlay at-Tayyib. That was as many years later as Allah willed. His state was a state of constant contraction. Allah had given him a tajalli-manifestation by His name the Withholder (al-Qabid).

One of his miracles that I saw was that one day I was with him together with one of my family who was very important. He had been his companion in the days of his travels. This man said to me, "We will marry you to so-and-so." He mentioned a young girl, a virgin, who was in his house. She was the daughter of one of the people he loved. I was also staying at his house and had been for about seven years since I was teaching the Immense Qur'an to his children. He was praising her and saying that she had goodness, beauty, good physique and proportions. "I will give you a third of all that Allah has given me." He had a lot of property. Then he mentioned his business with me, in the presence of Sayyidi Ibn Jami'. Then a tremendous state overcame Ibn Jami'. He withdrew from his senses for an hour and came back. He turned away from him and said to me, "This (man)," and he pointed with his hand at him, "if you put him in the heat of the hamam for seven days, not a drop of him will remain." What he told me was true, may Allah be pleased with him. The Sayyid whom I mentioned was one of my family. He was quite important. He was Mawlay 'Abdu'l

Hadi ad-Darqawi, known as Ibn 'Abdu'n-Nabi al-Hasani. He lived in the 'Uyun quarter in the city of Fez al-Bali.

I saw many of his miracles. One of them occurred when I was with him at his home. He said, may Allah be pleased with him, "Here is 'Abdullah! What has happened to him has happened." He repeated this several times. I listened to see whether I could hear anything. I could not hear a thing. Then we left the house and met our in-law, the sharif Sayyidi 'Abdullah as-Sarghini who had been freshly injured.

One of them occurred when I was reciting Qur'an with some students from a writing-board with the seven variants. "You will not obtain dutiful obedience. . .." When we reached the words of Allah-ta'ala, "Muhammad is only a Messenger. Messengers have passed away before him," Allah made a light shine in my heart. I did not show any ecstasy and it did not move me away from the recitation I was doing. Then he said to me, "Now your lights shine," as had happened to me. Allah is the authority for what we say.

One of them occurred when I was with him at the tribe of the Banu Yargha. We went from them to Madshar 'Azaba on a gloomy day with a lot of rain. When we reached Wadi 'Sbu, we found the water to be very wide. He entered it riding on a large black horse, and a very large horse it was! When he reached the middle of the river, he urged it onto a rock that was under a great cliff. He stopped there, mounted on his horse. Had he moved, he would have been killed. I despaired of rescuing him and only looked to see what Allah would do. Then there was a brilliant light from his face. That light distracted me from looking at him. Then suddenly he was safe on the edge of the ravine. Praise be to Allah! A group of people with us saw that. Allah is the authority for what we say.

One of the people who loved him told me that at one

time, he did not have any children. He took his wife to see this wali and asked him from where Allah would provide him with a child. He straightaway placed his blessed hand on her stomach. Then he told him, "Allah willing, she will give birth to a boy. However, one of his ears will be stuck to his head." What he had said was true as the man informed me, may Allah-ta'ala have mercy on him and be pleased with him.

One of his miracles was that he would not eat other people's food, no matter who they were, for a period of 50 years. He was extremely careful about eating permitted food. He continued to do this until he died. It is a great miracle which joins all miracles, and Allah knows best. I was his companion in one of his journeys for thirteen days. When his provisions which he had brought with him from his home had finished, he, may Allah be pleased with him and give us the benefit of his baraka, would eat only hedgehogs, partridges, and snails. Allah is the authority for what we say.

I knew Sayyidi Abu Bakr at-Tarabulisi who was known among the people of Fez as Abu Bakr b. Qalalash. I found him in the city of Fez when I made his acquaintance at the time the muslims entered al-Barija. He was a great majdhoub, withdrawn from his sensory experience all the time. The teacher, Abu 'Abdillah Sayyidi Muhammad b. 'Ali al-Laja'i told me about him that he said to one of the students, "Will you go with me?" He said, "Yes." They left together by the Bab al-Futuh. Then suddenly they were at one of the gates of Tripoli which was his home town. I have heard that he was one of the sons of the Bey who was there. When this Bey missed him he offered a reward for anyone who had news about him. The upshot was that they came to the city of Tripoli and traveled around in it as Allah willed. Neither of them spoke to each other. Then they left it and were suddenly at the Bab al-Futuh in Fez, and Allah knows best. The one who told me this, the teacher al-Laja'i was the student, and Allah knows best.

I used to know the wali of Allah-ta'ala, Sayyidi al-'Arabi al-Baqqal. He was a great majdhoub. Very rarely was his attraction accompanied by wayfaring. When he became sober from his intoxication, he would not neglect any of his actions. When he was near the end of his life, his intoxication was incredibly strong, and people stood in such awe of him that whoever saw him or spoke with him was filled with his love. One day I was traveling to the Hiyyaniyya tribe, and he was at a shop standing among the horsemen. He was utterly intoxicated, and people were gathered around him. No one except him was speaking. He saw me coming toward him and called me. I went up to him and he embraced me and put his tongue in my mouth. He said, "Suck, suck, suck!" Then he told me, "Go, we have given you nobility and nearness." I went to the Hiyyaniyya. When I came back from them, I found that he had died one or two days after that, may Allah have mercy on him, and Allah knows best. He left a will asking to be buried in the zawiyya of our shaykh at Ramila. Then our brothers the fuqara, the people of Fez, disagreed about that, so he was buried with his grandfather or uncle. That was the wali of Allah, Sayyidi Ahmad b. Nasir ad-Darawi near to the city of Ibn Safi.

As for visiting the dead, by Allah, when I was living in Fez, I could not stop visiting them and I was not lazy about it. Many times I visited the great Imam, Mawlay Idris the younger, Shaykh Sayyidi 'Abdullah at-Tawdi, Shaykh Sayyidi 'Ali b. Harazim, Shaykh Sayyidi Abu Bakr b. Al-'Arabi al-Mu'afiri, Shaykh Sayyidi Yusuf al-Fasi, and Shaykh Sayyidi Ahmad al-Yamani. I used to visit them when I lived in Fez, and I lived there for seven years. I visited them at the time the muslims entered al-Barija. I obtained the fullest portion and greatest share of good by the baraka of visiting them. Part of that good was that I recognised the shaykh, the famous realised wali, Abu'l-Hasan Sayyidi 'Ali al-Jamal, may Allah be pleased with him. By Allah, visiting the dead can be a reason for recognising the living, may Allah be pleased with

the living and the dead of the awliya of Allah-ta'ala. Oh
Allah! Be generous to us and to all who surrender to us as
You were generous to them, oh Most Generous of the
generous, oh Lord of the worlds!

Now we will mention those with whom we studied
Qur'an and from whom we benefited. It was my shaykh
and lord and master. We read Qur'an with my full brother,
Sayyidi 'Ali, may Allah have mercy on him, with all the
letters until we had finished two complete recitations by
the Ibn Kathir variant. Then I read with the faqih, Sayyidi
'Abdu's-Salam, the 'Imrani sharif from the sharifs of al-Misan
in the Banu Zarwal. He said to me one day, "May your
mother and father be delighted with you!" I have not seen
anyone among those I know who have 'ibada like his 'ibada.
He only did those deeds which were necessary, but he allowed himself no indulgence in them at all, no matter whether
it was summer, autumn, winter, or spring. I have also not seen
anyone among those I know who was lighter in his wudu and
ghusl while he did them perfectly. It is a very noble state.
Then I read with the faqih, Sayyidi Abu'l-Qasim b. Muhammad az-Zarwali. He was always in a state of cleanliness, allowing himself no indulgence in that as befits the people of
the Immense Qur'an. Then I read with the faqih, the teacher
Sayyidi 'Abdullah b. Fara'in. Then I read with the faqih, the
teacher Sayyidi 'Abdullah b. al-Hajj Hassun. Then I read with
the faqih, Abu 'Abdullah Sayyidi Muhammad al-Lahiyyani
al-Mazgaldi. Then I read with the faqih, Sayyidi at-Tahir al-
Gaydi al-Masmudi. Then I read with the faqih, the teacher
Abu Hafs Sayyidi 'Umar al-Jami'i al-'Aqri. Then I read with
the faqih, the teacher Abu 'Abdillah Sayyidi Muhammad b.
'Ali al- Laja'i. Then I read with the shaykh of the Fez con-
gregation, Abu Zayd Sayyidi 'Abdu'r-Rahman b. Idris
al-Manjari. I studied with him the recitation of the seven
from the Fatiha to the words of Allah-ta'ala, *"Fatigue does
not touch them in it and they do not leave it."* Then he
became ill. His situation became critical. He was only ill for

a day and a night, or a night and a morning, and Allah knows best. When his situation became critical and the word spread, many groups came to him – a group of the people of the Immense Qur'an, a group of the people of knowledge, a group of the sharifs, groups from zawiyyas and others. One group went in and another came out. I was near to him, but he did not speak. He motioned to me to look at him. He looked at me for a space of time and then he motioned to me. I went near to him and he kissed my brow. That was the last thing he did in this world, may Allah-ta'ala have mercy on him and be pleased with him! May He have mercy on all of our shaykhs we have mentioned and give us the benefit of their baraka.

One of his miracles is that when a man has a fever and visits his grave, he is immediately cured of it. I and others have experienced this. I was ill with a quartan fever for six months. One day, the teacher al-Gaydi said to me, "Don't you know that Shaykh Mawlay 'Abdu'r-Rahman disposes of it?" I visited his grave, and the fever left me and did not ever return to me after that day. May Allah have mercy on him and be pleased with him.

Also among his miracles was that his student, the great and famous realised teacher, Sayyidi Muhammad b. 'Abdi'r-Rahman, was on hajj. When he reached the bridge at Wadi 'Sbu with the group which was with him, it was said to him, "If you do not hurry, you will not reach your master Mawlay 'Abdu'r-Rahman while he is still alive." He hurried and reached him while he was still alive. Then he brought him a shroud sprinkled with zamzam water, and the embalming perfume. He died immediately. May Allah have mercy on both of them and be pleased with both of them.

People saw another of his miracles on the day of his death. His wife did not want him buried that day. It was early in the day. People were indulgent and tried to humour her, but she would not accept that. Then at the door of the room where he was, something moved three times. People rushed to the room and only found the corpse in it. All who saw that were warned by it, but she was not warned. They hurried then to make him ready and he was buried that day. That was Monday, and he was prayed over at the Qarawiyyin mosque. The Imam at the Qarawiyyin was one of our Fezi shaykhs, Sayyidi Abu Madyan b. Shaykh 'Abdu'l-Qadir al-Fasi. He was buried before the afternoon prayer at Qabab Mahrah, the garden in the West of our shaykhs. His funeral was like the funeral of Abu 'Umar ad-Dani. May Allah bless Sayyiduna Muhammad and his family and his Companions and grant them peace abundantly.

Peace

203

Attention is something very great and alertness is like that as well. Oh the happiness and good news of the one who takes notice and pays attention and constantly considers what he has from first to last! Then he is firm in what is correct action, and leaves error and does not return to it. We have not seen any of the people who love us or anyone else among those engaged in worldly means and those with practices who need anything like they need teaching. By Allah, by Allah, by Allah! He has not given any of us either knowledge or action beyond the adab he has given us.

> The adab of the slave is abasement and the slave should not abandon adab.
> If his abasement is perfect, he obtains love and draws near.

The people, may Allah be pleased with them! said, "Make your action salt and your adab flour." My brothers, always consider what you have from first to last. If it is correct action, then praise and thanks be to Allah! If it is error, then leave it and know, may Allah teach you good! that whoever neglects what he has so that he does not differentiate between correct action and error, or we could say, truth and falsehood, or the means by which reflection and all good is generated and the means which lead to immersion in darkness, ignorance and heedlessness, this one definitely has a false dark reality. We seek refuge with Allah! The first person, the one who has the means by which reflection and all good is generated, is the one who has a luminous reality. You absolutely must take notice and pay attention to what we tell you! Then you will obtain might, glory and victory, Allah willing. You must have the best intentions for each other and have concern for each other. Be full brothers always. Be on your guard against flagging himma. May Allah rescue you from flagging himma by the rank of the Prophet, peace be upon him! If you see a faqir from among you or someone else who does not make contact with his brothers, even once a month, does not attend the circle of dhikr with them, does not give them any share of his property from his provision, and so on, know that his himma is dull and asleep. Nothing comes from the one whose himma is dull and asleep.

Peace

204

I said to one of the brothers, may Allah be pleased with them: One of the benefits of breaking the habits of the self is breaking normal patterns. We think that the only one who will break the habits of his self is the one whom Allah takes by the hand. They are very few indeed, and Allah knows best. This is because whoever remembers himself — and we could say, his needs — constantly, forgets his Lord constantly. Whoever remembers his Lord constantly, forgets himself constantly. Whoever forgets himself constantly, has no need of the dhikr of the tongue. He is immersed in eye-witnessing. One of the people of this station, may Allah be pleased with them, said:

> I only have to remember You, and my spirit, my heart, and my secret begin to curse me in Your remembrance.
>
> It is almost as if there was a watcher from You calling to me, "Look out! Woe to you! Look out for remembrance!"
>
> Now you see that the witnesses of the Real shine, and all has reached your meaning from His meaning.

May Allah make us and you among the people of this station by the rank of the Prophet, peace be upon him! We said that whoever remembers his Lord constantly always forgets his self. The matter is like that except for the one who is as the great shaykh, Sayyidi Ibn 'Ata'Illah, may Allah be pleased with him, said in his Hikam, "A slave who drinks and it increases him in sobriety. He withdraws and it increases him in presence. His gathering does not veil him from his separation, nor his separation from his gatheredness. His annihilation does not veil him to his going-on nor does his going-on stop him from his annihilation. He gives everyone with a right his right, and he gives a full portion to every one with a portion."

You absolutely must break the habits of your self and cling to the sunna of your Prophet, may Allah bless him and grant him peace. Following him generates reflection and every good. This is well-known information. Listen to my answer to some of the fuqaha of Fez, when I was speaking to them about seeing the Messenger of Allah, may Allah bless him and grant him peace, while awake. I said to them, "Sayyidi so-and-so has seen him, Sayyidi so-and-so has seen him, and Sayyidi so-and-so has seen him," and I counted off for them as many as Allah willed of those who had seen him, may Allah be pleased with them. They completely rejected what I said. Since the time when I began to use my intellect,

I have believed that the awliya of Allah see him while awake, and I believed that one of them had died because of his yearning because he did not see him. Then they said to me, "How can you say this? The Messenger of Allah, may Allah bless him and grant him peace, is dead, and it has been more than 1200 years since his death!" I had no answer to this at all. "As far as dreams are concerned, that is not inconceivable. It is very close to the one Allah has honoured."

Then Allah made it easy for me to answer them by His overflowing favour and generosity. I said to them, "Listen to what I tell you, and think about it. May Allah-ta'ala open your inner eye!" They told me, "Tell us then." I said to them, "Those who see him are not like us. We are always plunging into our blameworthy appetites and we only leave that if Allah wills. No, by Allah! No, by Allah! No, by Allah! They have followed the Messenger of Allah, may Allah bless him and grant him peace! in his words and actions. Following him has resulted in reflection for them. Reflection has made them travel from the world of turbidity where we are to the world of purity which is the world of the spirits. They see him there, may Allah bless him and grant him peace. They see tremendous secrets which are beyond description. Only their forms are here with us in the world of turbidity. Their hearts – or we could say, their spirits – by Allah, are in the world of spirits with the spirits."

They were silent then and did not speak when I said that he is seen in the world of the spirits. They were exceedingly happy about what I had said since it agreed with them. When they were firmer in their opinion than they had been before, I said to them, "If you were to say, 'Where is the world of spirits in respect to the world of forms?' I would say that where the world of forms is, there is the world of spirits and there are all of the worlds. It is said that Allah has 18,000 worlds. Each world is like ours. This is in the Hilyatu'l-Awliya, may Allah be pleased with them!" They were silent and did not speak. Had they spoken, I would have spoken back to them. The truth overcomes, and is not overcome.

Peace

205

May Allah have mercy on you and be pleased with you! Know that by the power and strength of Allah, I guarantee that all who are concerned and pay attention to cleanliness, wudu, and freeing themselves of all traces of urine after going to the lavatory as is necessary, will have a tremendous opening like the opening which Allah gave to Shaykh Mawlay 'Abdu'l-Qadir al-Jilani, Shaykh Abu Madyan al-Ghawth, and Shaykh Sayyidi Abu'l-Hasan ash-Shadhili, may Allah be pleased with them and give us and you the benefit of their baraka! You absolutely must pay attention to what I have told you and do what your Lord has commanded you to do. Whenever you finish one good action, then start another one. Then you will completely abandon evil actions altogether. You must give your actions a sound foundation since the building is not sound and does not exist without the foundation. There is no doubt that cleanliness, wudu, and cleaning oneself of urine after the lavatory is a great foundation. We have only seen a very rare exception among people who is concerned with these three questions. There are very few people indeed who counsel themselves and are truly sincere in turning. Had we all counseled ourselves and been truly sincere in our turning, Allah would have given us an opening in the shortest possible time. We would have a tremendous affair. I advise you to oppose people by good character. If you have good character, the obligatory and confirmed sunna will be enough for you, especially those among you who are moderate and are bereft.

Peace

To all those who are our brothers in Allah and love us for His sake in the land of morocco, the people of the cities and the people of the deserts, those gainfully employed and those who are divested: Peace be upon you and the mercy of Allah-ta'ala and His baraka.

Whoever desires to save himself, to make himself happy, to make his affair easy, to veil his faults, to have his Lord's pleasure, to have his inner eye opened, to have gifts extended to him, to have a good end, high value, the death of his self, and the life of his heart, should be ashamed before his Lord and not delay the prayer from its proper time and not allow himself any indulgence in delaying it from its time. He should not pray alone as long as he is able to do otherwise. He should pray in a group. We see many people who delay the prayer from its proper time and allow themselves indulgence in delaying it from its proper time because they attach little importance to it. They pray alone while they are in a group. *"Very evil is what they do."* This is because making light of the command of Allah comes from lack of gnosis of Allah and lack of modesty, fear, and awe of Him, may His majesty be exalted! We see them immersed in anxiety, sorrow, constriction, hardships, and adversities. They do not know the origin of what has afflicted them. By Allah, what afflicts them has come from laxness in the deen and their total immersion in their own portions and desires. Had it not been for that, they would have been immersed, by Allah, in blessings and their hearts would have been brought to life after death. Allah-ta'ala said, *"Had the people of the cities believed and had taqwa, We would have opened baraka on them from the heaven and the earth."* *"Whoever has taqwa of Allah, He will make a way out for him, and provide for him from where he does not reckon."* *"Whoever has taqwa of Allah, Allah will make his affair ease."* There are more statements to that effect.

We also see that they do not distinguish between the prayer in the first row and the prayer in the last row. They do not straighten the row in the prayer although it is part of the completion of the prayer. It is also part of the excellence of the prayer as al-Bukhari mentioned in the Sahih. That is not because of their ignorance. It is because of their lack of concern about their deen. As for the prayer in the first row, everyone knows its excellence and they are not ignorant of it. We see that they do not care about cleanliness and are not concerned with it even though it is half of iman and the deen is based on it as it says in hadith. As far as freeing oneself from traces of urine is concerned, there are very few of them indeed who do that. The one who does not free himself of urine has no wudu. The one who has no wudu has no prayer. The one who has no prayer has no deen. The one who has no deen has no good.

My brothers, do what your Lord has commanded you. There is no way you can avoid the sunna of your Prophet, may Allah bless him and grant him peace at every moment, until certainty comes to you, i.e. death. Allah-ta'ala said, *"If you love Allah, then follow me and Allah will love you."* *"Take what the Messenger has brought you and leave what he has forbidden you."*

May Allah teach you good! Know that when the slave is subjected to his Lord, his Lord — may his majesty be exalted! subjects all created being to him and makes it obey him. Allah is the authority for what we say. Listen to what one of them said, may Allah be pleased with them:

If time obeys and people are slaves,
Then live every day of your life as if it were an eid day.

Peace

207

My brothers, whoever wants to obtain blessings beyond what his intellect can conceive of, should be ashamed before his Lord and should not deviate from the sunna of His Prophet, may Allah bless him and grant him peace. He should be firm in it and not be dislodged from it as long as he is alive and as much as he is able. Success is by Allah. We could say, whoever wants to be a master of his companions and a lamp for the people of his time should be ashamed before his Lord and not be lax in his deen.

Peace

208

My brothers, we have nothing to do with what people have of knowledge or actions. What we have — by the favour of Allah — is a profitable heart, sound intention, good opinion, love, true sincerity, yearning, passionate love, resolution, natural disposition, and high himma. All these are actions of the heart which we have from Allah as a divine gift and a favour and blessing from him. An atom's worth of the actions of the heart is better than mountains of the actions of the limbs.

Allah has slaves who do not obtain what they obtain by their knowledge or their action. They obtain what they obtain by the overflowing favour of their Lord on them, and nothing more. One of them was the great famous clear Imam, Sayyiduna Abu Bakr as-Siddiq, may Allah be pleased with him, about whom the Messenger of Allah, may Allah bless him and grant him peace, said, "The superiority of Abu Bakr over you is not because of much prayer and fasting. He is superior to you by something fixed in his breast." One of them was the famous great realised wali, Sayyidi Abu Ya'za, may Allah be pleased with him. He was illiterate and did not understand anything. It is said that he could not recognise his

own name when it was written down. Allah taught him what
he did not know and made him understand what he did not
understand. There are many of them among the awliya of
Allah, may Allah be pleased with them. This is well-known.
It reached us from one of the masters of the people of our
time that he said, "So-and-so does not recognise any knowledge. He and his disciples always mention majesty." He did
not know that Allah has slaves who do not obtain what they
obtain by any of the normal means. They obtain what they
obtain by the overflowing favour of the Generous, the Giving.
Sayyidi al-Busayri, may Allah be pleased with him! said:

> It is enough for you that knowledge in the illiterate is a
> miracle, as is good manners in orphans in the jahiliyya.

He said:

> The eye rejects the light of the sun because of ophthalmia.
> The mouth rejects the taste of water because of illness.

He did not know that Allah-ta'ala does not take an
ignorant wali without teaching him. It says in the Immense
Qur'an, *"We taught him,"* i.e. Sayyiduna al-Khidr, peace be
upon him, *"knowledge directly from Us."* There is disagreement about him. Some say that he is a wali. Some say that he
is a prophet. Some say that he is a messenger, and Allah
knows best about him. It also says in the Immense Qur'an,
"He taught man what he did not know." The upshot is,
and Allah knows His unseen world best, that the perfect
wali is like a lamp, or like the full moon, or like the sun,
or like the Night of Power, or he is beyond anything that
the intellect can conceive. One of them said, "Had the
reality of the wali been unveiled, he would have been worshipped." So then where in the world is the statement of
the one who said, "So-and-so does not recognise any knowledge?" We say to him, "Where is his knowledge in relation
to our knowledge? Where is his perception in relation to
our perception? How far apart these two are!" Sayyidi

al-Ghazali, may Allah be pleased with him! said:

> I used to assume that reaching You could be bought by
> precious property and profit.
> I supposed that Your love was easy, and that noble
> spirits are annihilated in it.
> Until I saw You selecting and singling out the one You
> choose with subtle gifts.
> Then I knew that You cannot be obtained by a trick,
> so I folded my head under my wing.
> I made my residence the nest of passion. I am always
> in it morning and evening.

It says in the Immense Qur'an, *"Had it not been for the
favour of Allah to you and His mercy, you would have
been among the losers." "Had it not been for the favour
of Allah to you and His mercy, you would have followed
shaytan except for a few." "Had it not been for the favour
of Allah to you and His mercy, none of you would ever
have been purified. But Allah purifies whomever he wills."*
It says in a hadith of the Messenger of Allah, may Allah
bless him and grant him peace, "None of you will enter the
Garden by his actions." When he said this, they said to him,
"Not even you, Messenger of Allah?" He said, "Not even me
unless my Lord covers me with His mercy."

Peace

209

My brothers, we do not think that anyone returns people
back to their Lord and Master, may His majesty be exalted!
after they have neglected Him except for the Companions,
the followers, the followers of the followers, our Imam
Sayyidi al-Junayd, our Imam Sayyidi al-Jilani, our Imam
Sayyidi al-Ghazali, our Imam Sayyidi ash-Shadhili, and their
likes since they, may Allah be pleased with them, are people
of knowledge and action. They join the shari'at of Muhammad

and the reality, and they are sober-intoxicated. As far as others are concerned, we do not think they have any merit in this respect except what Allah wills. We see many people at this time who take shaykhs in order to draw near to their own portions and desires, not to draw near to Allah. May Allah curse whoever lies to them! Many of them have come to me desiring the wird and extremely intent on taking it. Their intention is to become shaykhs over people or to ask them for this world by putting on our garments which indicates the outward state of divestment. It is not concealed from all of the people of North Africa. They also desire to restrict our teaching to the desire which we mentioned. This is all baseless and false. It is of no consequence whatsoever. I only mention it to you because of what we see of people's states and the corrupt goals that they have and their immersion in what is absolutely worthless. It is almost as if this world were empty of the people of outward knowledge and empty of the people of inward knowledge.

We seek refuge with Allah from it being empty of either group! It is filled with those who have hearts like Muhammad, hearts like Nuh, hearts like Hud, hearts like Da'ud, and Shu'ayb, Shith, Lut, Salih, Ibrahim, Musa, 'Isa, Khidr, and so on. Allah knows best, but we think that every wali of Allah-ta'ala has the hue of one of the prophets, peace be upon them and blessings and peace be upon our Prophet. Allah knows best, but we think that Allah has slaves who recognise Him and He recognises them. They love Him and He loves them. They exalt Him and He exalts them. They honour Him and He honours them. They respect Him and He respects them. He is with them wherever they are as they are with Him wherever He is. He, may his majesty be exalted! is everywhere because they are always in His presence. Shaykh Sayyidi Ibn 'Ata'Illah, may Allah be pleased with him, said, "The gnostic's need does not depart and he does not linger with other-than-Allah."

Peace

My brothers, the only thing which benefits and profits us is sound intention, good opinion, and submission to the slaves of Allah without bringing near the one who is far, or putting far away the one who is near. Allah-ta'ala said, *"None knows the armies of your Lord except Him."* The Powerful, may His majesty be exalted! is not powerless in anything at all. How many were like stone or harder still, and yet the fountains of wisdom gushed from their hearts and flowed on their tongues. This is well-known. Allah-ta'ala said, *"There are stones from which rivers gush forth, and there are stones that when they are split, water comes from them, and there are stones which fall down out of fear of Allah."*

My brothers, testify that I accept the statement of Shaykh Abu'l-'Abbas Sayyidi Ahmad Zarruq al-Fasi. He said, "There is no shaykh after this one except that we dislike him and think that he is unlikely. We did not like to hear it for a period of more than fifty years." I now recognise its true meaning. Praise and thanks be to Allah! Allah knows best, but it means that when he, may Allah be pleased with him, saw that there were an exceedingly large number of pretenders who claimed that they were shaykhs while not one of them recognised the rank of the shaykh or the rank of the murid, that depressed him and constricted his breast. Then he said what he said. Allah made his words to the point and strong by His overflowing favour to slaves like him. We seek refuge with Allah from his intention being that which most of the ignorant people understand. It is that the shaykhs of teaching are finished and only pretenders remain in this world. They did not hear the words of Allah-ta'ala, *"We do not abrogate an ayat or make it forgotten, but that We bring one better than it or like it. Do you not know that Allah has power over everything? Do you not know that Allah has the Kingdom of the heavens and the earth?"* Allah-ta'ala said, *"They want to put out the light of Allah with their mouths.*

*Allah has refused anything except that His light be complete,
even if the kafirun dislike it."*

My brothers, know that I think whoever understands the
words of the Shaykh Sayyidi Ahmad Zarruq differently from
what we understand, is ignorant, disappointed, in loss and
destroyed. He does not know that if there is one shaykh in
existence, he is enough for all of the slaves in existence
because he is like the sun which shines on everyone. It is
not enough for you to be attached to the shaykhs unless it
is someone who is truly a real shaykh. This is what we think
and it is what most people think, and Allah knows best.

Peace

211

My brothers, about fifty years ago, I said to one of the
brothers, "If you travel as I travel, you will have complete
power over whichever of your companions you like. Then
none of your brothers will be able to say anything." Many
years later, I said, "By Allah, if I had thought that I could
not make you reach your goal, I would not have begun with
you. I only began with you with the intention of making
you reach your goal." I said to them, "Now, if you hear me
and follow me, I will not leave any vertigo, inversion, or intoxication in you heads. I will leave you as shaykhs of yourselves and shaykhs of others. You will not have any need of
the people of your time. Whenever you need something, you
will find it with you. Allah is the authority for what we say."

Peace

212

My brothers, testify that I do not stipulate for people
what will confound their intellects and make their hearts turbid. I only stipulate for them what their intellects will accept

298

and what will expand their breasts. I have seen many fuqara, past and present, who talked about delicate meanings and wrote them down for people although they did not recognise their outward aspect, let alone their inward. We only make ourselves and others travel in enlargement and expansion. We do not travel in constriction. If man is truly sincere in his actions, he will obtain the cause which is recognised by all people. If he is not truly sincere in his actions, he will have no profit, no matter what he knows. The upshot is that whoever talks about delicate meanings — or we could say, rare meanings — while he does not recognise their outward aspect, is talking nonsense. His words are useless and of no consequence. He is ignorant or disappointed.

We say, may Allah make our words straight to the point! that we are supported by the Book and the Messenger's sunna. We also have the baraka of the Salaf because it goes to their successors. It came to us, praise be to Allah! when we were young. I was moved completely to the presence of my Lord about seven years after I reached puberty. Then I was not I. I was other than I after I had been I because I had been changed. My attribute was covered with the attribute of my Master, and my quality with His quality. I was Him and not I after I had been I. My incapacity became power, my weakness became strength, my poverty became richness, my abasement became might, my ignorance became knowledge, and so forth. I became an immense sea in knowledge. If I were asked about a thousand problems, I would have answered all of them with a concise, eloquent answer. Allah is the authority for what we say.

Part of Allah's favour to us and the baraka of the Salaf which came to us when we were young, is that about five years after I reached puberty, I saw my lord and master, the lord and master of all existence, our master, the Messenger of Allah, may Allah bless him and grant him peace, at the mosque of the wali of Allah-ta'ala, Sayyidi 'Abdu'l-Warith al-

Yalsuti az-Zarwali. Soon after I saw him, I saw his daughter, our lady Fatima az-Zahra, may Allah be pleased with her, in a dream which was almost as if I was awake. For about ten days after the vision, whenever I thought about her, I would weep copiously and there was an immense feeling of love and yearning in my heart. The Salaf who are our predecessors are the great predecessors and clear secret which has no like or rival: our lord and master, the lord and master of all existence, our master, the Messenger of Allah, may Allah bless him and grant him peace, and the pure good people of his house, may Allah be pleased with all of them. The Messenger of Allah, may Allah bless him and grant him peace, said about them, "The stars are an assurance of protection for the people of the heaven. The people of my house are an assurance of protection for the people of earth. When the stars leave the heaven, the people of heaven will be given what they have been promised. When the people of my house leave the earth, the people of earth will be given what they have been promised." May Allah be pleased with them! They are a large group, may Allah multiply their number and provide us with love of them! Each group of them has many perfect men, the people of knowledge and action who join the shari'at of Muhammad and the reality. They are sober-intoxicated.

The proof that the baraka of the Salaf comes to their successors is the word of Allah-ta'ala, *"As for the wall, it belonged to two orphan boys in the city. Under it was a treasure of theirs. Their father was a right-acting man. Your Lord wanted them to come of age and then remove their treasure as a mercy from your Lord."* As far as the people of knowledge are concerned, the father who is mentioned in the ayat is either the seventh ancestor or the fourteenth ancestor. Allah knows best, but I consider him to be the first right-acting predecessor. We have mentioned the baraka of permission (idhn) in earlier teaching.

Peace

213

My brothers, it is impossible that one of the slaves of Allah be straight and still lack the miracles of Allah which he bestows on His awliya, may Allah be pleased with them. We have seen many fuqara, past and present, who loved them and waited expectantly for them. When no trace of miracles appeared, their intention in their shaykhs and their Path was lost, their opinion became bad, and they were destroyed except for whomever Allah had mercy on. They did not know that the miracle only exists when you go straight. Shaykh Ibn 'Ata'Illah, may Allah be pleased with him, said, "It is better for you to look out for the faults that you have inside of you than to look for the unseen worlds which are veiled from you."

Peace

214

My brothers, if the murid does not have reverence, assumption of knowledge, modesty, awe, fear, respect, and esteem for the shaykh who is truly a real shaykh, then the murid does not benefit at all by him. If there is no benefit, then it is of no consequence to the shaykh or the murid. Neither of them has any profit. Listen to what I tell you and pay close attention to it as much as you possibly can, may Allah-ta'ala give you success and help you!

I was deeply absorbed in reading a particular book for a long time. I did not look at anything else. Then one of the brothers came and sat down in front of me with his face very near to mine. After a while, I became aware of him and that he was in front of me. I said to him, "How long have you been here?" He said, "Since the time you sat down here." I had been sitting for a very long time. I said to him, "Never mind." He said to me, "I have known you for 13 years and nothing has appeared to me." I said to him as soon as I heard what he said, "By Allah, you have not known me. You only know yourself. Where have you been for such a long time?" He said, "I have been in such-and-such a land." I said to him, "And where are your wife and children?" There were a number of them. That was a time of hardship, not a time of ease. He said to me, "In the tent." Then I confirmed what I had told him — that it was by success from Allah, and I knew from what he told me — that it was from the passions which play with man. Allah is the authority for what we say.

Peace

215

My brothers, I looked closely into the states of the men of Allah, may Allah be pleased with them. My state shone brilliantly and I saw in a way that was as if Allah had acquainted me with all of them, living and dead, past and present. That is not difficult for Allah. They are in three divisions. In the first division, their wayfaring is stronger than their attraction. These are very numerous. In the second division, their attraction is stronger than their wayfaring. These are less in number than the first group. The wine of the last group is accompanied by their intellects at all moments. Their wayfaring is not stronger than their attraction, and their attraction is not stronger than their wayfaring. They, may Allah be pleased with them, are sober-intoxicated. They always join intoxication and sobriety. Neither of them exceeds the other. These are very rare indeed in this world. They are matchless because their rank is a precious sublime rank. Not everyone perceives its end. Only one may perceive its end. That one person is called the unique one (al-fard), and Allah knows best, because he is isolated (tafarrad) with it. For that reason, the name the unique is true for him. You call so-and-so the unique of his time and the singular one of his age. The great famous realised wali, Sayyidi Ibn al-'Arabi al-Hatimi, may Allah be pleased with

302

him, said, "The fard is greater than the qutb in knowledge
of Allah-ta'ala.

Peace

216

My brothers, no action is better for us, after the shahada,
than the prayer. It is the first thing that Allah made obligatory for us and the first thing that He will ask us about on
the day of rising. Even if there are actions greater than it,
it is the first thing that he made obligatory for us. It has such
virtues that every man of intellect is left in bewilderment
concerning it. As far as its virtue is concerned, it is enough
for us that it forbids shameless action and the objectionable
as it says in the Immense Qur'an. Do not neglect it. You
must pay attention to it and to the conditions which make it
valid. May Allah-ta'ala give us and you success!

Peace

217

My brothers, if the murid does not have reverence, assumption of knowledge, modesty, fear, awe, respect and
esteem for the teaching Shaykh, then the murid does not
benefit at all by him. If there is no benefit, then it is of no
consequence to the shaykh or the murid. Neither of them
has any profit from each other. It is not correct behaviour
for the murid to say to his shaykh, "Give me permission to
divest myself, give me permission to engage in worldly
means, give me permission to do the dhikr of the Name, give
me permission to beg, or give me permission to wear the
patched robe or the turban, and so on." Correct behaviour
is to surrender your will about yourself to him so that you
are like a corpse in the hands of the washer. You should not
leave him until Allah gives you what you need, immediately

or after a while. The murid who desires the shaykh to follow him in what he thinks, he is the shaykh, and the shaykh is the murid. If this is the case, it is the very core of the realities in which the heretics are involved. The shaykh is also the imam of the murid, i.e. his master. The imam is set up as an imam so that he can be followed, as it says in the Sahih of al-Bukhari. This is what we think, and Allah knows best.

May Allah teach you the good and protect you from evil! Know that a certain person came to me at an odd hour and said to me, "We would like you to give us the wird." He desired to take it from me. I ignored him for a day and a night. Then he came back to me, so I gave it to him. As soon as I had given it to him, he said, "Give me permission to give the wird to other people." When I heard what he said, I immediately said, "Wait until you recognise me and I recognise you. Then there will be blessing." I mentioned the story of the praiser of the Prophet who was buried. As soon as he was buried, the two angels came to question him, peace be upon them. He said to them, "Blessings be upon my master Muhammad. Now how settled we are!" There is no objection in the murid asking him about his important affairs like marriage, the hajj, cultivation, building, and travel, and so on.

Peace

218

My brothers, the causes of happiness are very numerous. After the shahada, the greatest of them is the prayer. It is the first thing that Allah made obligatory for us. It is the first thing that He will ask us about on the Day of Rising. Even if there are actions greater than it, it is the first thing that He made obligatory for us. It has such virtues that every man of intellect is left in bewilderment concerning it. "The prayer at its proper time is better than this world and all that is in it," as the Messenger of Allah, may Allah bless him and grant him peace, said. As far as its virtue is concerned, it is enough for us that it forbids shameless action and the objectionable as it says in the Book of Allah-ta'ala, *"The prayer forbids shameless action and the objectionable."* One of the 'ulama, may Allah be pleased with him, said, "The relationship of the prayer to the deen is like the relationship of the head to the body. The relationship of sufism to the deen is like the relationship of the spirit to the body." We say as everyone else says, "The prayer is the buttress of the deen," as the Messenger of Allah, may Allah bless him and grant him peace, said. Do not neglect it. You must pay attention to it and to the conditions which make it valid with your utmost effort and as much as you possibly can as long as you are alive. May Allah-ta'ala give us and you success.

May Allah teach you good and shield you from evil! Know that we repeatedly performed many actions for several years like the prayer, recitation of Qur'an, la ilaha illa'llah, and the prayer on the Prophet, may Allah bless him and grant him peace. We found that they all had tremendous baraka. By Allah, we found that the baraka of repeating the prayer was above the baraka of every action, and Allah is the authority for what we say. Had it not been for the objection we heard in the words of the masters, may Allah be pleased with them!: "Whoever has no shaykh, shaytan is his shaykh", "Whoever has no shaykh, has no qibla", and "Whoever has no master, is idle. Dropping the means of arrival is unbalanced, and basing action on them is misguidance,", we would have said that the prayer dispenses with the shaykh. We would have said the same thing about recitation of Qur'an, saying la ilaha illa'llah, and the prayer on the Prophet, may Allah bless him and grant him peace. All would let us dispense with the shaykh, especially if we leave what does not concern us and what has no benefit for us and rely on our Lord, not on our actions, even if the actions are good and purely sincere. Our Lord is only worshipped by knowledge, so do not disregard it. You absolutely must do your utmost to pay attention to it as much as you possibly can while you are alive. Whoever disregards knowledge, the prayer, and what Allah has commanded, is completely disregarded and abandoned by Him.

Peace

219

My brothers, whoever wants to receive the gifts of Allah, or we could say, the fragrant breezes of Allah, should be ashamed before Allah and not deviate from the sunna of the Messenger of Allah, may Allah bless him and grant him peace. He should be firm in it and not be dislodged from it as long as he is alive and in so much as he is able, as we have said many times.

May Allah teach you good and shelter you from evil! Know that the last thing I heard from Shaykh Abu'l-Hasan Sayyidi 'Ali al-Jamal al-'Imrani, may Allah be pleased with him, was, "Expose yourselves to the fragrant breezes of Allah."

Peace

220

My brothers, when you recognise the excellence of knowledge and its baraka, it is easy to travel to it from the West to the East, and from the East to the West. That is nothing for the one who knows this, since our Lord is worshipped only by it. There is no truth and true sincerity among people except in the one who has knowledge. It says in a hadith of the Messenger of Allah, may Allah bless him and grant him peace, "When Allah desires good for someone, he gives him understanding in the deen." Success is by Allah.

Peace

My brothers, I strongly urge you not to read our book and the book of Sayyidi 'Ali, our Shaykh, may Allah be pleased with him, to the one who is not among the people of our discipline. This is necessary. If the envious hear the words of our shaykh and our words, they will certainly abuse us as they have abused those before us who were greater than us in knowledge, action, state, and station like Sayyidi ash-Shadhili, Sayyidi al-Hatimi, Sayyidi ash-Shar'ani, and their likes, may Allah be pleased with them. Whoever wants to know what has happened to them at the hands of the envious should look at al-Yawaqitu wa'l-Jawahiru fi Bayani 'Aqa'idi'l-Akabir (The Rubies and Jewels in the Clarification of the Beliefs of the Great) by Sayyidi ash-Shar'ani, may Allah be pleased with him. There are wonders and strange things in it which happened to our masters, the people of the Path, may Allah be pleased with them, in the way of injury at the hands of the envious. They – may Allah be kind to them – are only the wind of the people of true sincerity in reality. It is as one of the masters said, may Allah be pleased with him:

> My enemies are a favour and a blessing to me. May the
> Merciful not put my enemies far from me!
> They look for my error, so I avoid it. They compete
> with me, so I perform high actions.

Allah knows best, but I think that the injury which they inflict on our masters, the shaykhs of the Path, may Allah be pleased with them, comes before they are perfected. The perfect men are the people of knowledge and action who join the shari'at of Muhammad and the reality. They are sober-intoxicated. No one has any proof against them so that they could harm them, but they have a proof against everyone else so that it is not inconceivable for these others to be harmed. The most perfect of creation was Sayyiduna Muhammad, may Allah bless him and grant him peace, and he suffered great injury. So did Sayyiduna Ibrahim, Sayyiduna Musa, and others, blessings and peace be upon them, because the messengers are afflicted. Then they have the outcome as it says in the Sahih of al-Bukhari, may Allah be pleased with him.

Peace

222

To all our brothers in Allah and those who love us for His sake, in the land of morocco, may Allah make it flourish, the people of the cities and the people of the deserts, those with gainful employ and those who are divested: Peace be upon you and the mercy of Allah-ta'ala and His baraka.

I advise you for Allah and in Allah, and desiring Allah's pleasure. I advise you not to devote yourself to the recitation of the Immense Qur'an the way that the people of our mountains and others devote themselves to it so that you are only happy when you have memorised the recitation of the seven or the recitation of the ten and it is fixed in front of your eyes. This happens while many of you do not recognise the obligations and sunna, and are not good in the recitation of the Fatiha, or the adhan or the iqama. This is clearly a well-known error. Correct behaviour — or we could say, the truth — is that we cannot dispense with understanding of our deen. Allah knows best, but we have enough fiqh in the famous risala of the great shaykh, Sayyidi Muhammad b. Abi Zayd al-Qayrawani, or the Rab' al-'Ibada (Home of Worship) of Shaykh Khalil; or even the Murshid al-Mu'in (Helping Guide) of Shaykh Sayyidi 'Abdu'l-Wahid b. 'Ashir will be enough for us, Allah willing. In recitation of the Immense Qur'an, the Warsh recitation is enough for us. We do not dislike you reciting it in the recitation of all the variants of the reciters, may Allah be pleased with them and give us the benefit of their baraka. Indeed, we love i dearly. However, success is from Allah. There is no power nor strength except by Allah.

Listen to what I said to one of the brothers who asked for permission to go to Mazuna with the intention of studying knowledge after we had had some previous discussion. When you recognise the excellence of knowledge and its baraka, it is easy to travel in quest of it from the West to the East, and from the East to the West. That is nothing for the one who knows this, since our Lord is worshipped only by it. There is no truth nor true sincerity among people except for the one who has knowledge. It says in a hadith of the Messenger of Allah, may Allah bless him and grant him peace, "Seek knowledge, even in China." He said, may Allah bless him and grant him peace, "When Allah desires good for someone, he gives him understanding in the deen." In this is a door by which man learns knowledge which is better for him than this world, even if he had it all, lock, stock, and barrel. How remarkable is the one who hears about this great excellence which comes from the noble Prophet, may Allah bless him and grant him peace, without any doubt or dispute, and yet does not devote all the days of his life to studying knowledge. We think, and Allah knows best, that it is confirmed in respect to those who pray that they should always know the commentary of the suras which they use in their prayers. This is what we think, and it is what most people think, and Allah knows best. Certainly, 'ibada without knowledge is not valid at all. It says in the Book of Allah-ta'ala, *"I only created jinn and men to worship Me." "They are only commanded to worship Allah, making the deen sincerely His."* 'Ibada is certainly not valid at all without knowledge, as we all confirm.

How remarkable is the one who hears from the Messenger of Allah, may Allah bless him and grant him peace, as well as from the companions, the followers, and other imams of the deen, about the bliss in the Garden that Allah has prepared for those of taqwa, and does not devote all of the days of his life to obeying his Lord. Allah has prepared for those who have taqwa such bliss in the Garden as the eye has never seen, the ear has never heard, and as has never occurred to the heart of man. Even if those of taqwa only had human bliss in the Garden, 70,000 houris would serve them. They rise when they rise and sit when they sit. When they smile, the light of their smile extends for a distance of 500 years. That is enough. May Allah not deprive us and you by the rank of the Prophet, peace be upon him! May He not deprive any of the community of Sayyiduna Muhammad, may Allah bless him and grant him peace, and may He honour him, exalt him, glorify him, and greatly ennoble him until the day of reckoning. Peace be upon the messengers, and praise be to Allah, the Lord of the worlds.

Peace

223

I advise all of you, elite and common, men and women, old and young, slaves and free, to follow what Allah has commanded you. It is that you do not delay the prayer from its proper time, and that you allow yourself no indulgence in delaying it. You should pray in a group and not pray individually except with an excuse. Allah knows best, but the excuse is very rare indeed.

May Allah have mercy on you! Know that the reason which prompted me to say this to you is that I see many of the brothers who delay the prayer from its proper time. They allow themselves indulgence in its delay. They pray alone while they are a group. *"Very evil is what they do."* Even if they were among the lords of hearts, by Allah, they are sober. They are not intoxicated, withdrawn from their sensory experience so that they should do that. May Allah give you success! Therefore, you must be on your guard about this.

Forget remembering yourselves by remembering your Lord. Do not be the reverse and forget remembering your Lord by remembering yourselves. The one who remembers himself is the one who plunges into his appetites and is immersed in that. As for the one who remembers his Lord and forgets himself, he is only immersed in the meanings in which all of the awliya, may Allah be pleased with them, are immersed. They left their appetites and did not remain with them because they were ashamed that their Master should see them with something other than Him, so understand! May Allah make you understand! Avoid what you are forbidden and occupy yourselves with what you are commanded to do. May Allah give you success!

Know that I see many of the brothers who are always in anxiety, sorrow, distress and fraud. That is because they turn away from their Lord and turn to their passion. Had they been the opposite of that and turned to their Master and turned away from their passion, their anxiety, sorrow, grief, and turbidity would have left them. Allah-ta'ala said, *"Had the people of the cities believed and had taqwa, We would have opened up baraka on them from the heaven and the earth." "Whoever has taqwa of Allah, He will make a way out for him, and provide for him from where he does not reckon." "Whoever relies on Allah, He is enough for him. The command of Allah reaches the mark." "Whoever has taqwa of Allah, Allah will make his affair easy for him. That is from the command of Allah which He has sent down to you."* There are more ayat and hadith like this.

Peace

224

I advise you for Allah and in Allah, desiring the pleasure of Allah. I advise you to hold as tight as you possibly can to the Messenger's sunna which is the invincible fortress against every affliction. It is the ship of rescue and the treasury of secrets and blessings at every moment and time. Cling to it until certainty comes to you, i.e. death. If you are confused about any of your affairs and your breast is constricted and the matter is critical and you have exhausted all of your devices, then do not plunge into it — do not manage or choose as is the business of the people of heedlessness, may Allah be kind to us and them! Occupy yourself with what your Lord has commanded you. Either you pray as much as Allah wills, recite as much Qur'an as Allah wills, do the dhikr of la ilaha illa'llah as much as Allah wills, do the prayer on the Messenger of Allah, may Allah bless him and grant him peace, as much as Allah wills, or study knowledge as much as Allah wills, and so forth. Then Allah will give you a release and a way out as He has given to His awliya, may Allah be pleased with them and give us and you the benefit of their baraka.

May Allah teach you good and shield you from evil! Know that Shaykh Sayyidi Sahl b. 'Abdillah at-Tustari, may Allah be pleased with him! was one of the great sufis, may Allah be pleased with them. He said, "Beware of management and choice. They make people's lives turbid." I said that they both distract them from the remembrance of their Master. Dhikr is the fortress of the believer. During dhikr of Allah, peaceful calm descends so that the one who does dhikr does not choose, is not turbid, alarmed, anxious, or sorrowful. It says in the Immense Qur'an, *"Those who believe and whose hearts are peacefully calm by the dhikr of Allah. The hearts are made peacefully calm by the dhikr of Allah."* Certainly, peaceful calm descends during the dhikr of Allah. If you want to know that with certain knowledge, then persevere in dhikr of Allah with tranquility, gravity, esteem, respect, and a state of cleanliness based on the sunna while you rely on Allah. This is what we think and what most people think. Allah knows best.

Peace

312

If you lack anything of this world, then rejoice in a clear, well-known great blessing as the right-acting Salaf rejoiced in it. When this world left their hands, may Allah be pleased with them, they said, "Welcome to the token of the Salihun!" I heard from the lofty shaykh of noble value, our master Abu'l-Hasan Sayyidi 'Ali al-Jamal, may Allah be pleased with him! that he threshed three mudd of wheat at Wata Misfar at Wadi'l-Malih near Bab al-Gisa. He told his shaykh, Sayyidi Muhammad al-'Arabi b. 'Abdillah at the al-Makhfiyya quarter in Fez al-Bali after he did that. He said to him, "If you increase in the sensory, you decrease in the meanings." The shaykh, our master Sayyidi 'Ali, also had a low state and then went to a high state. His shaykh, Sayyidi al-'Arabi, saw him in a high state after he had been in a low one. He said to him, "You had 99 portions of might and one portion of abasement when you were low. Now you have 99 portions of abasement and one portion of might." Understand! May Allah make you and us understand! Wander in rapture in love of the Beloved and cast your cares aside! Say:

> Love is my deen and I do not desire any substitute for it. Beauty is a dominion to be obeyed, whether oppressive or just.
>
> The self is precious, but I spend it all for You. Abasement is bitter, but it is sweet in Your pleasure.
>
> You! My punishment is sweet and fresh in Your love. I do not complain of rejection or boredom from You.
>
> Abase yourself to the One you love — you will obtain might! How many men have obtained might by abasement!
>
> If the One you love is Mighty and you are not abased to Him, then say goodbye to arrival.
>
> If you are not steadfast in abasement, in passion, you will be parted from the One you love in spite of yourself.

The people of the Path have said much more about this meaning. May Allah honour us with their mention and place us among their party by his favour and openhandedness and by His pure generosity by the rank of the Messenger of Allah, may Allah bless him and grant him peace.

We urge Sayyidi Muhammad al-Harraq, the sharif with knowledge, to read this teaching of ours and others to all of the people who love us who are in your area. May Allah bless them all.

Peace

226

My brothers, whoever of you or others wants his fire to be transformed into a garden should not be dislodged from the sunna. It is the ship of rescue and the treasury of secrets and blessings. Whoever rides in it is saved. Whoever stays back and does not go on it is drowned. You should be gentle to your self in all matters and do not overburden it. The Prophet, blessings and peace be upon him, said, "I and those of my community who have taqwa are free of constraint." He said, blessings and peace be upon him, "Take on whatever action you are able to do. Allah does not slack off so you should not slack off." He should have what actions are heavy for the self, not what is light for it. Only the truth is heavy for it. It is swifter with the answer like the Greatest Name, the Name of majesty, "Alla . . . . h."

Among the conditions of doing this dhikr is doing what is heavy for the self, not what is light for it. That is cleanliness of the body, garment and place. It is visualising its five letters and being steady in visualising them before your eyes. Whenever you let their visualisation fade away, you should quickly visualise them again. If they fade away from you a hundred times, then return to them a hundred times. Stay with it by lengthening it. That is, that you say "Alla . . . . h," and not "Allah, Allah." You should leave what does not concern you because when you leave what does not concern you, a small amount of action will be enough for you.

Whoever does dhikr as we have described, and pays close attention to its conditions as we said, Allah will lift the veil between Him and him in three weeks or less. Whoever does dhikr as we have described and does it for more than seven weeks and Allah still has not lifted the veil between Him and him, he has no intention, no true sincerity, no love, no resolution, and no certainty. Allah is the authority for what we say. If he were to have good opinion, sound intention and other actions of the heart – and an atom's worth of actions of the heart is better than mountains of the actions of the limbs – the veil would be rent for him and the doors would be opened for him, and he would be immersed in correct behaviour by the overflowing favour of the Generous, the Giver. Glory be to Him! There is no god but Him!

The goal of visualising the letters of the Greatest Name and the method of doing its dhikr as we have mentioned is to imprison the self so that it does not plunge into the sensory and what is not correct behaviour. This is due to the fact that the sensory is opposite the meaning. Two opposites are never joined together. As soon as the one doing dhikr stops plunging into it, meanings will come to him from the unseen which he did not know before. They distract him from visualisation as plunging into sensory experience distracted him from it. If he leaves them and quickly returns to visualisation, then strong meanings will flow over him, becoming stronger and stronger. They will carry him to the presence of his Lord, glory be to Him! in the shortest possible time. There he will find secrets and blessings which no eye has ever seen, no ear has ever heard, and which have never occurred to the heart of any man. Allah is the authority for what we say. Only the very astute person travels this road, and not the entire tariqa. Allah is the authority for what we say.

Peace

227

The business of dhikr is vast. If you like, you can look at the meaning of the words of Allah-ta'ala, *"Oh you who believe! Remember Allah frequently"* with the people of commentary, may Allah be pleased with them. You will then find that the business of dhikr is vast as we have told you. As far as the dhikr of the Name itself alone is concerned, Allah knows best, but we think that the correct way is that the one doing dhikr mention it as I tell you; with tranquility, gravity, esteem, respect, and a state of cleanliness based on the noble sunna, while he relies on Allah. Also, he should not do the dhikr as "Allah, Allah, Allah" without any drawing out of the vowel at all. He should say, "Alla . . . . . h, Alla . . . . . h, Alla . . . . . h" with lengthening.

He must visualise its five letters and always keep their visualisation present with the eye of his heart. They are alif, two lams, the elided alif, and ha'. He should keep them present without writing them down on anything. Whenever he lets their visualisation fade, he should immediately return to it. If he lets it fade a thousand times, he should return to it a thousand times. Then the one doing dhikr will have the great opening in the shortest possible time. Allah knows best, but we think that it will not be more than three weeks. Some people say that it will not be more than one week. Some people say one night. Some people say less than that. That is not difficult for Allah provided that the one doing dhikr is as we have confirmed and said previously in another place.

Peaceful calm certainly descends during dhikr of Allah. Whoever wants to know that with real or certain knowledge should persevere in dhikr of Allah with tranquility, gravity, esteem, respect, and a state of cleanliness based on the noble sunna while he relies on Allah. The wayfarer must have this state in all he does. This is what we think and what most people think, and Allah knows best.

Peace

This is the last of what our noble master, the author of these works, dictated to us, may Allah be pleased with him, very near his death. We read them out to him while he listened. They had been read out to him many times before that. We wanted to add to these letters a letter which he had written to his brothers in Allah while he was in prison in 1236 since he, may Allah be pleased with him! did not remember it when he dictated the others to us which he wrote after being in prison. If he had remembered it, he would have recorded it with them, and Allah knows best. After praising Allah, the text follows.

THE LETTER FROM PRISON

To all of our brothers in Allah, the masters, the fuqara, peace be upon you and the mercy of Allah and His baraka.

My brothers, the affair belongs to Allah and to no one else. Whatever Allah wills, is. Whatever he does not will, is not. What happens to you should not make you turbid. This is absolutely imperative. What befalls you is none other than what has befallen our masters who had greater worth with Allah than us and others. They are the prophets, peace and blessings be upon them, and the awliya, may Allah be pleased with them. My brothers and people of my love, all of you, if something befell us that had not befallen them, it would make us troubled, anxious, sorrowful, alarmed and fearful. What befalls us has only befallen them, so we rejoice, are happy, and expanded. Harm departs from us. Allah is the authority for what we say.

May Allah have mercy on you! Know that we have knowledge from our masters, our shaykhs. Allah widened our constriction with it. Allah expanded our breast by it. Allah strengthened our weakness by it. Allah changed our turbidity for great purity by it. Allah is the authority for what we say.

I strongly recommend that you pay careful attention to the Messenger's sunna which is the invincible fortress against every affliction. It is the ship of rescue and the treasury of secrets and blessings. You should not be dislodged from it for any place else at any time and moment until certainty comes to you, i.e. death.

I strongly advise you have present the word 'Allah', the Mighty, the Majestic. "If a wound touches you, a like wound has touched the people." Allah-ta'ala said, *"Do you suppose that you will enter the Garden without there having come to you the like of what came to those who passed away before you?" "Do you suppose that you would enter the Garden without Allah knowing those who do jihad among you . . . ?" "Dutiful obedience is not that you turn your faces towards the East or the West . . . those, they are those who are truly sincere and those, they are the ones with taqwa."*

You should also remember the words of the people of the Path. They are our shaykhs and the shaykhs of others, may Allah be pleased with them and give us and you the benefit of their baraka in this world and the next. Amin. They said, "The Men of Allah are recognised from other men in the variation of states." "A man is exalted or humiliated in tribulation." They said, "Whoever claims to see beauty before he has adab with majesty, reject him, for he is a dajjal (imposter). " The Prophet, may Allah bless him and grant him peace, said to one of the Companions, and Allah knows best: "Are you balanced?" He said, "Messenger of Allah, how should I be balanced?" He said, "It is that giving and withholding, might and abasement, wealth and poverty, life and death, high and low are equal to you."

I said, my brothers, the sufi is the one who is not saddened when he lacks something, great or small. This is what I said, and it is not the statement of anyone else. Listen to the answer of the wali of Allah-ta'ala, Sayyidi Muhammad

Buzayyan, may Allah benefit us by his baraka, to the one who said to him, "May Allah spare the camel!" He said, may Allah be pleased with him, "Praise be to Allah! We have not missed dhuhr or 'asr!" There is also what he said to the one who told him, "The sultan has tried Sayyidi so-and-so and Sayyidi so-and-so and taken their goods. Are you not afraid of him?" He said, "Fear is for Allah. Water and qibla are two things which no one can eliminate. The rest can be left for the one who seeks it." There is more that the people of great certainty said, may Allah be pleased with them and give us and you the benefit of their baraka.

We urge you not to neglect sadaqa every day and night, if only with half of a fruit. It is the same with supplication since it is the core of 'ibada. It says in the Immense Qur'an, *"Say: My Lord would not have been concerned with you had it not been for your supplication."*

I recommend that you go wherever you like, i.e. each of you should go to his place. It is imperative. We are in the hand of Allah.

There is no god but Allah. There is no god but Allah. There is no god but Allah. Allah was and Allah remains. There is no god but Allah.

Praise be to Allah.

The end.

ALLAH

سـيـدنا رسول الله

sayyiduna

Muhammad

blessings and peace of Allah be upon him

Sayyiduna 'Ali bin Abi Talib

Sayyidi l Hasan bin Ali
Sayyidi Abu Muhammad Jabir
Sayyidi Sa id al Ghazwani
Sayyidi Fathu s 'su ud
Sayyidi Sa id
Sayyidi Sa id
Sayyidi Ahmad al Marwani
Sayyidi Ibrahim al Basri
Sayyidi Zaynu d Din al Qazwini
Sayyidi Muhammad Shamsu d Din
Sayyidi Muhammad Taju d Din
Sayyidi Nuru d Din Abu 'l Hasan Ali
Sayyidi Fakhuru d Din
Sayyidi Tuqayyu d Din
Sayyidi Abd ar Rahman al Attar

> And there came
> from the farthest part of the city
> a man running.
> He said, "O my people
> follow those who have been sent."

Sayyidi l Hasan al Basri
Sayyidi Habib al Ajami
Sayyidi Da ud at Ta i
Sayyidi Ma ruf al Karkhi
Sayyidi as Sarri as Saqti
Al Imam al Junayd
Sayyidi sh Shibli
Sayyidi t Tartusi
Sayyidi Abu l Hasan al Hukk ari
Sayyidi Abu Sa id al Mubarak
Mawlana Abd al Qadir al Jilani
Sayyidi Abu Madyan al Ghawth
Sayyidi Muhammad Salih
Sayyidi Muhammad bin Harazim

Sayyidi Abdu s Salam bin Mashish

Sayyidi Abu'l-Hasan ash-Shadhili

Sayyidi Abu l Abbas al Mursi
Sayyidi Ahmad Ibn Ata Illah
Sayyidi Da ud al Bakhili
Sayyidi Muhammad Wafa
Sayyidi Ali Wafa
Sayyidi Yahya al Qadiri
Sayyidi Ahmad al Hadrami
Sayyidi Ahmad az Zarruq
Sayyidi Ibrahim al Falham
Sayyidi Ali ad Dawwar
Sayyidi Abd ar Rahman al Majdhub
Sayyidi Yusuf al Fasi
Sayyidi Abdu r Rahman al Fasi
Sayyidi Muhammad bin Abdillah
Sayyidi Qasim al Khassasi
Sayyidi Ahmad bin Abdillah
Sayyidi l Arabi bin Abdillah
Sayyidi Ali al Jamal

ISNAD OF THE TARIQ

Mawlaya l Arabi bin Ahmad ad-Darqawi

Sayyidi   Sayyidi Abu Ya za al Muhaji
Muhammad bin Abd al Qadir al Basha
Sayyidi Muhammad bin Qudur
Sayyidi bin l Habib al Buzidi

Mawlana
Ahmad bin Mustafa al-'Alawi

Sayyidi Muhammad al Fayturi Hamuda

> In the Name of Allah,
> the Merciful, the Compassionate
> Say: He is Allah, One. Allah, as-Samad
> He has not begotten, nor was he begotten
> And no-one is like Him.

Sayyidi Ahmad al Badawi
Sayyidi Muhammad al Arabi
Sayyidi Arabi a Hawwari
Sayyidi Muhammad bin Ali

Sayyidi
Muhammad bin al-Habib

Sayyidi 'Abd al-Qadir as-Sufi

322

adab - inner courtesy coming out as graciousness in right action.

ahl as-suffa - the people of the bench. The poor and needy amongst the companions of the Prophet, may Allah bless him and grant him peace, who lived on a verandah in a courtyard next to the house of the Prophet in the mosque at Madinah.

Allah-ta'ala - Allah, the supreme and mighty Name, indicates the One, the Existent, the Creator, the Worshipped, the Lord of the Universe. There is no existent except Him and there is only Him in existence.

ayat - a phrase structure of Qur'an and also a sign, both in the linguistic and semiotic sense.

baraka - a subtle energy which flows through everything, in some places more than others, most of all in the human being. Purity permits its flow, for it is purity itself, which is light. Density of perception blocks it.

deen - the life transaction. Submission and obedience to a particular system of rules and practices.

dhikr - invocation of Allah. Declaring the unity of Allah, pro-strating, fasting, giving to the needy, pilgrimage. These are its foundation. Recitation of Qur'an is its heart, and invocation of the Single Name, Allah, is its end.

faqir (plural fuqara) - literally, the poor. These are the men of the path of knowledge.

fiqh - the formal study of knowledge, especially the practice of Islam.

fuqaha - the scholars of fiqh.

ghawth - a qutb who heals. A granter of requests, his followers always range in their thousands. He is characterised by vast generosity.

hajj - the pilgrimage to the Ka'aba, the House of Allah in Makkah, and the performance of the rites there.

hajjis - those who make the hajj.

hikam - wisdom. Also the title of the great work by the Shadhili Shaykh ibn 'Ata'Illah.

himma - yearning. It is by the heart's yearning that the goal is reached.

'ibada - acts of service.

iman - trust in the Real, a gift from Him.

imam - one who leads the communal prayers.

jellaba - a long hooded robe worn in north africa.

kufr/kafir - kufr means to cover up reality, the kafir is one does so.

majdhoub - a man who is mad-in-the-Divine.

malakut - the hidden world.

murid - the student of a shaykh of instruction. One who has abandoned his will to the teacher in order to discover who he is.

qibla - the direction that everyone turns to pray.

qutb - the pole or axis of the universe, only understood by the one who has attained it.

rajul - man of Allah, the gnostic.

sadaqa - gifts to the needy given voluntarily in good will seeking only Allah's pleasure.

salih (plural salihun) - a developed man. By definition, one who is in the right place at the right time.

sharif - a descendent of the Prophet, may Allah bless him and grant him peace.

shaytan - Iblis, the devil, may he be cursed.

sunna - the form or practice of the Messenger Muhammad, blessings and peace of Allah be upon him.

tajalli - a divine manifestation witnessed by the inner eye of the seeker.

taqwa - being careful. Knowing your place in the cosmos. Its proof is the experience of awe.

tawba - turning to face the Real whereas before one turned one's back.

tariqa - the Way.

tawhid - unity in its most profound sense.

'ulama (singular 'alim) - men of outward knowledge.

wali (plural awliya) - literally, the friend of Allah, referring to his station of knowledge of the Real by direct seeing.

warid (plural waridat) - that which descends on the awareness of the one performing dhikr or sitting in the company of the teacher. It is the first stage of awakening.

wird - a unit of dhikr constructed to contain in it certain patterns of knowledge and self-awakening.

zakat - the wealth tax obligatory on muslims each year, usually reckoned at 2½%.

zawiyya - literally, a corner. The building used as a meeting place by the shaykhs of instruction.